Formal specification of distributed multimedia systems

Formal specification of distributed multimedia systems

Gordon Blair
Lynne Blair
Amanda Chetwynd
University of Lancaster

Howard Bowman
University of Kent at Canterbury

UCL
PRESS

First published in 1998 by UCL Press

UCL Press Limited
1 Gunpowder Square
London
EC4A 3DE
UK

and

1900 Frost Road, Suite 101
Bristol
Pennsylvania 19007-1598
USA

The name of University College London (UCL) is a registered
trade mark used by UCL Press with the consent of the owner.

British Library Cataloguing-in-Publication Data
A CIP catalogue record for this book is available from the British Library.

Library of Congress Cataloging-in-Publication Data are available

ISBN: 1–85728–677–4 PB

Typeset in Palatino and Gill Sans.
Printed by Arrowhead Books Limited, Reading, UK.

Contents

Preface

Motivation for the book

The work reported in this book was carried out as part of the EPSRC/DTI sponsored Tempo Project at Lancaster University (in collaboration with BT Labs). The aim of the Tempo Project was to investigate formal specification and associated verification techniques to support the development of distributed multimedia systems. The initial idea for this research came about during discussions at Lancaster within the Distributed Multimedia Research Group. This group was involved in a number of projects concerned with the development of communications and distributed systems support for multimedia applications. In our discussions, it became apparent that there was a lack of available techniques to support the software development process for such complex systems. Most of the research at that time was concerned with prototypical development with consequently less attention given to software engineering techniques to support such developments.

As an example, consider the work on quality of service (QoS) management. Considerable progress has been made in developing quality of service architectures encompassing such functions as QoS specification, negotiation, monitoring, policing and adaptation. However, it is notable that such functions address the needs of quality of service management once the system is installed and operational. We believe that it is equally important to consider quality of service during the software development process. In particular, there is a need for additional QoS functions such as QoS requirements capture, QoS verification and QoS testing.

In parallel, we realised that there was a need for formal techniques to support this process. Formal techniques have the advantage that they enable the rigorous analysis of system behaviour. Equally importantly, they encourage the unambiguous expression of behaviour. This is particularly important in supporting the open systems ethos in communications and distributed systems. There is considerable interest in formal specification techniques in the open systems community, e.g. in the ISO committees for Open Systems Interconnection and Open Distributed Processing. However, existing techniques available are not suitable to meet the additional demands of multimedia.

The central issue in multimedia systems is dealing with real-time. In particular, there is a need for software development techniques that support the specification and verification of real-time properties. In the work in the Tempo Project, it became clear that existing techniques (and specifically formal techniques) do not fully support the specification and verification of real-time properties in distributed multimedia systems. We identified three crucial problems:

 i. There is a conflict in formal specification between the need to incorporate real-time and the need to retain abstraction in specifications (as required at early stages of the software lifecycle).
 ii. There is a similar conflict between the need to incorporate real-time into formal specification techniques and the need to retain mathematical tractability.
iii. Existing specification architectures do not support the isolation of real-time requirements and assumptions and their subsequent verification against the system behaviour.

Consequently, we developed a new approach based on the principle of maintaining a separation of concerns between the various components in the specification. This new approach is described in detail in this book. The book also expands on the arguments given above, providing a detailed rationale for the new approach. Finally, the book evaluates the new approach by presenting a number of worked examples taken from the domain of distributed multimedia systems.

Intended readership

The book is primarily a research monograph presenting a new approach to the formal specification of distributed multimedia systems. In addition, though, the book contains a considerable amount of survey and tutorial material. For example, Part II contains an overview of distributed multimedia systems and their requirements. Similarly, Part III contains a survey of existing formal specification techniques including LOTOS, Estelle, SDL, Petri Nets, Temporal Logics and the synchronous language Esterel. Particular attention is given to the treatment of real-time in Estelle, SDL, Esterel, LOTOS and timed extensions to LOTOS.

The book is consequently aimed at two distinct audiences. First, the book is aimed at researchers and advanced developers in the fields of distributed systems, telecommunications and formal methods as an evaluation of the potential impact of multimedia on (formal) software development techniques and as an introduction to a new approach to this problem. Secondly, the book is aimed at practitioners in the above fields who are concerned with gaining a more general insight into distributed multimedia systems, formal specification techniques and, especially, the relationship between these two fields.

The book is also of relevance to students of computer science or telecommunications. The book is particularly relevant for advanced courses, e.g. at a Masters level, or as a supplement to PhD studies.

Acknowledgements

The work reported in this book was sponsored by the EPSRC/DTI under grant number GR/G/01362 as part of the Specially Promoted Programme on Integrated Multi-Service Communication Networks. The authors would like to thank the EPSRC and DTI for this support, without which the book would not have been possible. The research was also carried out in collaboration with BT Labs. We would like to thank the many people at BT Labs who interacted in the research. Particular thanks are due to Elspeth Cusack, Tim Regan and Steve Rudkin. Thanks are also due to Phil Hughes, the monitoring officer for the project, for his enthusiastic and very helpful contributions to the research.

The authors would also like to thank Professor Doug Shepherd for his role in establishing the research and also Mark Madsen for his contributions at an early stage in the project. Stanislaw Budkowski and his research team at INT offered invaluable advice on specification in Estelle. Similarly, Jean-Bernard Stefani and his co-workers at CNET offered advice on Esterel specifications. In particular, we would like to thank François Horn for his assistance in developing the Esterel version of the multimedia stream example. Bengt Andersson also offered assistance with specification in SDL.

Thanks to the members of the Distributed Multimedia Research Group who contributed to many discussions throughout the lifetime of the project, especially Geoff Coulson, Nigel Davies, Frankie Garcia and Michael Papathomas. Thanks also to John Derrick for his many helpful comments on a draft of this book. Finally, thanks to the anonymous reviewers of the book and to the staff at UCL Press for their assistance during the development process. The support provided by Andrew Carrick and Rachel Blackman was particularly helpful.

Material from Chapters 11 and 12 has been reprinted from L. Blair, G. S. Blair, H. Bowman, A. G. Chetwynd, "Formal specification and verification of multimedia systems in open distributed processing", *Computer Standards and Interfaces* **17**, 413–16, 1995, with kind permission from Elsevier Science NL, Sara Burgerhartstraat 25, 1055 KV Amsterdam, The Netherlands.

Material from Chapter 5 has been reprinted from H. Bowman, G. S. Blair, L. Blair, A. G. Chetwynd, "Formal description of distributed multimedia systems: an assessment of the state of the art", *Computer Communications* **18**, 964–77, 1995, with kind permission from Elsevier Science NL, Sara Burgerhartstraat 25, 1055 KV Amsterdam, The Netherlands.

Material from Chapter 8 has been reprinted from H. Bowman, G. S. Blair, L. Blair, A. G. Chetwynd, "Time versus abstraction in formal description", *Formal description Techniques* **VI**, 467–82, 1994, with kind permission from Elsevier Science NL, Sara Burgerhartstraat 25, 1055 KV Amsterdam, The Netherlands.

Material from Chapters 9 and 12 has been reprinted from H. Bowman, G. S. Blair, L. Blair, A. G. Chetwynd, "A formal description technique supporting expression of quality of service and media synchronisation", *Lecture Notes in Computer Science* **882**, 145–67, 1994, with kind permission from Springer Verlag GmbH, Berlin Heidelberg, Germany.

PART I

Introduction

This first part of the book introduces the topic of the book and consists of one chapter (Ch. 1). This chapter presents an introduction to distributed multimedia computing and formal specification and then provides a motivation for bringing the two areas together. The difficulties of real-time specification in achieving this goal are highlighted. The important role of Open Distributed Processing standardization in the work is also emphasized.

CHAPTER 1

Motivation for the formal specification of distributed multimedia systems

1.1   Introduction

Distributed multimedia has grown rapidly into a major field of computing research and development. Most of the major developments in distributed multimedia computing have focused on constructing prototypical distributed multimedia applications, such as multimedia conferencing, video on demand, multimedia mail, video phones and teleworking. As is typical of rapidly expanding new fields of research, an applied (engineering) approach has been almost universally adopted. The emphasis has been placed on building systems, rather than formally defining the precise behaviour of developed systems.

However, a formal approach can benefit multimedia in a number of ways. For example, formal system development can aid the development of correct (error free) systems. In addition, the recent proliferation of multimedia technology suggests that *standardization* will be of considerable importance in the field of distributed multimedia computing. Formal description is of central importance in standardization. Less rigorous approaches lead to *unclear* and *ambiguous* expression of system behaviour, thus hindering interworking and openness of systems.

Formal specification and *verification techniques* have been extensively investigated, but these techniques have generally not addressed the requirements of distributed multimedia computing. This book responds to this deficiency by describing work directly targeted at the formal specification and validation of distributed multimedia systems.

This chapter motivates the work reported in this book. Trends in distributed multimedia systems are outlined in Section 1.2. Section 1.3 then discusses the motivation for adopting a formal specification approach. Following this, Section 1.4 discusses formal specification of distributed multimedia systems. Section 1.5 considers formal specification for the Open Distributed Processing (ODP) standardization framework; as a reflection of the importance of open systems solutions the work presented in this book will be performed within the context of emerging ODP standards. Section 1.6 then gives an overview of the rest of the book and Section 1.7 concludes with a short summary.

1.2   Distributed multimedia systems

1.2.1   Distributed systems

A distributed system is a system that consists of several co-operating components, each of which is connected through a communications network (Mullender 1994). Over the past decade, distributed systems have proved to be a major area of growth in computing and a significant amount of research and development in distributed systems has been performed. This interest can be attributed to two factors:

1. *Enterprise demands*   Most medium and large scale organizations are distributed with management, equipment, skilled personnel and administration spread across a number of geographically dispersed sites. Therefore, they have a great interest in techniques to integrate their computing and communication infrastructures and allow network-wide access to company resources.
2. *Technology developments*   Both computer and communication technology has advanced considerably over the past decade. It is now economically feasible to have a large number of workstations spread across a large organization. In addition, it is possible to connect such computer facilities with high speed local area and wide area digital communication systems.

As a consequence, there has been considerable research and development in distributed systems both in industry and in academia. Subjects such as communication networks, protocols, network management and distributed operating systems are now relatively well understood. Products such as Ethernet, X-25, Corba and DCE are available in the market place and standards to provide open communications are largely agreed.

1.2.2   Adding multimedia

Recently, the new field of distributed multimedia systems has emerged. Again, this can be seen as a natural development resulting from demands from industry/commerce and new technological developments (see Fig. 1.1).

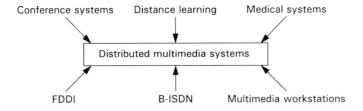

Figure 1.1 Emergence of distributed multimedia systems.

From above, there is a realization that facilities such as electronic mail and remote access to computing services are not enough. Industry and commerce are looking for more sophisticated communications infrastructures that will allow the *integration* of a range of communications services such as voice, image and video in addition to traditional text based services. A distributed environment supporting a range of *multimedia* services would enable the building of computer based collaborative systems in a wide range of areas not previously supported by text based systems. Multimedia collaboration has the potential to increase productivity in a distributed organization by improving the quality of communications between workers and by reducing costs by limiting the need to travel.

From below, technological developments are starting to make distributed, multimedia systems feasible. For example, local area network technologies such as FDDI and local Asynchronous Transfer Mode (ATM) networks have been developed. In addition, wide area Broadband Integrated Service Digital Networks (B-ISDN) is being extensively investigated, with considerable interest surrounding the standardization and construction of wide area ATM networks.

The emergence of multimedia has provided a great stimulus to distributed systems research. Multimedia systems add the extra requirement of predictable real-time behaviour. In most distributed systems or communications protocols, performance can degrade by a substantial amount without affecting the correctness of the system; the system will be slower but will still behave correctly. Multimedia systems however have certain real-time requirements that must be met or the system will fail to function correctly. The transmission of voice requires a certain guarantee of bandwidth for correct transmission. Similarly, synchronization between multiple continuous media transmissions places very strict real-time requirements on the underlying technology.

1.3   Formal specification

1.3.1   Rationale for formal specification

The virtues of taking a formal approach to system development is a hotly debated topic. However, the arguments for such approaches are strong. Positive arguments centre on the ability to reason formally about the system under development using proof and validation techniques. Furthermore, formal system development strategies force the system developers to think deeply about the system they are building at very early stages of system development. This is important since errors in system designs are increasingly expensive to rectify the later they are discovered during system development. An analogy in this respect can be drawn with design and planning in the traditional engineering disciplines. For example, consider the design of a bridge. An engineer would almost certainly develop a mathematical model of the bridge and then perform an initial validation on this model.

Design during the preliminary stages of system development is supported by the abstract non-implementation notations provided by formal methodologies. Thus, the focus is on abstract design rather than the practicalities of realization through coding. The discipline of rigorous investigation inherent in mathematics is also essential as it forces the system developer to investigate complex and difficult design issues thoroughly.

The virtues of a formal approach are highly significant in the distributed systems setting. The inherent complexity of distributed systems makes it important that abstract design methodologies are employed. In addition, formal description plays a vital role in standardization activities, as discussed below.

1.3.2   Approaches to formal specification

From within the theoretical community numerous specification notations and tools for validating system specifications have been developed and many of these have been targeted at specification of distributed systems. The spectrum of specification notations includes specification logics, process algebras, extended finite state machines, Petri nets and synchronous languages (Bowman et al. 1995a). In addition, validation tools are now commonly available. For example, tools are available that check a finite state description against logical requirements (Clarke et al. 1986), checking two specifications for equivalence (Garavel 1990, Fernandez & Mournier 1990), supporting rapid prototyping through simulated execution (Mañas 1992) and aiding logical reasoning about systems through theorem provers (Gordon & Melham 1993). The theoretical approach facilitates development of such tools by providing unambiguous semantic foundations that guarantee the validity of the analysis undertaken.

A particularly important set of formal specification techniques are those developed within the standards community. Here the importance of formal specification was recognized as long ago as 1979 when the ISO organization founded an ad-hoc group to make formal descriptions of OSI protocols possible. Initially this work was targeted at Formal Description Techniques (FDTs)[1] for communications protocols. The goals of the initial work were to provide a basis for:

1. the unambiguous and clear specification of protocol standards,
2. verification of specifications in order to find errors and prove properties,
3. functional analysis of specifications in order to detect unintended but correct behaviours of the specifications, and
4. implementation of a specification and testing of this implementation (e.g. for conformance).

Considerable work has now been done in this area, in particular, three FDTs have been standardized: LOTOS (ISO 1988), Estelle (ISO 1987) and SDL (CCITT 1988). The first of these is based upon the process algebra paradigm, while the latter two are both finite state machine based. LOTOS and Estelle were standardized by ISO in order to specify OSI protocols, while SDL was standardized by CCITT (now the ITU) in order to specify telecommunications protocols.

1.4   Formal specification and distributed multimedia systems

1.4.1   The space of real-time

As emphasized previously in this chapter the major added requirement arising from the move from distributed systems to distributed multimedia systems is the need to support real-time. A considerable amount of research has been targeted at real-time systems, but the description and construction of such systems remains a difficult area of computer science.

There are a number of different types of time to be found in computer systems, as illustrated in the following list:

1. *Pure event ordering*   All programming and formal specification languages provide for event ordering. This class of time simply enables the relative order in which events will occur to be defined; there is no reference to any quantitative measure of time. Consequently, this class

---

1. In common with a number of authors we will use the term FDT specifically to refer to the three standardized FDTs: SDL, Estelle and LOTOS. We use the term formal specification techniques more broadly to encompass all formal notations.

of timing is often referred to as *qualitative time*. In addition, the part of a system that can be specified solely using event ordering is commonly called the *functional* part of the system (see Appendix A for a clarification of terminology). Concurrent event ordering is often defined in a branching form. For example, concurrency is commonly represented using interleaving, e.g. the computation $a ; (b \parallel c)$ (where a, b and c are atomic events, ; expresses sequential composition and $\parallel$ expresses parallel composition), would be represented as,

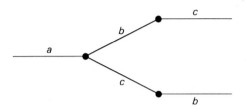

Figure 1.2 Pure event ordering.

i.e. the event a is followed by a choice of either b and then c or c and then b. Thus, concurrency is mapped to sequential behaviour using interleaving semantics. Algorithms defined using simple ordering of events are *temporally closed*, i.e. algorithm execution times have no external constraints. Critically, this means that target performance speeds do not have to be resolved against external timing requirements.

2. *Quantitative time* This class extends pure event ordering with a quantitative measure of time. As an illustration, the computation, $\sigma; a ; \sigma^2; (b \parallel c)$ (where σ denotes a delay of one unit of time, i.e. a single tick) could be semantically modelled as:

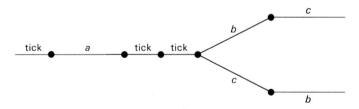

Figure 1.3 Timed event ordering.

Importantly though, the simple incorporation of quantitative time does not necessarily offer an external view of time. A tick may simply be an internal measure, corresponding to an internal system clock, which measures a tick as, for example, one processor cycle. A simple internal timeout to handle message loss is a good example. This class of time is still temporally closed, since external time constraints do not need to be met, i.e. the successful behaviour of the system is measured logically, not in terms of real-time.

3. *Real-time*   Real-time is non-system, human time, such as 5 seconds or 5 o'clock. In systems that exhibit real-time behaviour, the correctness of the system depends on both the logical results of computation and the (real-)time at which the results are produced, i.e. one is interested in both logical properties, such as *safety* and *liveness*, and the physical property of *timeliness* (see Appendix A for a clarification of terminology). Examples of such systems are factory control systems, aircraft control systems, robotics and many vision systems. Real-time systems are *temporally open*, i.e. speed of execution is an external issue and run-time performance must be externally related to (real-)timing constraints. In temporally closed systems there is a separation between correctness and performance. In temporally open systems, performance and correctness are very tightly related. More specifically, performance is one correctness variable.

4. *Soft and hard real-time*   Soft real-time systems exhibit weak failure conditions, i.e. there is a certain degree of flexibility in their timing behaviour. In contrast, hard real-time systems exhibit strong failure conditions. An example is a control system for a nuclear power station that, if it does not respond in a timely fashion to signals of a core failure, could lead to a catastrophic disaster. Timing constraints must be strictly adhered to in such systems and approximate solutions are not satisfactory.

Distributed multimedia systems are real-time systems and examples of such systems can fall into either the soft or hard real-time classes, depending upon the consequences of the timing requirements of the system not being met. However, generally multimedia systems are examples of soft real-time systems; if timing constraints are lost, the results, although not optimal, are not catastrophic.

1.4.2   Formal specification and real-time

Often the only way to confirm the real-time properties of a system is to build a prototype and monitor its performance. This is unacceptable in a distributed, multimedia system where the cost of implementation is high. Therefore it is important that tools can be provided which allow the validation of timing properties of a distributed processing system at early stages of system development. Such early validation of systems is especially advantageous in the real-time setting, for which there are numerous examples of systems that have been found not to meet their real-time requirements once developed and have thus been rendered worthless (Berryman

1993). There is thus a pressing need to develop formal specification and validation techniques applicable to real-time systems.

Although, as indicated in Section 1.3.2, there has been considerable work on formal specification and validation of distributed systems, support for formal specification and validation of distributed real-time systems is still limited. Considerable current activity is attempting to rectify this situation and numerous enhancements of existing techniques to support real-time have been made. For example, timed extensions to all the major specification paradigms have been considered, e.g. to process algebras (Davies 1993), Petri nets (Merlin & Farber 1976), finite state machines (ISO 1987) and specification logics (Alur & Henzinger 1991). In addition, validation tools have been extended to support real-time, e.g. real-time model checking (Henzinger et al. 1992). However, very little of this work addresses the specific class of real-time specification and validation arising from distributed multimedia systems.

1.4.3   Why is real-time so difficult?

In general, formal specification of real-time systems has proved to be a hard topic. One reason for this is that the resolution of performance and timing requirements critical to such systems contradicts the abstraction levels so central to formal description. Specifically, performance is an implementation issue of the lowest level of system development. In contrast, formal specification is the highest level of software development and prides itself on its level of abstraction (i.e. avoidance of consideration of implementation issues). Real-time requires the highest level to be reconciled against the lowest level, i.e. the highest level can only be developed while considering lowest level implementation issues. We will return to this issue in Chapter 8; it will serve as a strong motivation for the new approach that we will propose in that chapter.

We finish off this section with a highly appropriate quotation from Stankovic & Ramamritham (1988):

> A major challenge is to solve the dilemma that verification techniques abstract away from the implementation, but it is the implementation and environment which provide the true timing constraints.

1.5   Focus on Open Distributed Processing

One of the most important issues in modern distributed systems is how to ensure openness of developed systems, i.e. systems will be built with components from many different vendors and it is essential that these components can interwork. In the area of distributed multimedia computing this is accentuated by the recent proliferation of multimedia technology. As a reflection of the importance of open systems solutions, the approaches that we develop in this book will be placed within the context of emerging standards for Open Distributed Processing (ODP). Throughout the book the requirements of formal specification in ODP will be used as a yardstick for the approaches we propose. The next two sections introduce the basic concepts of ODP.

1.5.1   The ODP model

The ISO Basic Reference Model for Open Systems Interconnection is now mature. In addition, standards have been agreed for such diverse services as Office Document Architecture (ODA), the Remote Operations Service Element (ROSE) and the Commitment, Concurrency, Control and Recovery Service Element (CCR). However, it is recognized that such standards are primarily concerned with communication *between* end systems. In a full distributed system, it is also important to consider standards *within* end systems thus allowing the full functionality of a distributed system to be described (Linington 1995). In recognition of this, ISO established a work program to define a Reference Model for Open Distributed Processing (RM-ODP). The terms of reference of this work are as follows (ISO/ITU-T X.901 1995):

> The objective of ODP standardization is the development of standards that allow the benefits of distribution of information processing services to be realized in an environment of heterogeneous IT resources and multiple organizational domains.

One of the most important aspects of the work on the RM-ODP has been the recognition that a distributed system can usefully be considered from a number of different perspectives depending on the interests of the viewer. Such perspectives are referred to as *viewpoints* in ODP terminology. Five viewpoints have been proposed:
- *Enterprise viewpoint*   The enterprise viewpoint describes the distributed processing system in terms of what it has to do in the enterprise concerned. This viewpoint captures global requirements that justify and orientate the design of the distributed system.
- *Information viewpoint*   The information viewpoint concentrates on information, and information processing requirements of distributed processing systems. The common information structures and information flows of the system are modelled.

11

- *Computational viewpoint* The computational viewpoint provides a functional model of the system in terms of application objects and the interaction between objects at interfaces. It concerns the structuring of applications independent of the computer systems and networks on which they run.
- *Engineering viewpoint* The engineering viewpoint describes the system in terms of the engineering necessary to support the distributed nature of the processing. Thus, engineering structures are provided which realize the enterprise, information and computational specifications. For example, interaction in the computational viewpoint is realized using concrete engineering communication channels.
- *Technology viewpoint* The technology viewpoint concentrates on the technical artifacts from which the distributed processing system is built. It must identify the hardware and software that comprise the local operating system, the input/output devices, storage, points of access to communications services, etc.

A primary motivation for the viewpoints models is to enable the system to be observed at a level of abstraction that is appropriate to each particular viewer. So, for example, the information viewpoint is directed towards the systems analyst while the computational viewpoint is intended for application developers and programmers.

The ODP reference model (ISO/ITU-T X.901–4 1995) defines *viewpoint languages*, one for each viewpoint. These describe the concepts involved in the specification of each viewpoint. However, the reference model does not define actual notations for expressing these viewpoint specifications. It is anticipated that particular existing specification notations will be used to realize the viewpoint languages. Thus, the concepts defined in each viewpoint language will be instantiated in the chosen specification notation.

One of the most important aspects of the ODP model is that it supports specification of multimedia applications. All the ODP viewpoints are in some way involved in the specification of such applications. As a reflection of such modelling of multimedia structures it is assumed that viewpoint languages will support real-time specification.

1.5.2   Formal specification for ODP

There are three main areas of ODP where formal specification can be used (Bowman et al. 1995b):

- *Viewpoint languages* Some non-formal languages have been considered as vehicles for instantiating viewpoint languages. However, the suitability of a wide spectrum of formal specification techniques is also being assessed, e.g. LOTOS, Estelle, SDL and Z. It is now well accepted that different specification techniques are applicable to different viewpoints, because the features of the specification techniques variously support the required specification style of each particular viewpoint.

- *Conformance assessment*   Formal specification techniques also underpin work on conformance assessment within ODP. They do so by enabling rigorous system development to be undertaken from formal specifications (e.g. automatic test case generation). A formal approach to conformance facilitates the development of such tools.
- *Architectural semantics*   A large amount of work has also been undertaken on defining an architectural semantics for ODP. This work seeks to formalize the ODP modelling concepts. The architectural semantics (Pt 4 of the reference model (ISO/ITU-T X.904 1995)) define an interpretation of the ODP model in four different formal specification techniques, LOTOS, Estelle, SDL and Z. They thus act as a bridge between the ODP model and the semantic models of formal specification techniques. The architectural semantics will enable formal descriptions of standards for ODP systems to be developed in a sound and uniform way.

ODP imposes a number of demanding requirements on formal specification techniques, e.g. *object-based* specification, *dynamic reconfiguration* and, as indicated already, *real-time*. We will return to these requirements in Chapter 4.

1.6   Book overview

1.6.1   Objectives

The overall aim of the book is to examine the potential impact of multimedia on the formal specification of distributed systems. Particular attention will be given to the specification and verification of real-time properties relating to quality of service and real-time synchronization. In more detail, the book has the following objectives:

- (a) to highlight the requirements for formal specification and verification of distributed multimedia systems,
- (b) to evaluate existing formal specification techniques against the identified requirements,
- (c) to develop a new approach specifically targeted at the identified requirements, and
- (d) to evaluate the new approach through a number of worked examples.

In addition, the work described in the book is biased towards approaches to distributed systems development that comply with the ISO standard for Open Distributed Processing.

1.6.2 Structure of the book

The book is divided into a number of logically distinct parts as discussed below:

Part I *Motivation for the formal specification of distributed multimedia systems*
This first part of the book provides an introduction to the topics of formal specification and distributed multimedia systems and illustrates the importance of bringing these two areas together. Part I consists of one chapter:
1 *Introduction* (i.e. this chapter) describes the target domain and motivates the remainder of the book.

Part II *An introduction to distributed multimedia computing*
This part concentrates on defining what is meant by distributed multimedia systems and highlighting the issues raised by such systems (e.g. supporting continuous media, quality of service and synchronization). The part is divided into three chapters:
2 *The nature of multimedia* describes the emergence of multimedia, key aspects of the field and the major application areas.
3 *Underlying technology* discusses the central technologies that facilitate distributed multimedia computing. A wide range of technologies are covered, ranging from telecommunications networks through to user interface toolkits.
4 *Detailed requirements* presents the major requirements for formal description of distributed multimedia systems. Particular emphasis is placed on the requirements to support end-to-end quality of service and real-time synchronization.

Part III *Existing approaches*
This part surveys and assesses the suitability of a wide spectrum of existing formal description techniques. The chapters are sequenced to be increasingly specific.
5 *Broad survey: the spectrum of formal specification techniques* presents a broad survey of existing formal description techniques and assesses them against the general requirements laid out in Part II.
6 *Assessment of specific formal specification techniques* focuses on three classes of technique, extended finite state machines, synchronous languages and process algebras, which in the light of the general review work presented in Chapter 5, can be seen to be the most likely techniques to satisfy our requirements.
7 *Evaluation of LOTOS based techniques* focuses directly on the field of timed process algebras (in fact specifically, on a number of timed extensions to LOTOS that have been developed). A number of prominent timed extensions to LOTOS are compared.

Part IV *A new approach*

This part describes a new approach to formal description of distributed systems that is specifically developed to support multimedia properties.

8 *Introducing the new approach* presents the motivation for the development of a new, LOTOS based, approach to timed formal description. This new approach has been developed in direct response to the perceived state of the art of timed formal description (as presented in Pt III).

9 *The design of the logic QTL* describes the real-time temporal logic that is at the heart of the new formal specification technique.

10 *Verification with the LOTOS/QTL approach* presents an approach to the verification of LOTOS/QTL specifications.

Part V *Applying the LOTOS/QTL approach*

This part presents examples of the LOTOS/QTL approach.

11 *Simple examples* presents a number of simple examples of real-time and multimedia specifications with the LOTOS/QTL approach.

12 *A larger comparative example* compares the LOTOS/QTL specification of a lip synchronization algorithm with the specification of the same system in a timed LOTOS.

Part VI *Conclusions*

This part presents the conclusions and consists of one chapter.

13 *Conclusions* summarizes the arguments in the book and highlights the major contributions of the book. The chapter also revisits the requirements from Chapter 4 and presents some future research directions.

In addition, the book contains two appendices. Appendix A contains some notes on terminology and Appendix B contains formal specifications of a multimedia stream in a number of different formal specification techniques (these are referred to throughout Ch. 6).

1.6.3   How to read the book

The overall structure of the book is depicted in Figure 1.4. This diagram shows the overall part structure, the individual chapters and, importantly, the dependencies between chapters. From this diagram, it can be seen that the key chapters are chapters 1, 4, 5, 8 and 13. These chapters collectively provide a minimal path through the book for readers interested in the general approach. This can then be supplemented by additional material depending on the background and interests of the reader:

(a) To obtain more background information on distributed multimedia computing readers should refer to Chapters 2 and 3 of Part II (as background to Ch. 4).

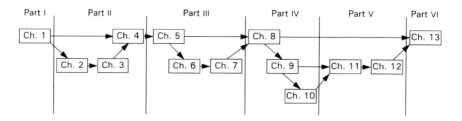

Figure 1.4   Structure of the book.

> (b) To obtain a detailed analysis of the state of the art in formal specifica-
> tion techniques readers should refer to Chapters 6 and 7 of Part III
> (amplifying the analysis of Ch. 5).
> (c) To obtain details of the particular logic adopted and of verification
> methods for the new approach, the reader should refer to Chapters 9
> and 10 of Part IV (building on the overall approach described in Ch. 8).
> (d) To obtain an evaluation of the new approach, the reader should refer
> to Chapters 11 and 12 of Part V.

1.7   Summary

This chapter has provided an overall motivation for the work that follows
in this book. The chapter started by discussing the separate topics of distributed multimedia computing and formal specification techniques. The
chapter then considered the application of formal specification techniques
to the area of distributed multimedia systems. The problems introduced
by the specification and verification of real-time behaviour were highlighted. The importance of Open Distributed Processing in realizing open
systems solutions was also discussed. Finally, the structure of the book was
reviewed.

Each of these issues will be elaborated on throughout this book. Particular emphasis will be placed on responding to the perceived conflict
between abstract specification and real-time specification. A resolution of
this conflict is at the heart of the new approach to formal specification that
we propose in Part IV.

PART II

An introduction to distributed multimedia computing

This part concentrates on defining what is meant by distributed multi-media systems and highlighting the issues raised by such systems (e.g. supporting continuous media, quality of service and synchronization). The part is divided into three chapters. Chapter 2 describes the emergence of multimedia, key aspects of the field and the major application areas. Chapter 3 then discusses the central technologies that facilitate distributed multimedia computing. A wide range of technology is covered, ranging from telecommunications networks through to user interface toolkits. Finally, Chapter 4 presents the major requirements for the formal description of distributed multimedia systems. Particular emphasis is placed on the requirements to support end-to-end quality of service and real-time synchronization.

CHAPTER 2

The nature of multimedia

2.1   Introduction

Multimedia computing is motivated by the wide range of potential applications made feasible by combining information sources such as voice,
graphics, hi-fi quality audio and video. Most of the work to date has centred on the stand-alone multimedia workstation, and a variety of software
packages is now available in areas such as music composition, computer-
aided learning and interactive video.

The combination of multimedia computing with distributed systems
support offers even greater potential. A wide variety of application areas
for distributed multimedia systems has been identified, such as office
information systems, scientific collaboration, conferencing systems and
distance learning. However, distributed multimedia systems are still at an
early stage of development and many of the proposed applications have
yet to be realized.

To achieve the potential promised by distributed multimedia it is important to ensure that the developers of distributed systems fully understand
the requirements of distributed multimedia applications. This chapter
introduces multimedia computing and describes the characteristics of
multimedia information. Those application areas where this new technology is having a significant impact are also discussed along with an evaluation of the current state of the art.

The chapter is structured as follows. Section 2.2 charts the emergence of
distributed multimedia computing and Section 2.3 provides some key definitions. Section 2.4 then presents an analysis of the key characteristics of
multimedia. A number of application areas are described in Section 2.5.
Finally, Section 2.6 presents some concluding remarks.

2.2   The emergence of multimedia

2.2.1   The end user perspective

In understanding the motivations behind multimedia computing, it is important to consider information technology from the point of view of the end user (as opposed to the technologist). To an end user, information technology is concerned with access to various forms of information and the ability to co-operate through these forms of information. Any actual technology that helps in this task is merely a means to an end.

From this perspective, it is possible to identify two separate aspects of information technology, namely the *forms of media* available to an end user and the ability to *communicate* efficiently using these media forms. In both these areas, the modern user of information is coming under increased pressure. This pressure is discussed in more detail below.

Forms of media
In recent years, there has been a dramatic increase in the range of media used to convey information. This trend is illustrated in Figure 2.1.

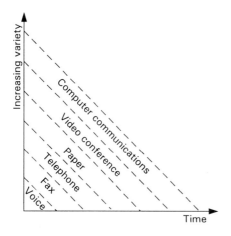

Figure 2.1   End user perspective.

Throughout history, there has been a steady trend towards the development of richer and more varied forms of media. This century has witnessed the introduction of a wide variety of media types such as the telephone and visual forms. In the latter part of the century, this trend has accelerated. There is now a staggering range of media types available to convey information.

These advances provide a great opportunity for new developments in a range of areas such as education and commerce. However, there are also a number of problems associated with the growth of information in society. In particular, there is a great danger of creating *information overload*. This problem can be seen, for example, in business where executives are required to make decisions based on an ever increasing variety and volume of information. Similar problems are also occurring in areas such as government, health care and education.

Problems of communication

The other great trend in information technology from a user perspective is the decentralization of information. Most modern day organizations are large and tend to consist of a number of separate institutions spread across a wide geographical area. These institutions typically co-operate through the sharing and exchange of information. Thus, communication is a vital concern for most organizations. Efficient communications can make the difference between successful operation and failure. Without appropriate forms of communication, there is a danger of *information starvation*, i.e. decision makers do not have the right information to make the correct decisions.

Requirement for information technology

The end user is faced with the two problems of information overload and information starvation. They may either have too much information or may not have the right information. There is, therefore, a need to help the end user to *manage* information to ease the burden created by the increasing importance of information. Essentially, the end user needs support in order to get the right information to the right people at the right time. This clearly cannot be achieved by manual systems. Thus, there is a requirement for automation in the process of information management.

2.2.2   The technology perspective

From a technology perspective, information technology is concerned with the processing of information and the ability to communicate information between different sites. More specifically, information technology is seen as a combination of computing technology and communications infrastructures. The aim of this technology is essentially to manage information for the end user. The most noticeable trend in information technology from a technology perspective has been the increasing *integration* of media. This is illustrated in Figure 2.2.

Traditionally, computer systems have dealt exclusively with textual and numerical information. Communications technologies, therefore, have developed to support the transmission of textual and numerical data. More recently, there has been a dramatic increase in the range of media types

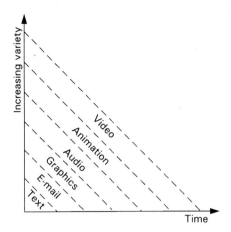

Figure 2.2 Technology perspective.

supported by computers and communications technologies. Significant steps have been taken in integrating graphics into computer workstations and communications technologies. Researchers are now tackling the harder problems presented by audio and video.

2.3 Definitions

2.3.1 Media

The term *media* refers to storage, transmission, interchange, presentation, representation and perception of different information (data types) such as text, graphics, voice, audio and video. The following explanation clarifies the different usages of the word media (Kretz 1990):

- *Storage media* The term *storage media* refers to the type of physical means to store data (e.g. magnetic tape, hard disk, optical disk, etc).
- *Transmission media* The term *transmission media* refers to the type of physical means to transmit data (e.g. coaxial cable, twisted pair, fibre optic, etc.).
- *Interchange media* The term *interchange media* refers to the means of interchanging data; this can be by storage media, transmission media or a combination of both.
- *Presentation media* The term *presentation media* is used to describe the type of physical means to reproduce information to the user or to acquire information from the user, e.g. speakers, video windows, keyboard or mouse.

- *Representation media* The term *representation media* is related to how information is described (*represented*) in an abstract form, for use within an electronic system. For example, to *present* text to the user, the text can be coded (represented) in raster graphics, in graphics primitives or in simple ASCII characters. Thus, the presentation can be the same but with different representations. Other examples of abstract media are ASN.1 and SGML.
- *Perception media* The term *perception media* is used to describe the nature of information as perceived by the user, e.g. speech, music and film.

Because of these different aspects of media, it is important not to use the word in isolation. Rather, it is more correct to use terms such as *interchange media* for storage and transmission, *representation media* for an abstract description of the media, etc.

2.3.2 Multimedia

The previous sections have highlighted important trends in information technology from both the end user and technology perspective. Two themes have emerged from this discussion. First, the *variety* of media types is an important feature of modern information systems. Secondly, in order to deal with the variety, *integration* is a critical concern. These observations provide a good working definition of multimedia:

Multimedia = Variety + Integration

It is *necessary* for a multimedia system to support a variety of media types, i.e. support in terms of storage, transmission, presentation, representation and perception. The range of media types could be as modest as text and graphics or as rich as animation, audio and video. However, this alone is not *sufficient* for a multimedia environment. It is also important that the various sources of media types are integrated into a single system framework. A *multimedia system* is then one that allows end users to *store, transmit, interchange, present, represent and perceive a variety of forms of information in an integrated manner.*

In essence, multimedia systems are attempting to solve the problems of information management by integrating the various forms of media into the computer/communications infrastructure. There are two benefits of achieving this level of integration:

1. the computer can help in the task of managing and processing the information,
2. information users only have to deal with one integrated environment rather than a number of separate information subsystems.

This is the great benefit of multimedia information systems and is the main motivation behind the current research on the subject.

2.3.3   Distributed multimedia computing

Multimedia systems have received a great deal of attention recently, and a number of successful prototypes have been developed. Some systems are also now available commercially. However, it is important to draw a distinction between multimedia systems that operate on a single computer workstation and those that can span a networked environment. As mentioned earlier, most of the developments to date have been on single workstations. There has been much less work on networked systems.

The term *distributed multimedia system* is introduced to describe the general case of a number of *multimedia workstations* interconnected by one or more *multi-service networks*, i.e. networks that offer a variety of services such as data and voice (see Ch. 3, Section 3.2). In addition, a *distributed multimedia application* is defined as an application that runs over a distributed multimedia system. The problems of managing multimedia in a distributed system are great and introduce a number of unresolved research problems. In contrast, the technological problems of multimedia workstations and multiservice networks are much better understood.

2.4   Characteristics of multimedia information

The previous section outlined the need to integrate a variety of media types into a distributed system. In the following sections we discuss a range of media types, outline their characteristics and discuss some of the issues that arise when attempting to integrate them into a computing environment.

2.4.1   Media types

As indicated previously, early computer applications tended to deal exclusively with single media types. For example, word processors were text-based, CAD packages manipulated vector drawings and paint packages produced bit-mapped images. The advent of new application areas such as desk-top publishing, however, led to the integration of textual and graphical media. The usefulness of integrating such media types is now self-evident. However, studies of potential multimedia application areas (Williams & Blair 1994) have demonstrated that significant gains may be made by further integration of new media types including audio and video.

The various forms of media can be categorized as either discrete or continuous. The term discrete media is used to refer to media that do not have a temporal dimension. In contrast, continuous media have an implied temporal dimension, i.e. they are presented at a particular rate for a particular length of time. Continuous media types, therefore, demand a continuing commitment from the underlying system in terms of services provided. A summary of the media types in these two categories is provided below.

1. *Discrete media*
   "Plain" data (data without any structure such as binary files)
   Raw ASCII
   Numerical (data units of fixed length such as integer, real, etc.)
   Encoded text (character strings of arbitrary length with embedded font control)
   Vector graphics
   Bit map images
   Special forms (e.g. mathematical or chemical formulae)
2. *Continuous media*
   Audio data (digitized speech and high quality audio)
   Formatted audio data (e.g. MIDI)
   Video data (digitized video information)
   Formatted video data (e.g. compressed video)
   Animation data (sequences of vector graphics primitives)
   "Live" data (interactive data)

2.4.2 Representations of media types

Continuous media types such as audio and video may be represented in either digital or analogue format. Many early multimedia systems such as MINOS (Christodoulakis et al. 1986) manipulated analogue representations of continuous media data. In particular the developers of MINOS constructed voice and video stores built around existing analogue storage devices that could be controlled by computer. Output from these storage devices was transmitted in analogue form and presented using analogue devices. This use of analogue technology allowed much pioneering work in the assessment of the potential benefits of multimedia systems to be carried out, since existing hardware already provided the necessary functionality at a reasonable cost.

Recently however there has been a general move towards digital representations of all forms of media. This move has been particularly prevalent in industries which repeatedly manipulate data, such as the music and film industries. From a computing perspective, there is a more significant reason for promoting the use of digital representations of all media types: it allows the full integration of existing media types, and the comparatively easy integration of new media types. For example, analogue systems providing support for media types such as voice and video require separate cabling and devices for these media types when compared to more traditional media types such as text and graphics. The use of digital representations of all media types allows all forms of information to be fully integrated. However, it must be understood that the support of digital representations of continuous media places considerable demands on the underlying technologies.

2.4.3 Demands of digital media

Given the range of media types, it is possible to calculate each of their basic data requirements. Calculations for a cross-section of media types are presented below, with the results summarized in Figure 2.3.

- *Encoded text*   *Assuming*: screen size of 768 * 512 pixels, character size of 8 * 8 pixels, 2 bytes per character for representation.
  No. of character positions on screen = (768/8) * (512/8) = 6144
  $\Rightarrow$ one page of text requires = 6144 * (2 * 8) = 96 Kbits
  i.e. storage for one full page of encoded text = 12 Kbytes
- *Vector graphics*   The storage requirement of an image in vector graphics format is a product of the number of lines required to construct the image and the average amount of information needed to reproduce each line. Each line can be represented by a quintuple of the form *<start-x, start-y, end-x, end-y, attributes>* where the *attributes* component stores information pertaining to a line's colour and thickness etc. *Assuming*: screen size of 768 * 512 pixels, 1 byte per line for attributes.
  $\Rightarrow$ storage per line = (10 * 2) + (9 * 2) + 8 bits = 46 bits
  Stating the storage requirements of a "page" of vector graphics is meaningless without stating some parameter values. Therefore, to provide an indicator of the overheads of handling vector graphics, we can approximate the cost of what might be considered a non-trivial image, i.e. an image consisting of several hundred lines:
  *i.e. storage requirements per 500 lines of vector graphics $\approx$ (500*46 bits)*
  $\approx$ *2.8 Kbytes*
- *Bit Map images*   *Assuming*: screen size of 768 * 512 pixels, character size of 8 * 8 pixels, 256 colours per pixel.
  $\Rightarrow$ storage requirements of a bit mapped screen = 768 * 512 * $\log_2$ (256)
  = 3072 Kbits
  i.e. storage for one bit mapped page = 384 Kbytes
- Digitized speech   *Assuming:* an analogue bandwidth of 4 KHz, 8 bit sample size.
  $\Rightarrow$ Sample rate must be at least 8 KHz
  Hence, storage for one second of voice is 8 KHz * 8 bits = 64 Kbits
  i.e. storage requirements for digitized voice = 8 Kbytes per second
- Digitized high quality audio   *Assuming*: an analogue bandwidth of 22 KHz, 16 bit sample size.
  $\Rightarrow$ Sample rate must be at least 44 KHz
  Hence, storage for one second of digitized audio = 44 KHz * 16 bits
  = 704 Kbits

i.e. storage requirements for digitized audio = 88 Kbytes per second
- Digitized video *Assuming*: a Phase Alternate Line (PAL) encoded signal with a vision bandwidth of 5 MHz, a frame rate of 25 frames per second, and a sample size of 24 bits.
Analogue bandwidth = 5 MHz,
$\Rightarrow$ Sample rate must be at least 10 MHz
Hence, storage for one digitized frame = (10MHz / 25) * 24
$= 9.6$Mbits $= 1.2$ Mbytes
Hence, storage for video = (1.2 * 25) Mbytes per second
i.e. storage requirements for digitized video = 30 Mbytes per second

The figures presented in Figure 2.3 are calculated according to the provision of a particular *quality of service*. The notion of quality of service is fundamental to multimedia computing and will be revisited in more depth in Chapter 4.

Text: storage for one page of text ≈ 12 Kbytes

Vector graphics: storage per 500 lines of graphics ≈ 2.8 Kbytes

Bit map images: storage for one bit mapped page ≈ 384 Kbytes

Digitized voice: storage for digitized voice ≈ 8 Kbytes/sec

Digitized audio: storage for digitized audio ≈ 88 Kbytes/sec

Digitized video: storage for digitized video ≈ 30 Mbytes/sec

Figure 2.3 A summary of the requirements of key media types.

2.5 Multimedia applications

There are many areas of application where the introduction of multimedia can enhance the utility of existing systems. Similarly, there are many new areas of application made possible by the emergence of multimedia. This section examines some of the potential application areas of multimedia (with particular emphasis on distributed multimedia applications).

The section first considers the role of distributed multimedia applications in supporting organizations; this part of the study considers *generic* tools that can benefit all organizations in managing and, more generally, in supporting co-operative activity between potentially geographically dispersed employees. The survey then examines specific economic sectors where distributed multimedia applications are likely to have the most impact. The areas considered are the service industries, retail industries, home entertainment and, finally, arts and culture. This structure is illustrated in Figure 2.4.

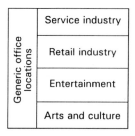

Figure 2.4 Structure of the applications study.

2.5.1   Office applications

It can be envisaged that office applications will be a major beneficiary of distributed multimedia applications. Offices produce and consume large amounts of information which can take many forms. They also rely on communication for co-ordination and management and, more generally, for co-operative working between potentially geographically dispersed groups of employees. It is not surprising, therefore, that office systems have been widely targeted for pilot multimedia applications. The requirements of office systems have also been addressed by researchers in the field of Computer Support for Co-operative Work (CSCW) (Bannon & Schmidt 1991) because of the emphasis on co-ordination and group working mentioned above. A number of the application areas mentioned below are derived from research in this field.

We group office applications into four areas:

  (a) multimedia documents,
  (b) multimedia mail,
  (c) multimedia conferencing, and
  (d) teleworking.

These are discussed in turn below.

Multimedia documents
Document production was one of the first application areas to be affected by the advent of multimedia computing. The integrated text/graphics word processor has been a commercial product for several years and has achieved widespread success through the popularity of desktop publishing. The extension of documents to incorporate audio and video is the obvious development path for this type of application.

   Recently, *multimedia document editors* have been constructed that attempt to provide the functionality required by end users of multimedia technology (Christodoulakis & Graham 1988, Scholler & Casner 1989). This research has concentrated on the methods of viewing, editing, and manipulating various media types. Multimedia documents generally have a hierarchical structure with leaf nodes being of a variety of media types. For example, a multimedia document could consist of a number of sections, where sections consist of paragraphs including text paragraphs, graphics or sequences of video. More general graph structures have also been proposed leading to the concept of *hypermedia* (Ritchie 1989), where nodes of different media types are connected together to form a general information base.

Standardization is extremely important in this area as documents provide the basic unit for the exchange of information. There are a wide number of activities in this area (Liu 1994). For example, the International Standards Organisation (ISO) is developing a range of standards for document processing and communications, including:

(a) HyTime – a hypermedia-based document structuring language,
(b) HyperODA – hypermedia extensions to the Open Document Architecture standard (ODA),
(c) MHEG – a multimedia and hypermedia expert group standard for the interchange of multimedia and hypermedia documents, and
(d) PREMO – a presentation environment for multimedia (graphical) objects.

Multimedia electronic mail

Multimedia electronic mail is an application area which will be applicable to a number of multimedia environments (Postel et al. 1988, Reynolds et al. 1985). Unlike text mail, however, multimedia messages can be extremely large and difficult to manage (Huitema 1989). The size of mail messages for example, may range from a few kilobytes to many megabytes (Davies & Nicol 1991). The storage requirements, therefore, are extremely variable and difficult to foresee.

As well as being large, multimedia messages may also be highly structured. For example, a mail message is a prime example of a multimedia document that consists of a number of different information components. Mail applications will have to be able to understand the structure of messages sent from a range of different systems. The necessity for standards which describe how messages can be structured, therefore, is an important issue in the development of multimedia mail applications.

The two most important multimedia mail standards are MIME and X.400. MIME (Multipurpose Internet Mail Extensions) is a de facto standard developed by the Internet community (Borenstein 1993). The protocol takes an evolutionary approach to supporting multimedia by extending the existing Internet Simple Mail Transfer Protocol (SMTP) with additional structuring to the message body. The two main extensions are content type (with associated subtypes) and content transfer encodings. Example content types and content transfer encodings are given in Tables 2.1 and 2.2 respectively.

Table 2.1 Example MIME content types.

Content-Type	Subtype	Description
Text	Plain	Simple ASCII text
	Richtext	Formatted text
Multipart	—	Used to combine multiple body parts
Application	PostScript	PostScript format
	RTF	RTF interchange format
	MSWORD	Microsoft Word format
Message	Partial	E-mail message fragment
	External	Body referenced but not included
Image	JPEG	JPEG compressed image
	GIF	GIF compressed image
Audio	—	Audio data
Video	MPEG	MPEG compressed video
	Quicktime	Quicktime format video

Table 2.2 Example MIME content transfer encodings.

Encoding	Description
7-bit	ASCII encoding
8-bit	ASCII plus some non-ASCII characters
BASE64	Three bytes mapped to 4 ASCII characters
QUOTED-PRINTABLE	ASCII but with an additional escape mechanism
BINARY	Binary (i.e. no) encoding

X.400 is an ISO/ITU-T standard for electronic mail (ISO/ITU-T X.400 1988). In contrast to SMTP/MIME, X.400 was designed from the start with multimedia support. X.400 defines a number of standard body parts such as text, voice, fax and multipart, and also a set of extended body parts based on these (including ODA documents). In addition, X.400 provides a language for specifying abstract syntax of body parts (ASN.1 (ISO/ITU-T X.208 1988)) and an associated set of basic encoding rules (BER (ISO/ITU-T X.209 1987)) to encode the abstract syntax.

Multimedia and desktop conferencing

Desktop conferencing systems stem from the merging of workstation technology and real-time computer conferencing. Such systems enable groups of users to interact simultaneously with one or more applications; voice and video facilities are also often provided. Two main approaches have been identified: collaboration-transparent and collaboration-aware conferencing.

Collaboration-transparent systems enable existing applications to be viewed in a group setting (examples include Rapport (Ahuja et al. 1988), SharedX (Garfinkel et al. 1989) and MMConf (Crowley et al. 1990)). As the application is unaware of the presence of more than one user, it is necessary to multicast display output and multidrop user input so that the application deals with a single stream of output and input events. To avoid confusion, users must take turns in interacting with the application; this is achieved by adopting an appropriate floor control policy.

In contrast, collaboration aware solutions provide facilities to manage explicitly the sharing of information, allowing sharing to be presented in a variety of different ways to different users. The management of sharing is often embedded in the application itself. Such applications are often referred to as *multi-user applications* and represent the emerging generation of desktop conferencing applications (these include Cognoter (Stefik et al. 1987), Grove (Ellis & Gibbs 1989) and Meade (Bentley et al. 1992)).

In addition, a number of multimedia conferencing systems have also been developed with the intent of forming distributed shared *media spaces* across a user community (Gaver et al. 1992, Root 1988). These systems use multimedia communication facilities to simulate the everyday environment within which people work. Perhaps the best known example is the experiment at Xerox PARC linking two coffee rooms with a shared video wall (Olson & Bly 1991). A variety of other systems have been reported including Cruiser, developed at Bellcore, and the more asynchronous system Portholes (Dourish & Bly 1992), developed at EuroPARC. Recent work has focused on extending the ability to explore the remote spaces through techniques such as using multiple cameras with moving fields of view (Gaver et al. 1992).

Teleworking
Teleworking services allow users to work in their homes rather than travel to a place of work. They simulate the environment found in the office by enabling remote access to information services, providing audio and video communications with others in the organization, allowing the transmission of faxes and electronic mail, etc. They are therefore more of an application area for the technologies discussed above, rather than a source of new services. It is likely though that teleworking will become increasingly popular, especially given the congestion in the transport infrastructures in many cities around the world.

2.5.2   Service industry applications

The service sector consists of organizations whose main concern is running a service for the public. Important examples of such services include education and health. Both these services have always been large consumers of computing technology. It is not surprising, therefore, that both of these areas are investigating the potential of multimedia for enhancing the services they provide.

Education

The use of multimedia in education has been widespread for many years. In schools and colleges there has been a continuous move towards computing support for teaching since the introduction of the home computer in the 1970s. This inexpensive technology has the capability to use text, image, and sound to supplement and enhance the more traditional teaching methods.

An additional breakthrough in educational multimedia came with the introduction of optical disk technology. The use of optical disks as information sources with interactive teaching applications has been highly useful in both schools and commercial training institutions (Loveria & Kinstler 1990). With the initial lack of communications support, however, the full use of this type of application was constrained by the high cost of producing the information and the relatively low ability for its distribution. The emergence of the required communications technology is now allowing research to investigate the potential for teaching and training applications where central information sources can be accessed from remote sites. Livenet (Beckwith et al. 1990), for example, is providing remote access to course information for students.

Other important areas for education include technology support for *distance learning* where students can study a range of educational material from their own homes and *just-in-time* learning where clients (normally in industry) can be trained in a particular technique just before they are due to apply this technique. Just-in-time learning could be used, for example, in providing some instant training for the use of scientific instrumentation.

Health

The health service consists of a wide range of equipment that produces high volumes of information in various forms. Scanning equipment, for example, produces video output while x-ray machines produce high quality images. The quality of the information available to medical staff and its accessibility are highly important when patients' lives are at stake. To enhance this information and its access methods, therefore, is an important objective.

Distributed multimedia computing provides the support infrastructure to build medical systems that can hold many forms of information and allow access to this information both quickly and easily from any location. Information systems with this level of processing and communications power will have great benefits for the health industry. The MUSIC project (Goldberg et al. 1989) and the BERKOM Heart Hospital (Hehmann et al. 1991) are particular examples where a distributed multimedia system is enhancing the communication of information within a medical environment. Other research (Mavridis & Weser May 1990) is looking at the management and control of medical data within automated information systems.

2.5.3   Retail applications

Multimedia provides opportunities in many retail areas where the technology can be applied to provide customers with comprehensive, up to date information. The information provided may either describe a product or be the product itself and can be made available at a wide range of locations, including domestic properties. The potential of multimedia in the retail industry is being investigated in a number of areas as discussed below.

Publishing
Multimedia technology has the potential to affect the publishing industry in a variety of ways. Newspaper publishers, for example, have a need for systems that can be used to obtain and collate multimedia information from a number of sources. The most important application area created by multimedia computing, although, is *electronic publishing* (Brailsford & Beach 1989, Koo 1989), i.e. the production of newspapers, magazines, and books in electronic form enabling publishers to utilize audio and video in addition to text and image. On-line publications are able to provide readers with current information in a highly dynamic and interactive form. Many examples of such interactive publications are already available via the World-Wide Web. Further advances in on-line publishing can also be anticipated with the advent of high-speed networks; the BERKOM tele-publishing system (Hehmann et al. 1991) has already investigated the use of high speed networking to support electronic publishing.

Finance
The finance industry is regarded as one of the world's main consumers of information. The success of a financial organization is dependent upon the effectiveness of its information gathering and communication systems. The nature of the financial markets requires that relevant information is quickly filtered out and made available to those people making investment decisions based on market conditions. The information received may be from a number of different sources, e.g. company reports and political statements, which may include a variety of media types. It is important, therefore, that the system receiving, communicating, and presenting the information is capable of handling the various forms of information it may encounter.

Travel and property
The publishing industry has been mentioned as an area where multimedia technology can help replace paper based products with electronic alternatives. Electronic information has the advantage of being more comprehensive, up to date, and interactive. The travel industry would also benefit from this advanced method of presenting information. Customers could be provided with access points to information systems with audio and video

descriptions of holiday locations. If accessed via a hypermedia style interface, this capability would allow customers to browse at leisure through suitable holiday resorts and be presented with descriptions far superior to those currently provided in magazines. Many people travel to holiday resorts only to find they are disappointed with the eventual location. More informative information systems which provide customer specific information through selective browsing would reduce this type of problem.

The property market is a further area where information is currently presented through paper based media. Property is initially viewed through a magazine or newspaper that gives little indication of the location, condition, and internal layout. A multimedia information system, utilizing audio and video, would provide a means of showing potential customers much more detail than presently available. The extra information accessible through a computer system thus reduces the need for numerous visits to unsuitable properties. Distribution of the information would allow customers to view properties from anywhere in the country, from a local source, possibly even their own home. The benefits to buyers, vendors, and property agents would be high, due to the large reduction in time wasted over visiting numerous properties. GTE Laboratories have assessed the use of distributed multimedia systems within the property market (Sasnett et al. 1994).

Others

The introduction of communication technologies capable of transmitting multimedia to domestic properties is providing the necessary infrastructure for home users to access a wide range of information services. Home shopping, cookery lessons, home maintenance, and home safety are examples of information that could be made available.

Finally, distributed multimedia technology is enabling the development of a new area of retailing, namely commercial information services. As mentioned earlier, communications infrastructures such as the Internet offer connectivity to a substantial user community. There are also now sophisticated tools such as World-Wide Web providing access to a range of services available in the network. For example, the World-Wide Web currently offers international access to a range of services as diverse as the RAL-Durham particle database, the Legal Information Institute's hypertext archive of American Law, and a database of restaurants in Palo Alto (Berners-Lee et al. 1994). At present, many of these services are free. However, it is likely in the future that services will be offered commercially especially given the increasing use of the Internet by commercial organizations.

2.5.4   Entertainment

Interactive television

For many years the main communication methods used to access domestic properties have been mail, telephone, radio, and television. Each of these communication systems have limitations regarding their support for inter-action and information selection. Television and telephone companies have attempted to address this limitation with the use of teletext (in the case of television) and information lines (in the case of telephones). Both systems attempt to provide a range of information that can be selectively browsed. The limiting factors of these systems are their restricted media types and methods of interaction. It is also likely that interactive television will become a reality in the near future.

Video-on-demand

Video-on-demand systems allow users to watch their choice of videos in their own home at their own preferred time. Such systems are already being piloted world-wide. It is also anticipated (as mentioned earlier) that systems could grow to as many as 1.5 million customers.

   According to Gelman et al. (1991), at least three categories of video-on-demand systems can be envisaged:

(a) *Quasi video-on-demand*   In such systems, users are grouped according to their interests. Users can perform rudimentary temporal control by switching to a different group.

(b) *Near video-on-demand*   In near video-on-demand systems, the user can select a film from a proposed set of films and can also perform functions such as forward and reverse within discrete time intervals (say 5 minutes). This capability can be provided by having multiple channels with the same programme skewed in time.

(c) *True video-on-demand*   In true video-on-demand systems, the user has complete control over the session. They can choose when to start the film and can then have the full range of VCR capabilities such as for-ward, reverse, pause, fast forward, etc.

Such services mark a convergence of computers, communications and broadcasting. A good discussion of video-on-demand services can be found in Little & Venkatesh (1994).

Virtual reality

Virtual reality is a further major growth area in computing. In the early days, most virtual reality systems were developed on stand-alone workstations, However, more recently, a number of people have become interested in the potential of distributed virtual reality (Fahlén et al. 1993). Such systems involve a range of media types, most specifically 3-D graph-ics, animation and sound and can hence be considered as distributed multimedia applications.

The potential of this technology in the entertainment industry is considerable. For example, a range of games has been developed that allows users to interact through the shared virtual world. Note however that this technology can be used in a wide range of areas other than entertainment; applications are envisaged in such diverse areas as industrial training, education, co-operative design and medicine.

2.5.5   Arts and culture

Arts and culture is an area with immense potential for multimedia due to its high use of visual information. A number of research organizations are investigating the possibilities for multimedia technology in this domain. With the range of information types available, it is possible to imagine applications that will allow art galleries and museums to enhance their exhibits with a multimedia information system. The European Museums Network (RACE 1994), for example, has developed a pilot scheme for displaying exhibits at several sites simultaneously. The number of people able to view these exhibits would, therefore, increase dramatically.

More specifically for the art world, multimedia computing provides artists with a tool for constructing, storing, and displaying their creations. It may not be uncommon to see multimedia workstations in art galleries using the range of available media types to display audio/visual art. Teaching art and supporting design processes will be a future use of multimedia technology.

2.6   Summary

This chapter has presented an introduction to the expanding field of distributed multimedia computing. The rationale for the emergence of distributed multimedia has been explored, some key definitions introduced and the characteristics of various media types have been examined. The range of potential applications for distributed multimedia computing has also been examined. The range of applications highlights the potential for multimedia and the need for distributed system designers to recognize the particular requirements of these applications.

CHAPTER 3

Underlying multimedia technology

3.1   Introduction

This chapter discusses the key technologies underlying distributed multi-media computing. Such a survey covers a wide range of technologies ranging from telecommunications networks through to user interface toolkits. To structure the discussion, we therefore partition the technologies into four areas as illustrated in Figure 3.1.

User interfaces		
Hypermedia	Multimedia window systems	
Integrative standards and technologies		
OMG CORBA	ODP	TINA
End systems technologies		
Multimedia workstations	Compression storage	Protocols OS support
Communications networks		
ISDN	B-ISDN/ATM	GSM

Figure 3.1   Underlying technologies for distributed multimedia computing.

The bottom level in this diagram is the underlying communications networks offering services for the transmission of the range of media types. End systems technologies are then layered on top of this offering multimedia facilities at the desktop. Integrative standards then deal with the interconnection of large scale systems consisting of heterogeneous networks and end systems technologies. Finally, multimedia user interfaces allow the presentation of a range of media types to the user. This diagram can be thought of as a high level architecture for distributed multimedia systems. The four layers of this diagram are considered in turn (Sections 3.2 to 3.5). Section 3.6 then summarizes the chapter.

3.2 Communications networks

3.2.1 Emerging high-speed multi-service networks

Rationale
Most of today's telecommunication networks tend to be specialized and designed to carry one type of service only. For example, standard telephony is generally transported via a Public Switched Telephone Network (PSTN). Computer data are transported in the public domain by either a Public Switched Data Network (PSDN) based on X.25 or by a Circuit Switched Data Network (CSDN) based on X.21. In the private domain computer data are carried by local area networks (LANs) such as Ethernet and, more recently, high speed local area networks (HSLANs). Television signals can be transported in three ways: broadcast via radio, by cable (CATV) or by satellite. With the interest in multimedia applications, however, there is now considerable interest in the development of high speed multi-service networks that can achieve integration of these various services at the networking level.

Local/metropolitan area networks
In the local/metropolitan area, the central technologies are the Fibre Digital Data Interface (FDDI) (Ross 1990) and Distributed Queues Dual Bus (DQDB) (IEEE 1990) networks. FDDI is an ANSI standardized 100 Mbits/sec token ring based metropolitan area network that supports about 500 workstations over a distance of 200 km. The more recent FDDI-II standard explicitly supports continuous media data by partitioning the available bandwidth into *isochronous* (for continuous media) and *non-isochronous* (for conventional data) parts. DQDB is an IEEE standardized network that uses a pair of optical fibre buses for added reliability. Again, support is provided for both isochronous multimedia data and more bursty asynchronous traffic. Both types of network also support multicast communications in order to support applications structured around groups of users.

Wide area networks
In the wide area, the integrated services digital network (ISDN) (de Prycker 1989) is becoming widely supported by telecommunications providers. ISDN is a digital network standard intended to replace current telephone

networks, and to carry a variety of multimedia data in addition to digital telephone signals. Basic rate ISDN, intended for domestic use, provides a pair of 64 Kbps channels for data and a 16 Kbps or 64 Kbps channel intended for control traffic. Primary rate ISDN is intended for consumers with heavier requirements and specifies either 30 Kbps x 64 Kbps channels (Europe) or 23 Kbps x 64 Kbps channels (USA) together with a signalling channel. Broadband ISDN (B-ISDN) (Spears 1988) is a development of ISDN that offers far higher data rates (e.g. 150 Mbps or 620 Mbps). B-ISDN is implemented with Asynchronous Transfer Mode (ATM) packet switiching (de Prycker 1991) that uses small fixed sized packets (or *cells*) and allows variable numbers and capacities of connection, each with varying QoS properties. ATM uses a connection oriented call set up procedure; at connection time, resources are allocated in network switches to support the particular throughput, latency and cell loss requirements of each connection. Higher level services called ATM Adaptation Layers (AALs) are also defined. These are specifically tailored for particular media types and offer facilities such as fragmentation and reassembly of large packets into/from ATM cells, error checking and correction, and a choice of isochronous or non isochronous delivery.

Finally, SMDS (Switched Multimegabit Data Service) is a network service being developed by Bellcore in the USA that has caused strong interest among the European telecommunications operators. It is an example of a frame relay type of service, in which the complexities of network protocols are brought out to the edges of the network, leaving only simple switches inside the network. Using this approach, information can be switched more rapidly and cheaply. Presently, SMDS is being piloted at 1.5 Mbit/s or 2 Mbit/s, but is soon expected to offer 34 Mbit/s or 45 Mbit/s end-to-end capabilities.

3.2.2   Mobile networks

Significant developments are also taking place in the field of mobile communications. In wide area mobile communications, *cellular* radio based systems (Walker & Gardner 1990) are becoming prevalent. In these systems, the geographical area covered by the network is divided into small areas (cells) each equipped with a base station. Each mobile station communicates with the nearest base station that subsequently relays the message, typically via a wire-based network, to another base station and hence to another mobile.

The most important cellular based network at the present time is the second generation pan-European digital service commonly referred to as GSM (Groupe Spéciale Mobile). This is intended to provide continent-wide mobile communications mainly for voice but also for data communications. GSM is based on digital time division multiplexing and has a raw data rate of 13.8 Kbps (with error checking this is reduced to 9.6 Kbps). Third generation mobile communications services are also now envisaged. For example, it is expected that Mobile Broadband Systems (or MBS) will be available by the year 2000. Such systems will provide a full range of multimedia services over radio networks. However, deployment will require substantial technological advances and the requirement to support multimedia services must be reconciled with the need to support an ever increasing number of regular subscribers. One way of addressing these concerns is to reduce the cell size significantly, thus allowing more effective radio spectrum re-use (future radio networks may well include cells that occupy less space than a typical building). The negative aspects of small cell sizes are increases in deployment costs and increased complexity of call routers. The *practical* bandwidth of third generation radio networks will depend, at least in part, on the successful resolution of these issues.

3.2.3 Summary

A large number of digital networks have been discussed above, ranging from low bandwidth public switched telephone and data networks through to high bandwidth multi-service networks such as B-ISDN. The capabilities of the various networks are summarized in Table 3.1.

Table 3.1 An overview of current networking technologies.

Network	Service	Bandwidth (Mbit/s)
GSM	Data+Voice	0.01
PSTN	Voice	0.01
PSDN	Data	0.05
LAN/ HSLAN	Data	1–100
CATV	Video	0.064-5
FDDI	Multi-service LAN	100
DQDB	Multi-service MAN	150
Basic Rate ISDN	Multi-service WAN	0.128
Primary Rate ISDN	Multi-service WAN	1.9
SMDS	Multi-service WAN	1-45
Broadband ISDN	Multi-service WAN	150–1200

3.3   End systems technologies

3.3.1   Multimedia workstations

A multimedia workstation is a workstation capable of creating, displaying, storing and processing and transmitting a variety of media types. A typical multimedia workstation is shown in Figure 3.2.

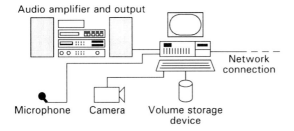

Audio amplifier and output

Network connection

Microphone   Camera   Volume storage device

Figure 3.2 A typical multimedia workstation.

Hardware support for audio and video is now quite sophisticated; this work builds on recent developments in audio and video compression techniques as discussed in Section 3.3.2 below. The major outstanding research issue in multimedia workstations is in interfacing to high speed networks; this issue is discussed in more detail below.

Current workstation architectures are severely limited in that they are able to handle very few continuous media connections before suffering CPU/bus overload. Initial efforts at overcoming the host system bottleneck took the approach of off-loading the processing and bandwidth requirements of multimedia applications from the computer's main CPU/bus on to a front end *multimedia enhancement unit*. Examples of such units are the Pandora Box (Hopper 1990) and the Multimedia Network Interface (Blair et al. 1993) developed at Cambridge and Lancaster Universities respectively. These units are placed between the host computer and the network and directly generate and consume all continuous media streams coming from/arriving at the host. All multimedia peripherals supported by the host (e.g. video frame buffer, camera, audio hardware) are directly connected to the network interface so that continuous media data do not need to flow across the system bus. In the enhancement unit approach, the host computer's role is to supervise streams of data rather than directly handling the multimedia streams itself.

More recently, a new approach has been investigated that can be viewed as extending the scope of the ATM network inside the end-system (Hayter & McAuley 1991, Lunn et al. 1994). In this approach, the host computer is configured as a set of nodes (e.g. the main CPU(s), multimedia peripherals and external network interface) connected by an internal ATM switch; the various nodes then communicate with each other and with the outside world using ATM cells. This approach offers an elegant integration of network and end-system architectures but has the disadvantage that it is not so easily applied to existing commercial workstations.

There has also recently been some interesting work on network interfaces for mobile computers (Hager et al. 1993). This work has resulted in

41

the development of the MINT router which enables mobile computers to exploit the services offered dynamically by a number of networks and supports seamless transition between network types (in particular between mobile and fixed networks).

3.3.2 Compression technology

An introduction to compression
As already discussed, multimedia systems impose considerable demands on the underlying communications and storage subsystems. This is particularly true for video: without compression, full motion video (24 frames per second, 800 pixels x 600 pixels, 256 colours per pixel) requires a transfer rate of 90 Mbits per second and would require over 600 Mbytes of storage for each minute of the film. This would make the storage and transfer of digitized video infeasible for the majority of applications. The objective of compression is therefore to reduce the quantity of data by removing *redundancy*. The success of this process can be measured by the *compression ratio* achieved.

Note that we focus the discussion below on compression techniques for image and video. A number of techniques have also been reported for audio, e.g. Pulse Code Modulation (PCM), non-linear PCM, adaptive PCM and differential PCM. Such techniques have provided the basis for a number of commercially available audio codecs. The interested reader is referred to Tanenbaum (1989) for more information.

Existing compression techniques exhibit a range of characteristics. The key differences are highlighted below:

(a) *Lossy vs lossless schemes* Compression techniques are either lossy or lossless depending on whether information is fully recovered on decompression. Lossless techniques are essential for a number of media types such as text. However, continuous media types such as audio and video can normally tolerate the loss of information, particularly if they are being presented live to the user. Obviously, the degree of loss has to be carefully controlled.

(b) *Symmetrical vs asymmmetrical schemes* In symmetrical techniques, the same algorithm is used both to compress and (in reverse) decompress the information. In contrast, asymmetrical schemes employ different algorithms for the two phases. It is generally true that asymmetrical techniques offer higher compression ratios.

(c) *Real-time or non-real-time processing* Compression algorithms are often extremely complex. One important issue is therefore whether the algorithms can compress and decompress in real-time. This is affected by whether the technique is symmetrical or asymmmetrical. Symmetrical techniques take the same amount of (real-) time to compress and decompress data (assuming the same hardware performance).

However, asymmetrical techniques are often designed to take far more time in compression than in decompression to allow for the real-time decompression and presentation of data. In both cases, specific hardware is often provided to enable real-time processing of data.

Compression principles

The two simplest compression techniques for video are *spatial* and *temporal* compression, where the number of pixel elements forming the image are reduced (creating a more coarse grained image) and where the number of frames per second are reduced, respectively. Although simplistic, both these techniques can give acceptable results in quite a wide range of application areas, and also have the advantage of being achievable in software on reasonably powerful workstations.

More generally, currently available compression techniques can be categorized as either intra-frame or inter-frame. These are discussed in turn below.

- *Intra-frame coding* Intra-frame coding techniques rely on the relationship that often exists between neighbouring pixels in an image. It is often possible to remove redundancy by detecting repetition of patterns across the image. This class of coding includes run-length encoding where adjacent pixels of similar colour are coded as a colour and run-length pair, the run-length giving the number of adjacent pixels of the specified colour. Run-length encoding is particularly suited to computer generated images where the variation in colour tends to be restricted. The best results are achieved by the matrix transformation techniques where the distribution of colour and luminance within the image are analyzed in order to produce a more intelligent removal of information from the image. Many of these transformations are based around fast Fourier or discrete cosine transformations of the image, possibly coupled with other compression algorithms or statistical coding; this achieves the best compression factor with the minimum perceivable loss in image quality. A relatively new approach to intra-frame compression has been the use of fractal techniques to achieve vast compression ratios. A problem with this approach is the speed at which this compression is able to transform the data, as an immense amount of processing may be needed to obtain the best results.

- *Inter-frame coding* Inter-frame coding allows a reduction in the volume of data forming a single video frame, but a better solution to the more general problem of reducing the quantity of data forming a complete video sequence can often be found by analyzing the differences between a number of successive frames. This class of inter-frame coding has had a dramatic impact on video-conferencing due to the fairly small movements found around the "conference table". In this situation, only very small amounts of data are required to transmit the differences between frames; therefore, a video picture can be transmitted over a basic rate ISDN consisting of just two 64 Kbits/s channels. The problem is, of course, that a large amount of movement, such as a person standing up, can lead to the image being broken up for a considerable time while the appropriate section of the frame store is transmitted in its entirety. Inter-frame coding techniques also introduce variable bit rate data streams (VBR) as opposed to constant bit rate data streams (CBR).

Note that it is also possible to have compression techniques that employ a combination of intra- and inter-frame codings (as seen below).

Compression techniques and standards

The three most important compression techniques for image and video are JPEG, MPEG and H.261:

- *JPEG*   JPEG (Joint Photographic Experts Group) is a collaboration between ISO and CCITT that resulted in the publication of the JPEG standard for image information in 1991. As JPEG is designed for still images, it employs an intra-frame compression technique. The technique can also be used for video by applying the compression algorithm on successive frames (Motion JPEG). The compression ratio for both images and video is up to 70:1. JPEG is a symmetrical compression technique. It also has the attractive feature that the degree of loss can be traded off against the compression ratio achieved.

- *MPEG*   MPEG (Motion Pictures Experts Group) has developed a compression standard within ISO specifically designed for the compression of video and its associated audio track. MPEG-I was standardized in 1992 and uses both intra- and inter-frame techniques. It is designed specifically for data streams of 1.5 Mbits per second (intended to support data from a CD ROM device) and can achieve compression ratios of up to 200:1. MPEG-II is also currently under development. This is designed for the high quality coding of either standard or High Definition Television (HDTV) and is targeted towards high performance networks such as ATM. MPEG-II also offers a compression ratio of up to 200:1. Both techniques are asymmetrical and (as with JPEG) allow the degree of loss to be controlled.

- *H.261*   The H.261 standard, or px64, was adopted by CCITT in 1990. It is designed specifically for videophones and videoconferencing over digital networks offering between 64 Kbits to 2 Mbits per second. It uses both intra- and inter-frame coding techniques to achieve compression ratios sufficient to map to ISDN networks offering px64 Kbits/s channels, where $p = 1, 2, \ldots, 30$ (hence the alternate name). This technique is also asymmetrical. To enable interoperability across different networks, the standard also specifies an intermediate video format known as the Common Intermediate Format or CIF, with

Table 3.2 Characteristics of the major compression techniques.

Standard	Standardization	Symmetry	Coding	Compression ratio
JPEG	ISO/CCITT, 1990	symmetrical	intra-frame	<70:1
MPEG-I	ISO, 1992	asymmetrical	intra- and inter-frame	<200:1
MPEG-II	ISO Work item	asymmetrical	intra- and inter-frame	<200:1
H.261	CCITT, 1990	asymmetrical	intra- and inter-frame	100:1-2000:1

352x288 pixels per frame and 30 frames per second. A special inter-mediate format for videophones has also been specified as Quarter CIF (QCIF) that offers a lower quality and frame rate.

The characteristics of the various compression standards are summarized in Table 3.2. There are also a number of proprietary compression techniques such as Intel's Digital Video Interactive (DVI) or Apple's RPZ-RPZ used with their QuickTime software. An excellent and comprehensive discussion on compression technologies can be found in Steinmetz (1994).

3.3.3 The storage subsystem

Storage technologies

The data-intensive nature of media types such as digital video and audio imposes two stringent requirements on the technology required to store them persistently:

(a) *large volumes* of storage capacity must be available to accommodate data of such media types even when stored in compressed form, and

(b) the storage technology must be capable of providing sufficient *data transfer bandwidth* to support the real-time retrieval of multimedia data.

A number of possible storage media are available for use in multimedia systems. We focus our discussion on digital solutions as they provide more general and flexible solutions for the future.

Digital storage techniques can be divided into three categories, namely *magnetic, optical* and *magneto-optical*. Current magnetic hard disk drives are capable of delivering transfer rates in excess of 1 Mbyte/sec and have capacities in the region of several hundreds of Mbytes. They also have the big advantage that they provide random read–write access. They are therefore suitable for the storage of a wide variety of media types including audio. However, they are unable to provide the required storage capacity or data transfer bandwidth for high-cost media types, especially in environments where multiple applications compete for resources. For example, in the extreme case, an otherwise empty 600 Mbyte magnetic disk could provide storage for approximately 20 seconds of uncompressed, full motion colour video, and will take up to 16 minutes to retrieve the information. Compression can ease this problem; however, limitations on storage capacity still remain. For this reason, a number of manufacturers have recently developed RAID technology (Redundant Arrays of Inexpensive Disks) (Chen et al. 1994). With this technology, storage is provided by an array of hundreds or possibly thousands of magnetic disk drives capable of parallel operation. This new technology can, in theory, provide storage capacities of up to 1 Tbyte and bandwidths of up to 100 Mbytes/sec.

Storage devices based on optical technology offer low-cost mass storage and provide what is presently considered to be reasonable data transfer bandwidth. They also have the advantage that, unlike magnetic solutions, the quality of information does not degrade over time. A number of commercial solutions based on optical technology are now available. The most notable of these are Digital Video Interactive (DVI), Compact Disc-Interactive (CD-I), CD-Read Only Memory (CD-ROM) and its successor CD-ROM XA that all offer full multimedia capabilities including video playback. Optical jukeboxes have also recently been introduced offering very large capacities by having racks of optical discs available for selection and playback. However, there remain two fundamental problems with current optical devices. First, optical disks are predominantly read-only or write-once-read-many (WORM) devices. Secondly, although high data transfer rates can be obtained, seek times are high. This stems from the nature of optical disk drives. In general, a single laser is used to read the disk and this is moved to and fro across the disk. The laser apparatus and the supporting hardware are necessarily large and it is the movement of this arrangement across the disk that limits the seek times. To remedy this problem, emerging optical disk players use a system of mirrors which allow tracks adjacent to the head to be read without moving the head. This provides rapid access to data stored in adjacent tracks.

In order to overcome the problems of optical storage, new discs have been developed using a combination of magnetic and optical techniques. The result is a rewritable mass storage technology, referred to as magneto-optical discs. Such devices offer capacities of between 500 Mbytes and 5000 Mbytes and have the advantage that they can be read to and written from freely. The range of storage technology for multimedia is summarized in Table 3.3.

One interesting new development is the emergence of storage hierarchies. Such systems are motivated by the requirements of large scale, large capacity video-on-demand systems. Such systems provide a hierarchy of storage servers, for example a large capacity, on-line film archive, a more regional cache of the most popular films and local storage capacity to store portions of the currently accessed film. The advantage of such a scheme is that the most appropriate storage technology can be used for each level of the hierarchy. It is anticipated that storage hierarchies can meet the demand of realistic commercial video-on-demand services with large numbers of films and in the order of one million subscribers.

Table 3.3 An overview of current digital storage technologies

Technology	Technique	Attributes	Bandwidth (Mbytes/s)	Capacity (Mbytes)
Magnetic disks	magnetic	read/write	1.0–5.0	100–4000
RAID	magnetic	read/write	100	1 000 000
CD ROM	optical	read only	0.15–0.6	650
CD ROM/XA	optical	read only	0.15–0.6	650
WORM	optical	write once read many	0.15–0.6	10 000
MO	magneto-optical	read/write	0.2–0.2	500–5 000
Jukeboxes	optical	read	0.1–0.6	10x650

File handling techniques
The development of new file handling techniques is now becoming recognized as an additional means of helping to overcome the data transfer bottleneck presented by existing storage systems. It is now recognized that existing file systems are not suited to continuous media data transfer. The main problem is lack of throughput. For example, most UNIX file systems can deliver only a very few continuous media streams simultaneously. However, bandwidth is not the only problem; the deterministic requirements of continuous media are also not well served by existing technology. For example, conventional disk caching strategies do not work well with continuous media files as they are optimized for access to data that exhibit temporal locality. In contrast, access to continuous media data is normally sequential. Most of the work in continuous media storage servers has concentrated on disk layout and disk head scheduling. The aim is to optimize the layout of continuous media data on the disk to minimize disk head movements. Examples of research in this area are the Video-on-Demand service designed at the University of California at San Diego (Vin & Rangan 1993), the Continuous Media File System developed at the University of California at Berkeley (Anderson et al. 1992), and the Lancaster Continuous Media Storage Server (Lougher & Shepherd 1993). In addition, the latter two systems use the technique of *disk striping* whereby successive segments of a continuous media stream are stored on separate discs arranged in an array. This technique enables n discs to provide a throughput approaching n times that of a single disc. Note, however, that these techniques have so far failed to produce fully *scaleable* solutions for the simultaneous retrieval of large numbers of continuous media streams.

Further improvements are also possible. For example, Ousterhout & Douglis (1989) have reported that seek times account for a considerable percentage of the total time taken to retrieve a given data item from disk and that any reduction in the seek time will lead to a significant reduction in the overall data transfer delay. It is worth noting that this observation becomes particularly relevant when one recalls the poor seek times of current optical storage technology. They then propose a new approach to reducing seek times through the use of *log-structured files*, a technique that makes use of large cache stores to practically eliminate reads from the disk and allow writes simply to be appended to a log for recovery purposes. During the operation of a log-structured file system, the head is rarely moved and hence the seek time is generally close to zero.

Although most of this work is research-oriented, a number of multimedia storage servers have been released commercially. For example, Hewlett Packard have announced a multimedia storage server capable of supporting a substantial number of simultaneous audio and video streams.

3.3.4   The communications subsystem

A number of experiments have been carried out in using existing communications protocols for multimedia. For example, the Multicast Backbone (or MBONE) is now in regular use by a large number of users of the Internet (Eriksson 1994). MBONE provides a multicasting service to subscribers including both audio and video channels. A number of applications have also been developed, including *ivs* (INRIA videoconferencing system) and *nv* (network video). MBONE uses existing Internet protocols, in particular UDP and IP. Note that many of the applications rely on a layer of software known as RTP (Real-Time Protocol) for real-time data such as continuous media.

A number of researchers argue that the present generation of communications protocols, i.e. the OSI protocols and the US Internet protocol family, are not suitable for the new environment of high speed networks and more demanding applications (Shepherd & Salmony 1990). Consequently, there has been considerable research and development activity directed towards the development of communication architectures for multimedia systems. Early work addressed the provision of new transport services designed to operate over high speed networks, e.g. XTP (Chesson 1988) and NetBlt (Clark et al. 1987). Such protocols are often referred to as "rate based" because of their reliance on clock driven rather than window-based flow control. XTP in particular has attracted considerable commercial interest .

More recently, a number of protocols have emerged that are designed specifically to meet the needs of continuous media, e.g. TPX (Baguette 1992) and HeiTS (Hehmann et al. 1992). In addition, a new version of XTP (XTPX) has recently been developed by the Technical University of Berlin (Miloucheva et al. 1993). These protocols are generally configurable in terms of quality of service specification for use by a range of different media types.

Other significant work on QoS provision at the transport layer has come from the Tenet Group at the University of California at Berkeley. This group has developed a family of protocols (Wolfinger & Moran 1992) that run over an experimental wide area ATM network known as Aurora (Clark et al. 1991). The protocol family includes the Real-Time Internet Protocol (RTIP), the Continuous Media Transport Protocol (CMTP) and the Real-time Channel Administration Protocol (RCAP). The latter provides generic connection establishment, resource reservation, and signalling functions for the rest of the protocol family. CMTP is explicitly designed for continuous media support. It is a lightweight protocol that runs on top of RTIP and provides sequenced and periodic delivery of continuous media samples with QoS control over throughput, delays and error bounds. Notification of all undelivered and/or corrupted data can optionally be provided to the client. The client interface to CMTP includes facilities to specify traffic characteristics in terms of burstiness (useful for variable bit rate encoding techniques) and workahead (which allows the protocol to deliver faster than the nominal rate if data is available). CMTP also permits dynamic QoS renegotiation by sending a special *on* transport protocol data unit that contains the new QoS parameters at the start of a new stream, and an *off* transport protocol data unit to signal the onset of a silent period.

The technique of *orchestration* has also been proposed to support continuous synchronization in the communication architecture (Campbell et al. 1992). Finally, a number of widely agreed implementation principles are beginning to emerge, including the minimization of data copying and the avoidance of multiplexing (Tennenhouse 1990).

It is interesting to note that ISO have recently set up a new work item on Enhanced Communication Functions and Facilities (ECFF), which will address, amongst other things, multimedia services over high speed networks.

3.3.5   Operating system support

In terms of multimedia, the most important requirement at the operating system level is to provide predictable real-time behaviour for the processing of a range of media types. Unfortunately, popular workstation operating systems such as UNIX are not able to provide such predictable performance because of their essentially non-deterministic nature (Nieh et al. 1994). For example, a UNIX process attempting to meet a particular real-time deadline can be blocked for arbitrary lengths of time in functions such as I/O operations, system calls or page faults. Most of the research on operating systems is attempting to extend UNIX-like systems to meet the demands of multimedia. Two main approaches can be identified:
 (a) modifying existing UNIX implementations, or
 (b) completely re-implementing UNIX.

In the first approach, alterations are made to the existing UNIX kernel to provide more predictable behaviour. For example, work is currently underway at Sun MicroSystems in this area. The position adopted by SUN is that today's workstations have ample CPU power but their weaknesses lie in inappropriate resource management. Their proposal is for *time driven resource management* (Hanko et al. 1992), which allows applications to signal their likely forthcoming resource requirements in terms of parameters such as quantity, deadline and priority. The system will not attempt to guarantee performance, but will instead bias available resources in the requested directions and concentrate on graceful degradation of service, optionally accompanied by notification of degradation to the affected process. It is argued that this is an appropriate strategy in general purpose, multiprogrammed workstations.

The second approach is to preserve the standard UNIX interface, but re-implement the traditional kernel structures in terms of the *micro-kernel* model. Examples of micro-kernels capable of supporting UNIX interfaces are Chorus (Bricker et al. 1991), Mach (Accetta et al. 1986) and Amoeba (Tanenbaum et al. 1988). Work is being carried out at Lancaster University using Chorus as the basis of a distributed system with end-to-end continuous media support (Coulson et al. 1994). In addition, work has been carried out in a Mach environment to provide processor scheduling more appropriate to continuous media (Govindan & Anderson 1991). Finally, work has been undertaken at CWI, Amsterdam to support continuous media in an Amoeba based UNIX environment. The approach is to use co-processor based intelligent device controllers and to give applications controlled direct access to physical devices (Bulterman & van Liere 1992).

There have also been significant developments in specific operating system components, especially in the area of scheduling. It is now recognized that currently used scheduling policies, primarily priority based algorithms, are too static and coarse grained to support multiple continuous media sessions in a dynamic environment. A prevalent view is that *earliest deadline first* scheduling (Liu & Layland 1973) is the appropriate approach (Coulson et al. 1994). This is particularly true for continuous media support as each information unit in a continuous media stream has an implicit deadline; hence, it is natural to schedule the processes handling these units on the basis of such deadlines. Recent research has proposed the use of *split level scheduling* for the processing of continuous media (Govindan & Anderson 1991). In such schemes, the application programmer is presented with the abstraction of multiple user level threads of control (or simply threads) in a single address space (the use of user level threads has the advantage of minimizing context switches in a concurrent application). Responsibility for the scheduling of user level threads is split between a user level scheduler and a kernel level scheduler. The two schedulers communicate, through an area of shared memory, to ensure that globally appropriate scheduling decisions are made.

3.4   Integrative standards and technologies

Heterogeneity is one of the dominant characteristics of multimedia environments (see Ch. 1). For example, it is likely that networking infrastructures will be heterogeneous, consisting of a variety of different local, metropolitan and wide area technologies. Similarly, end systems are likely to be heterogeneous in terms of both the workstation architecture and the operating system. Hence, in order to develop multimedia applications, it is necessary to have standards and technologies that enable inter-working across such heterogeneous platforms and enable services to be accessed in a platform-independent manner.

A number of distributed platforms have been developed for this purpose, masking out details of underlying hardware architectures, communications architectures and systems implementations. Examples of such systems include CORBA (The Object Management Group 1991), ANSAware (APM 1993) and DCE (The Open Software Foundation 1992). International activity is also developing standards for Open Distributed Processing (ODP) (ISO/ITU-T X.901–4 1995).

There is a general consensus that distributed systems platforms should offer an object-based environment where applications consist of a set of interacting objects. Object interaction is provided by an invocation mechanism that hides the location of objects from the programmer. Facilities are also provided to locate and manage objects in the distributed environment.

There is a clear need for such distributed systems platforms to support multimedia applications. However, most of the existing technologies were developed before the emergence of distributed multimedia computing. A number of projects have therefore looked at extending such platforms with multimedia facilities. Previous research at Lancaster developed extensions to the ANSAware architecture to support multimedia (Coulson et al. 1992). The extensions include:

(a) the introduction of a stream abstraction to allow users to interface QoS controlled transport services,

(b) the addition of quality of service annotations on object interfaces, and

(c) the introduction of synchronization managers to implement real-time synchronization constraints.

Similar work on extending ANSAware has been carried out by APM Ltd., Cambridge (Nicolaou 1991), by the University of Kent at Canterbury (Pinto & Linington 1994) and by France Telecom's CNET (Stefani 1993).

From these activities, proposals have emerged for extensions to ODP to meet the requirements of multimedia (Coulson et al. 1995). These extensions are now largely included in the standard providing a framework for the development of open technologies to support the development of multimedia applications.

There has also been considerable work in the telecommunications community in providing platforms for the development of multimedia applications. Researchers at Bellcore have built a number of interactive distributed multimedia applications (e.g. Cruiser (Fish 1989) and Rendezvous (Patterson & Hill 1990)). Cruiser, for example, allows users to browse along a "virtual corridor" in an office building and visit office occupants who leave their virtual door open. This results in an audiovisual conference connection being made between the browser and the occupant. The initial implementation of these applications was built directly on to the operating system and external hardware. This was later realized to be limiting from the point of view of extensibility and wider applicability, and therefore a generic platform architecture known as the Touring Machine (Bates & Segal 1990) was designed. The Touring Machine architecture consists of *station objects*, which encapsulate all the multimedia sources and sinks at a single multimedia workstation, and *call objects*, which represent a particular connection topology between stations. This architecture has been heavily influenced by the telecommunications background in which it was developed. In particular, a careful separation is maintained between resources owned by the network provider (call object) and resources owned by the customer (station object). This is a significant consideration in a wide area networking environment due to the necessity of tariffing structures and divisions of responsibility (Ruston et al. 1992).

Work in this area is now continuing in the TINA Project (Telecommunications Information Networking Architecture) (Leopold et al. 1994). TINA is a collaborative project to define a standard framework for telecommunications networking in the context of new multi-service networks, multimedia and real-time applications, telecommunications services and ISO standards. Telecommunications companies throughout Europe and the USA are represented. Support for multimedia services is one of the key concerns in this work. It is interesting to note that the TINA consortium has adopted many of the ideas from ODP in their work.

3.5   User interfaces

Most modern workstations or PCs provide a graphical user interface featuring windows, icons, menus and pointers (WIMP interfaces). With the advent of multimedia, these interfaces are now being extended with support for additional media types such as audio and video. For example, video windows are now supported on the Apple Macintosh, PCs with MS Windows and UNIX machines running X-Windows. This is normally achieved through the use of a specialized video card. Such cards communicate with the windowing system and direct the video output to the appropriate region of the screen. More sophisticated changes are also being made to X-Windows to support general multimedia interfaces. In addition, Macintosh have released Quicktime which is designed to provide general support for the co-ordination of multimedia user interfaces.

Hypermedia has proved to be a particularly attractive user interface for multimedia information systems. In hypermedia, information is structured as nodes and links. Nodes represent the basic components in the information model and could be a piece of text, a segment of sound, a video clip or an animation. Links represent relations between components and allow the user to browse freely through the information base. Research in hypermedia is now entering a period of consolidation with the development of the Dexter Hypertext Model; this model represents a technical consensus on the state of the art in hypertext and is intended to "provide a principled basis for comparing systems as well as for developing interchange and interoperability standards" (Halasz & Schwartz 1994). This latter aspect is particularly important for distributed systems. Proposals have also been made to extend the Dexter Hypertext Model towards generalized hypermedia structures featuring the full range of media types.

There is also considerable interest in developing hypermedia systems in networked environments (Leggett & Schnase 1994). The most notable development in this respect is the success of the World-Wide Web information service (Berners-Lee et al. 1994) on the Internet. In the standards arena, the Multimedia and Hypermedia information coding Expert Group (MHEG) has been established by ISO to produce appropriate standards for the representation of audio and moving image, for multimedia synchronization, for hypermedia navigation, and for reusability and interoperability within and between applications.

Finally, there has been considerable research on cognitive aspects of multimedia and multi-modal user interfaces. This research addresses issues such as user perception of different media types and criteria for the design of multimedia user interfaces. This work is beyond the scope of this book; the interested reader is referred to the literature for further discussion of these issues (Blattner & Dannenberg 1992, Blattner 1994).

3.6   Summary

This chapter has discussed the key technologies required to support distributed multimedia applications. The following key technologies were identified and discussed:
- high performance multi-service networks and network interfaces
- multi-service mobile networks
- multimedia workstations
- compression technology for both audio and video
- storage technology and file handling techniques

- communications protocols
- new operating system techniques to support the processing of multi-media data
- integrative standards and technologies
- multimedia user interfaces

Having looked in some detail at distributed multimedia computing in this chapter and the previous chapter, we now consider the potential impact of the area on formal specification techniques.

CHAPTER 4

Detailed requirements

4.1   Introduction

This chapter presents a detailed requirements analysis for the formal specification of distributed multimedia systems. The chapter is structured as follows. Section 4.2 examines the fundamental characteristics of distributed multimedia systems. This is followed, in Section 4.3, with an examination of the requirements for the specification of distributed multimedia systems (extracted from the previously identified characteristics). Section 4.4 then introduces some typical scenarios found in distributed multimedia systems; these scenarios are selected to illustrate the particular requirements of distributed multimedia systems and will provide the basis for examples later in the book. Finally, Section 4.5 summarizes the results of the requirements analysis and comments on the state of the art in the formal specification of distributed multimedia systems.

4.2   Characteristics of distributed multimedia systems

4.2.1   Characteristics of distributed systems

There are a number of features that characterize distributed systems. First, distributed systems are inherently *concurrent* since distributed nodes generally run autonomously in parallel. A second characteristic is that, since interaction will occur between different nodes, distributed systems must provide some form of *communication* between these nodes (for example, through synchronous/asynchronous message passing or broadcast communication). This interaction will typically be *unpredictable*, since messages between nodes may be lost (or corrupted) during transmission and the exact time taken for the transmission of messages can rarely be guaranteed.

Another important consideration for distributed systems is that components of such systems should be *open* and *inter-operable*, i.e. it must be possible for components implemented by different manufacturers to be connected and to inter-work. In order to achieve this, it is necessary to comply to standards for distributed systems. In this book, we are interested in compliance to ODP standardization. As mentioned in Chapter 1, the concept of *viewpoints* is central to ODP. Viewpoints address the breadth and complexity of distributed systems by offering different perspectives on a distributed system development. We are particularly concerned with the Computational and Engineering Viewpoints (i.e. the viewpoints which focus on the concurrent and distributed nature of the system).

Object-based paradigms (Blair et al. 1991) have been employed within ODP to describe distributed systems. In such approaches, systems are described in terms of objects that abstract over lower level implementation issues, in particular, distribution. Consequently, object-based paradigms can be used to provide a uniform platform for the application user and to mask out the underlying implementation details and to hide heterogeneity.

Finally, a further characteristic of distributed systems is that they are typically *dynamically reconfigurable*, e.g. objects within a system may be created dynamically and may also alter their communication paths dynamically. Dynamic reconfiguration is crucial in modern distributed systems to support evolution and fault tolerance. In terms of evolution, new services can be introduced or existing services upgraded. In terms of fault tolerance, the system can react to a failure by providing a backup service.

4.2.2   Adding multimedia to distributed systems

Supporting continuous media

The most fundamental characteristic of multimedia systems is that they incorporate continuous media such as voice, video and animated graphics. The use of such media in distributed systems implies the need for *continuous data transfers* over relatively long periods of time, e.g. playout of video from a remote surveillance camera. Furthermore, the timeliness of such media transmissions must be maintained as an ongoing commitment for the duration of the continuous media presentation.

A further problem arising from the consideration of continuous media is that traditional forms of interaction, such as synchronous or asynchronous communication (see Appendix A) or remote procedure calls, are inadequate to model the concept of the required ongoing transmission of data. Consequently, new communication models must be developed for multimedia systems employing continuous media types. The term *streams* is now widely used to refer to the mechanisms for supporting continuous media transmissions (Coulson et al. 1992). In ODP, the term *flow* is used for an individual continuous media channel; the term stream is then used for a potentially composite continuous media communication involving one or more flows (ISO/ITU-T X.903 1995).

Continuous media also imposes additional requirements on distributed systems in terms of quality of service and real-time synchronization as discussed below.

Quality of service
The second requirement of distributed multimedia applications (in common with other real-time and safety critical applications) is the need for sophisticated support for *quality of service* (QoS). Quality of service embraces all the non-functional properties of the system (see Appendix A for clarification of terminology). Such quality of service support applies both to continuous media communications and also to discrete modes of interaction including message passing and remote procedure calls.

A number of different *categories* of quality of service can be identified including reliability, timeliness and volume. Within each category, it is also possible to isolate individual *dimensions* along which the quality of service can be quantified and measured. For example, the reliability category could contain system-related dimensions such as mean time between failure (MTBF) or mean time to repair (MTTR). Another reliability category relating more particularly to the field of multimedia and real-time distributed systems may contain dimensions relating to, for example, the permitted percentage of loss of media frames in a flow or the permitted bit error rate in ATM cells.

In distributed multimedia systems, the timeliness category would contain dimensions relating to the end-to-end delay of either messages or continuous media packets. Examples of such dimensions are *latency*, measured in milliseconds and defined as the time taken from the generation of a media frame to its eventual display, and *jitter*, also measured in milliseconds and defined as the variation in latency suffered by packets in the same stream. The volume category would then contain dimensions that refer to the throughput of data. At the user level, an appropriate QoS dimension may be video frames delivered per second. Alternatively, at the ATM layer, a typical volume QoS dimension would quantify throughput in terms of *peak-rate* throughput and *statistical* throughput measured in cells per second. These examples illustrate that certain dimensions are often only applicable at certain system layers and imply that a complete category should contain dimensions for each system layer involved in the support of that category.

The list of dimensions and categories given above is summarized in Table 4.1. Note however that this list is far from exhaustive. Other categories worthy of mention are *criticality*, which relates to the assignment of relative priority levels between activities, *quality of perception*, which is

Table 4.1 Example categories and dimensions

Categories of QoS	Example dimensions
Reliability	Mean time between failure
	Mean time to repair
	Percentage loss of frames
	Bit error rate in ATM cells
Timeliness	End-to-end latency of frames
	Permitted jitter on latency
Volume	Perceived throughput in frames per second
	Peak rate throughput in cells per second

concerned with dimensions such as screen resolution or sound quality, and *logical time* which is concerned with the degree to which all nodes in a distributed system see the same events in an identical order. *Cost* is another important category. This may contain dimensions such as the rental cost of a network link per month, the cost of transmitting a single media frame in a flow, or the cost of a multiparty, multimedia conference call.

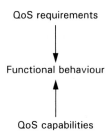

Figure 4.1 Requirements and capabilities.

Quality of service embraces both requirements and capabilities (see Fig. 4.1). Broadly speaking, in quality of service architectures, QoS requirements flow downwards from the user and QoS capabilities flow upwards from the supporting infrastructure. QoS requirements express the non-functional constraints demanded by the user, while QoS capabilities state the timing constraints enforced by the infrastructure, i.e. the performance the infrastructure is capable of providing. QoS capabilities are associated with service offers and a process of negotiation is undertaken in order to reconcile the clients QoS requirements with the service capabilities.

In multimedia systems, quality of service requirements can vary considerably between the different media types. For example, video connections require consistently high throughput, but can tolerate reasonable levels of jitter and bit or packet errors. In contrast, audio does not require such high bandwidth, but places tight restrictions on jitter and error rates. A summary of media types and typical quality of service requirements is given in Table 4.2 (taken from Hehmann et al. 1990).

Table 4.2 Typical quality of service requirements.

QoS	Maximum delay (s)	Maximum jitter (ms)	Average (Mbit/s)	Acceptable bit throughput error rate	Acceptable packet error rate
Voice	0.25	10	0.064	$<10^{-3}$	$<10^{-4}$
Video (TV quality)	0.25	100	100	10^{-2}	10^{-3}
Compressed video	0.25	100	2–10	10^{-6}	10^{-9}
Data (file transfer)	1	—	2–100	0	0
Real time data	0.001–1	—	<10	0	0
Image	1	—	2–10	10^{-4}	10^{-9}

Quality of service management encompasses a number of *different functions* including static aspects such as quality of service specification, negotiation, resource allocation and admission control, and more dynamic aspects such as quality of service monitoring and re-negotiation. Furthermore, this management will be required at a number of *different levels* of the system (e.g. network, transport and operating system) with appropriate mappings between the various layers. At the highest level, quality of service should be more user-oriented and declarative (e.g. a HDTV display) whereas, at lower levels, the descriptions are more system-oriented and prescriptive (e.g. 10 ms maximum delay). Finally, it is important to stress that, in distributed systems, quality of service should be end-to-end from the information source to the information sink. In order to achieve this, co-ordination is necessary between the end system and the network infrastructure.

Further discussion on quality of service management in distributed systems can be found in Hutchison et al. (1994).

Real-time synchronization

One of the key characteristics of distributed multimedia applications is the need to maintain, often complex, *real-time synchronization* constraints. Consensus has still not been reached on the precise nature of mechanisms to meet such constraints. In our view, though, the following requirements must be addressed:

(a) *Intra- and inter-media synchronization*   Various styles of real-time synchronization must be supported covering both *intra-* and *inter-media* synchronization (Little & Ghafoor 1990). Intra-media synchronization refers to the maintenance of real-time constraints across a continuous media stream. For example, intra-media synchronization would be required to ensure that both audio and video are presented with the required throughput, jitter and latency characteristics. This corresponds directly to quality of service requirements for continuous media as discussed above. In contrast, inter-media synchronization refers to the maintenance of real-time constraints across more than one media type. Examples of inter-media synchronization include

59

lip-synchronization between an audio and a video channel, synchronization of stereo audio channels and synchronization of text subtitles and video sequences. Note that the first two inter-media examples refer to constraints between continuous media types; the third example illustrates inter-media synchronization between a continuous media type and a discrete type.

(b) *The impact of distribution*   It is important to stress that synchronization mechanisms must operate correctly in a distributed environment, potentially involving both local and wide area networks. This adds considerably to the complexity of providing such mechanisms. For example, it is necessary to ensure that intra-media synchronization is maintained between the producer and consumer of the media type when they are on different nodes. Similarly, in inter-media synchronization, real-time constraints must be met even when producers are on different nodes, e.g. audio and video transmitted from separate storage servers. Finally, some applications demand that media presentations are synchronized even though each of many producers and each of many consumers are all on different nodes, e.g. a co-ordinated multimedia presentation across multiple nodes.

(c) *Varying levels of commitment*   As discussed in Chapter 1, multimedia is often viewed as being "soft" real-time, i.e. there is no need for absolute guarantees on real-time performance. However, this is only partially true. Many multimedia applications can be satisfied by soft guarantees. However, other multimedia applications require more rigid guarantees, for example in safety critical areas such as medical or scientific systems. We therefore feel that there is a requirement to offer varying levels of commitment over meeting real-time constraints (Ferrari et al. 1993). In particular, the following levels are required: *best effort* (where the system attempts to provide the required quality of service) and *guaranteed* (where the system pre-allocates resources to ensure that real-time constraints are met).

(d) *The requirement for a dynamic approach*   It is required that the specification of real-time synchronization can be altered at run-time. There are two reasons for this. First, multimedia applications are typically interactive and hence the precise real-time requirements cannot be predicted in advance. Secondly, the quality of service offered by the network and underlying systems software may change, for example due to temporary overloading. For both these reasons, static schemes, such as those based on pre-allocated timestamps on media objects (e.g. Little & Ghafoor 1991), are problematical. For a fully general solution, it is necessary to provide a general purpose *language* to enable arbitrary synchronization policies to be specified.

In summary, distributed multimedia applications require mechanisms to enable the expression of arbitrary intra- and inter-media real-time synchronization constraints. The supporting infrastructure must then provide the required level of service in the distributed environment.

4.2.3 Summary

The above discussion has highlighted some of the characteristics of distributed multimedia systems. Briefly, distributed systems are *concurrent* systems which must provide some form of *communication* between distributed nodes (this communication typically exhibits *unpredictable* behaviour); they should be *interoperable* (hence the importance of ODP standardization activities) and are typically *dynamically reconfigurable*. Additionally, because of the complexity and diversity of distributed systems, a number of different views of a system exist (reflected by the ODP *viewpoints*), each intended for a different class of application user. Finally, *object-based paradigms* have been widely used to model distributed systems.

It is the integration of *continuous media* (e.g. voice and video) which provides the most fundamental distinction between multimedia systems and traditional systems. Importantly, the transfer of continuous media requires a *sustained* level of support from the underlying system. Data must be delivered and presented according to certain *real-time constraints* that represent an *ongoing commitment* for the duration of the continuous media presentation. *Quality of service* (QoS) *requirements*, such as throughput and jitter, can be identified which describe the standard of media transmission to be maintained in a system; similarly, the *QoS capabilities* of the underlying infrastructure must be modelled. Finally, mechanisms that allow *real-time synchronization* must be provided in distributed multimedia systems; this is necessary to permit the temporal integrity of media transmissions to be maintained (e.g. to maintain lip-synchronization between an audio and video data transmission).

4.3 Requirements imposed on formal specification techniques

We now consider requirements imposed by distributed multimedia computing on formal specification techniques. A number of requirements can be derived directly from the characteristics of distributed multimedia systems that we have discussed above. Section 4.3.2 considers the requirements for the specification of distributed systems. Additional requirements imposed by the integration of multimedia into such systems are then considered in Section 4.3.3. First, however, some general requirements that we believe should apply to all application domains are discussed (Section 4.3.1). The collected requirements provide a set of criteria against which the suitability of different specification techniques can be judged; these requirements will be returned to at later stages of the book (specifically Chs 8 and 13).

4.3.1   General requirements

An initial requirement, which should be true of any formal specification technique, is that of *usability*, i.e. it should offer sufficient facilities for the complete specification of potentially complex systems. Typical properties that we require formal specification technique to possess are a complete data manipulation component and facilities to enable modularity and compositionality in specification.

In addition, we impose the more subjective requirement that formal techniques are, in some sense, *natural*, i.e. they are a natural vehicle for expressing the class of specifications we are interested in. Naturalness implies that resultant specifications are easy to read and understand.

We also require that techniques avoid *over specification*, i.e. implementation decisions should be postponed and valid implementations should not be excluded. This is an important aspect of formal techniques. For example, such an attribute is clearly important in order to enable standards to be implementation non-specific. Critically, the requirement not to over specify suggests that techniques should support *abstract* specification.

Finally, we require that specifications developed with the techniques can be efficiently analyzed and used. In particular, this requires that viable *validation* techniques must be available (e.g. to validate quality of service requirements) and that efficient implementations can be *synthesized* from specifications.

4.3.2   Specifying distributed systems

In this section, the key characteristics of distributed systems that have been raised above will be considered with respect to the requirements they place on formal specification techniques.

Concurrency

The formal specification technique must be capable of specifying concurrent behaviour. Concurrency is usually achieved in formal specification techniques by mapping concurrent behaviour to sequential behaviour using interleaving semantics (in effect, concurrency is modelled by a choice between different sequential behaviours). However, alternative approaches exist that provide a notion of true concurrency (Manna & Pnueli 1989) (see Appendix A).

Interaction

Most formal specification techniques incorporate one of three primitive means of interaction: synchronous message passing, asynchronous message passing, or broadcast communication. Since communication between nodes of a distributed system is inherently asynchronous, it is essential to be able to model this style of communication in a formal specification technique. Note that asynchronous communication can be simulated in techniques exhibiting synchronous message passing by explicitly modelling a medium/queue.

Additionally, interactions between distributed nodes are typically unpredictable. Consequently, a mechanism should be provided in the formal specification technique to permit the expression of unpredictable behaviour. One way in which unpredictable behaviour can be specified is by offering a non-deterministic choice between different possible behaviours. This approach is particularly attractive as non-determinism can also be used to provide a level of abstraction in a specification and hence can help to avoid the problem of over specification (see below).

Openness and inter-operability

As explained above, standardization is important in achieving openness and inter-operability between distributed systems (or between components of distributed systems). This has two implications for formal specification. First, it is important that formal specification techniques adopted are compatible with distributed systems standards (and, in particular, ODP standards), i.e. formal specification techniques should be able to express the various concepts defined in the standard. Secondly, it is helpful if the formal specification techniques used are themselves standardized. This ensures that specifications are stable. Without standardization, the specification could be rendered obsolete by redefinition of the language. Consequently, in considering techniques for the specification of distributed multimedia systems, special consideration should be given to the standardized formal specification techniques LOTOS, Estelle, SDL and Z (standardization for Z is currently in progress).

An additional, essential requirement is that formal specification techniques should allow systems to be specified in a completely *implementation independent* way. In other words, it should be possible to specify systems abstractly; over prescriptive specification may obstruct the freedom of implementation and may jeopardize the goal of openness in distributed systems.

Object-based paradigms

As mentioned earlier, object-based paradigms are now heavily used in distributed systems. Their use should therefore extend to the specification of distributed systems. A number of object-based and object-oriented[1]

---

1. Object-based techniques support encapsulation and data abstraction. Object-oriented techniques extend this by also featuring the concepts of class and inheritance (Wegner 1987). Distributed systems have a minimal requirement of object-based specification.

extensions to formal specification techniques have been proposed. For example, Clark (1992) and Mayr (1989) present an object-based and an object-oriented LOTOS respectively; Sijelmassi & Gaudette (1989) describe an object-oriented Estelle, and Færgemand & Olsen (1992) describe an extended object-oriented SDL called SDL-92. Object-based techniques such as these should be used, where possible, for the specification of distributed systems.

Dynamic reconfiguration

To model distributed systems, a formal description technique must provide a mechanism for specifying objects that are created dynamically and that change their communication paths dynamically. Very few formal specification techniques directly support full dynamic reconfiguration. For example, event gates in LOTOS, which are often used to model the endpoints of communication channels, must be allocated statically and cannot be passed as parameters or changed dynamically.

ODP Viewpoints

The diverse nature of distributed systems and the existence of different views of the same system imply that a number of formal specification techniques are likely to be necessary, each one particularly suited to the expression of properties of a different viewpoint. However, if different languages are used to specify a system in different viewpoints, consistency must be maintained between the resulting specifications (Bowman et al. 1996a,b). As mentioned earlier, in this book we will particularly emphasize techniques that are suitable for the specification of distributed systems when viewed from the Computational or Engineering Viewpoints.

4.3.3   Specifying multimedia behaviour

The integration of multimedia into distributed systems imposes additional requirements on formal specification techniques. These are discussed below.

Continuous media

The integration of *continuous media* is the most fundamental characteristic of multimedia systems. Consequently, formal specification techniques must provide support for continuous media, i.e. it must be possible to specify concepts such as streams or flows. This data must be delivered and presented according to certain *real-time constraints* that must be maintained for the duration of the continuous media presentation.

Quality of service (QoS)

Quality of service parameters describe the standard of media transmission to be maintained in a system. Since these parameters typically make reference to *real-time constraints*, it must be possible to specify such real-time constraints and verify whether or not these constraints can be met. Additionally, QoS parameters may change through system development. For example, QoS requirements may be refined as the specification evolves. Similarly, it might be necessary to set QoS capabilities experimentally to observe the impact on requirements. Finally, QoS capabilities may change completely if the underlying components (e.g. the network to be used) changes. Hence, it is important that these parameters should be *easily identifiable* in a specification and should be *easy to change*.

As seen previously, quality of service parameters may be probabilistic. The formal specification technique should therefore provide some mechanism for the specification and verification of probabilistic statements.

Real-time synchronization

Finally, formal specification techniques must provide mechanisms that allow *real-time synchronization* to be achieved. Two examples of real-time synchronization have been given, namely intra-media synchronization and inter-media synchronization. To achieve both of these, it must be possible to express real-time constraints over concurrent behaviour and to verify that they can be met.

4.3.4   Summary

A number of requirements on formal specification techniques have been identified by considering the characteristics of distributed multimedia systems. These are briefly summarized below:

(a) usability and naturalness;

(b) concurrency;

(c) interaction (particularly unpredictable and asynchronous communication);

(d) openness and inter-operability;

(e) implementation independent specification (avoiding over-specification);

(f) object-based techniques;

(g) dynamic reconfiguration;

(h) co-existence of different languages for different ODP viewpoints;

(i) specification of real-time constraints (for real-time QoS requirements/ capabilities and real-time synchronization);

(j) specification of probabilistic constraints (for probabilistic QoS statements);

(k) easy to identify and change real-time constraints;

(l) validation, including validation of real-time constraints.

4.4   Example scenarios

This section introduces some typical scenarios found in distributed multi-media systems. These scenarios have been selected to illustrate the most important aspects of distributed multimedia systems as discussed above. The scenarios will provide the basis of examples later in the book (in Chs 11 and 12).

For each example, we firstly introduce the problem and then consider a set of assumptions and requirements. Note that assumptions correspond closely to QoS capabilities whereas requirements correspond to QoS requirements (see Section 4.2.2). As will be seen later, this format mirrors the formal specification architecture introduced in this book (see Ch. 8).

4.4.1   Bounded invocation

The first example considered is a specification of bounded invocation using a simple RPC protocol. Figure 4.2 illustrates the structure of a remote procedure call.

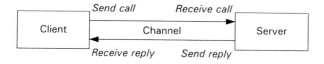

Figure 4.2   The basic concept of a remote procedure call.

This figure shows two (remote) processes, the client and the server, which are connected over a communication channel. The client sends a call to the server requesting the remote execution of a procedure. Upon receiving this call, the server processes it and returns a reply containing the results of this execution.

The *assumed* behaviour of the invocation service and associated protocol can be informally described as follows:

- All communication between the client and the server is over the net-work (i.e. an asynchronous medium).
- The network is unreliable (hence messages may get lost) and mes-sages may be re-ordered during transmission.
- Any successful transmission over the network (either client to server or server to client) takes a maximum of 2 ms.

- After receiving and executing a call, the server sends a reply back to the client; the server will take at most 1ms to process any call.
- After sending a call, the client waits for a reply. If no reply arrives within 6 ms, the client times out and re-sends the call (the timeout value is based on the estimated two-way transmission delay of 4 ms and a processing time of 1 ms by the server).
- After timing out, the client takes 1ms to reset the clock and prepare to re-send the call.
- Repeated timeouts cause the client to report an error and stop execution; it is assumed that after 5 timeouts an error will be reported immediately.

In addition, the *required* behaviour of the bounded invocation service is as follows:

- The maximum response time for the protocol should be 45 ms, i.e. after sending a call, either a reply should be received or an error reported within 45 ms.
- For each distinct call sent, the server should execute the request at most once (repeated requests are ignored/discarded). This is known as *at-most-once* semantics (note that this requirement makes no reference to real-time).

These represent the *quality of service requirements* for the invocation service.

With this scenario, we would like to be able to specify the behaviour of the bounded invocation, capturing the assumptions given above. It would also be desirable to specify formally the quality of service requirements and then verify the requirements against the behaviour.

4.4.2 Multimedia stream

The second scenario is that of a multimedia stream. As mentioned previously, a stream is a multimedia structure that links a continuous media data source and corresponding data sink. In this example, the source and the sink are assumed to be communicating asynchronously over an appropriate medium, as shown in Figure 4.3.

Suppose that the stream exhibits the following assumed behaviour (real-time values have been arbitrarily chosen):

- All communication between the data source and the data sink is asynchronous (it is assumed that the queue at the data sink is unbounded).

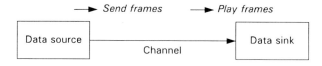

Figure 4.3   A multimedia stream.

- The channel over which frames are transmitted is unreliable and may result in the re-ordering of messages.
- The data source repeatedly transmits data frames every 50 ms (i.e. 20 frames per second).
- After the generation of a frame, 5 ms elapse before it is transmitted.
- Successfully transmitted frames arrive at the data sink between 80 ms and 90 ms after their transmission (channel latency).
- If the number of frames arriving at the data sink is not within 15 to 20 frames per second (channel throughput), then an error should be reported.
- The time taken by the data sink to process a frame is 5 ms (i.e. the time between receiving a frame and being able to play it).

The stream then has a number of *quality of service requirements* in terms of latency, jitter and throughput:

- The *end-to-end latency* should be between 100 ms and 120 ms (this requirement incorporates the acceptable jitter on latency). Consequently, a frame taking longer than 120 ms can be assumed to have been lost during transmission.
- The *end-to-end throughput* should remain between 15 and 20 frames per second.

As with the bounded invocation example, we would like to specify formally the behaviour and quality of service requirements and then verify the requirements against the behaviour.

4.4.3 Adding compression to the multimedia stream

To illustrate a process of refinement, we consider a second stream implemented using MPEG compression and decompression as shown in Figure 4.4 (implying that a lower bandwidth channel can be used).

We assume the use of MPEG compression and decompression carries an overhead of 3 ms at each end but achieves a compression ratio of, say, 200:1. All other assumptions and requirements remain as above (see Section 4.4.2).

Again, we would like to specify this refined behaviour, demonstrate that this refined behaviour is compatible with the initial behaviour and verify that the refined behaviour can still meet the requirements.

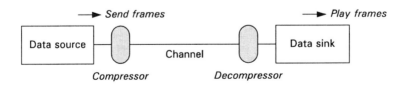

Figure 4.4 A compressed stream.

4.4.4   Achieving lip synchronization

Suppose that there are two data streams, one carrying video frames and the other carrying voice packets, which are transmitted to a common data sink from two independent data sources. At the data sink, these two data streams must be played out in a manner such that lip-synchronization is achieved between the video and the voice. In order to meet this requirement, certain real-time constraints that relate (synchronize) the two streams must be maintained (all numbers have been kept consistent with those presented in Stefani et al. (1992) and Regan (1993)). The requirements for lip synchronization are described below.

The first requirements are that both sound and video data should be presented at regular intervals. Note that, as in Stefani et al. (1992) and Regan (1993), no jitter (variance in presentation time) is permitted on the sound presentation; however, jitter is permitted on the video presentation.

1. *Sound intervals*   Sound packets must be presented every 30 milliseconds (ms).

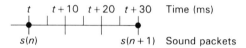

2. *Video intervals*   Video packets should be presented every 40ms, but a jitter of ±5 ms is permitted (i.e. video packets must be presented between 35 ms and 45 ms after the previous packet).

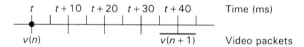

The third (and final) requirement for achieving lip-synchronization is that the presentation of the sound and video data must be synchronized, that is, the presentation of one media type must not lag or precede the presentation of the other media type by more than a certain amount. The constraints on the synchronization between the sound and video presentations are described below. Note that in this example, no jitter is permitted on the sound presentation. Therefore, it is only the jitter on the video data that can cause the presentation to drift out of synchronization (for example, if video frames repeatedly arrive late).

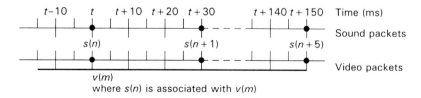

3. *Synchronization of sound and video*
   i. The video presentation must not lag the associated sound presentation by more than 150ms.
   ii. The video presentation must not precede the associated sound presentation by more than 15ms.

If these real-time constraints (requirements) cannot be met or are broken at some stage in the data presentation, then lip-synchronization has not been achieved.

In this example, we would like to specify the behaviour of a lip synchronization algorithm together with a formal specification of the three requirements identified above. We would then like to verify that the algorithm meets the requirements.

4.4.5 Summary

In this section, we have introduced four typical scenarios from distributed multimedia applications:

- The first scenario is bounded invocation, i.e. placing real-time bounds on operations. This example illustrates the need for the specification of some simple quality of service properties.
- The second scenario is that of a continuous media stream. This example illustrates the need for the specification of continuous media behaviour and the subsequent specification of quality of service properties.
- The third scenario is a refinement of the above, introducing compression. This example illustrates the issues raised by refinement of specifications.
- The final scenario is lip synchronization, i.e. inter-media synchronization between audio and video. This example illustrates the need for the specification of both intra- and inter-media real-time synchronization properties in that both the audio and video must be presented with the required quality of service and the two streams must also be synchronized together.

The examples also collectively illustrate typical distributed system requirements such as concurrency, asynchronous interaction and the need to avoid over-specification.

4.5 Summary

This chapter has highlighted a number of requirements for the specification of distributed multimedia systems. These requirements are repeated below:

(a) usability and naturalness;

(b) concurrency;

(c) interaction (particularly unpredictable and asynchronous communication);

(d) openness and inter-operability;

(e) implementation independent specifications (avoiding over-specification);

(f) object-based techniques;

(g) dynamic reconfiguration;

(h) co-existence of different languages for different ODP viewpoints;

(i) specification of real-time constraints (for real-time QoS requirements/ capabilities and real-time synchronization);

(j) specification of probabilistic constraints (for probabilistic QoS statements);

(k) easy to identify and change real-time constraints;

(l) validation, including validation of real-time constraints.

While some of these requirements can be met by existing formal specification techniques, it is clear that other aspects are beyond the state of the art. This should not be surprising. Existing formal specification techniques (e.g. the ISO standard formal description techniques Estelle, SDL and LOTOS) were designed for the domain of communication protocols and only partially reflect the more general requirements of distributed multimedia computing. More specifically, existing techniques provide support for requirements (a), (b) and (c). A number of techniques also address (d), (e), (f), (g) and (i). Other requirements such as (h), (j) and (k) remain research issues. In addition, major difficulties remain in the area of validation of real-time systems (l). The following section of the book will focus on the state of the art in formal specification techniques in more detail, including a more thorough assessment of the ability to meet our requirements. Because of the wide nature of the above requirements, particular attention will be given to the specification and verification of real-time properties. We view this as the most crucial requirement of distributed multimedia systems. Other open issues such as the ease of identifying real-time constraints will also be given prominence. However, some issues such as object-based techniques, dynamic reconfiguration, co-existence and probabilistic specification are considered beyond the scope of this book.

PART III

Existing approaches

This part has two main functions: to review the existing spectrum of formal specification techniques in the light of the requirements highlighted in Chapter 4 and to introduce techniques we will need in later parts of the book. The part is divided into three chapters. The chapters are sequenced to be increasingly specific. The first chapter (Ch. 5) presents a broad survey of existing formal specification techniques. Then, in Chapter 6, we focus on three classes of technique, extended finite state machines (EFSM), synchronous languages and process algebras, which in the light of the general review presented in Chapter 5, can be seen to be the most likely techniques to satisfy our requirements. Particular examples of each class of technique are highlighted and compared in this chapter. Finally, Chapter 7 focuses directly on LOTOS and its timed extensions. The chapter motivates the need to extend LOTOS with real-time and describes the main design issues involved in this extension. The chapter concludes by relating one of the prominent timed extensions to LOTOS back to the four techniques discussed in Chapter 6.

CHAPTER 5

Broad survey: the spectrum of formal specification techniques

5.1   Introduction

This chapter gives a broad assessment of the applicability of existing formal specification techniques to the field of distributed multimedia systems. The major part of the chapter is a survey of existing formal specification techniques, which assesses the suitability of each particular technique against the requirements set out in Chapter 4.

The central requirement for distributed multimedia systems is the modelling of real-time behaviour. More specifically, it is important that strict timing constraints are maintained in order to guarantee that continuous media types such as audio and video are presented with an acceptable quality of service and real-time synchronization. In order to describe such properties formally, timed formal specification techniques must be considered. This is now an extensively investigated topic and a wealth of timed techniques have been proposed. However, there is still considerable debate between workers in this field regarding the relative benefits of different techniques. Typical issues that generate debate are:

1. Which timing paradigm is most expressive?
2. Which timing paradigm is mathematically most elegant?
3. Where should time be incorporated (directly in the language or outside)?
4. Which time domain should be used: discrete, dense or continuous?
5. What role do probabilities play and what is the relationship between time and probabilities?

One relationship which is clear, and indicates why this area is so problematic, is the conflict between usability and rigour. This is a characteristic common in formal computer science. It is relatively straightforward to define specification notations that are very expressive, i.e. enable many features to be specified, e.g. mobility, object orientation, real-time, etc. However, it is a much harder task to define well founded and tractable semantics for such notations. Furthermore, it is clear that if the full benefits of formal specification are to be realized, such rigorous foundations must be provided. The incorporation of time into formal specification techniques is an example of this conflict. Specifically, untimed notations can easily be extended with a notation to express real-time constraints, but reconciling such extensions with the existing semantic underpinnings of the untimed notation is invariably very hard. Thus, new mathematical models have to be defined in order to support the new features. A consequence of this is that in a new application area, such as multimedia, development of mathematically well founded approaches often lags behind more pragmatic less rigorous approaches. The conflict between usability and rigour is a theme that will recur throughout this chapter.

5.2 Scope of the survey

A large number of formal specification techniques can be found in the literature. We will initially highlight a broad spectrum of techniques, and then focus on the techniques that most closely satisfy our requirements. The techniques we will consider are:

1. *Specification logics*   Mathematical logics have been proposed as specification notations. An important motivation behind this proposal is that logics abstract completely from methods of solution and thus support highly abstract description of computer systems. Such specification logics have been especially recommended for requirements specification. Examples are temporal logic (Manna & Pnueli 1992) and modal logic (Milner 1989).

2. *Process algebra based*   The process algebra approach was developed within the concurrency theory community (Milner 1980) and is supported by a wealth of work on the formal properties of concurrent systems. The two archetypal process algebras are: CCS (Milner 1989) and CSP (Hoare 1985). In addition, many other process algebras have been proposed; SCCS (Milner 1983), ACP (Bergstra & Klop 1986) and CIRCAL (Milne 1985) are some of the most important. The process algebra that has moved most significantly out of the theoretical domain is LOTOS. This is partially because of its position within the standards community.

   A wealth of work on timed process algebras has also been performed. Timed extensions for all the main process algebras exist, e.g. TCCS (Tofts 1988) and TPL (Regan 1991) for CCS, TCSP (Reed et al. 1991) for CSP and TLOTOS (Leduc & Léonard 1993) and LOTOS-T (Miguel et al. 1993) for LOTOS.

3. *Finite state machine based*   These techniques are based around the

finite state machine paradigm, usually extended finite state machines. The two most notable techniques are: Estelle, which has been standardized by ISO (1987), and SDL, which has been standardized by the CCITT (now the ITU) (CCITT 1988). Other interesting approaches include Statecharts (Harel 1987) and TTM (Ostroff 1990).

4. *Petri nets* Petri nets (Reisig 1985) are one of the earliest theoretical models of concurrency. Furthermore, most of the early attempts to integrate quantitative time into a formal model of concurrency employed Petri nets as their basis. Thus, many of the issues concerning real-time extension of formal specification were first investigated with regard to Petri nets.

5. *Synchronous languages* In contrast to the previously highlighted formal specification techniques this class of technique has approached the problem of formal description from an applied angle, i.e. a primary objective of these techniques is executability. Thus, in general, synchronous languages are closer to programming notations. Such languages employ a specific paradigm for simplifying the development of real-time reactive systems, known as the *synchrony hypothesis* (see Appendix A). Signal (Gautier et al. 1986), Lustre (Halbwachs et al. 1990) and Esterel (Berry & Gonthier 1988) are examples of synchronous languages; Statecharts also conform to the principles of the synchrony hypothesis.

6. *Other techniques* A number of other techniques, which have been developed for purely software engineering reasons, are also important, e.g. Z (Spivey 1989), VDM (Jones 1990) and Raise (Raise Language Group 1992). With the exception of Raise, these techniques do not explicitly consider concurrency issues.

We now present the survey of existing techniques for the specification and validation of distributed real-time systems. We include subsections on all the six classes of techniques listed above. Each subsection follows the same pattern; we introduce the main features of the technique, focus on the model of time and then analyze the capabilities for the specification and validation of distributed multimedia systems.

5.3   Specification logics

5.3.1   The basic approach

Background on logics
Consideration of logic based mathematical notations has been fuelled by the argument that specification should totally avoid reference to methods of solution, and that it should describe the desired behaviour in an abstract non-operational manner. These techniques are aimed at capturing what or

how well a system should perform and not how or by what means it should perform it.

There are many different classes of logic, as discussed below,

- *Propositional logic*   Propositional logic is built up from expressions that take either the value true or the value false (propositions). It makes use of the logical operators $\wedge$, $\vee$, $\neg$, $\rightarrow$ and $\leftrightarrow$ (conjunction, disjunction, negation, implication and equivalence respectively) and applies them over constants and Boolean variables.
- *Predicate logic*   Predicate logic is an extension to propositional logic in that, through the use of variables, it allows relations or properties of objects to be expressed (for example, the relation $x<5$). The truth of predicates typically depends on the value of variables.
- *First-order logic*   A first-order logic is a logic that permits quantification over variables. This term is normally applied to a predicate logic extended with quantification.
- *Modal logics*   A basic modal logic is a classical propositional logic that has been extended with modal operators such as $[a]$ (referred to as box-a) and $\langle a \rangle$ (diamond-a) (Stirling 1991). In such a logic, the formula $[a]p$ expresses the fact that after every action a, proposition p holds while the formula $\langle a \rangle p$ expresses the fact that after one action a, p holds. Milner's logic $\mathcal{PL}$ (Milner 1989) is a good example of a modal logic.
- *Temporal logics*   Temporal logics are a subclass of modal logics. It was in the pioneering work of Amir Pnueli during the 1970s that temporal logic was first applied to computer science (Pnueli 1977). In a similar way to modal logics, temporal logics add new operators to classical logics. These operators allow reasoning about the qualitative time at which events occur. We will introduce the new operators shortly.

Because of its extensive application in computer science, particularly in the field of distributed and concurrent computer systems, temporal logics will play a central role in the remainder of this book. As a reflection of their importance, we will devote the next subsection to a more in depth introduction to the paradigm.

Temporal logics

The need for, and the benefit of using, a temporal logic is made clear in Pnueli (1977). In this work, Pnueli points out that, while a first-order logic is sufficient for the expression of safety properties (something undesirable never happens), extensions such as those provided by temporal logics are needed to express liveness properties (something desirable eventually happens). (See Appendix A for a clarification of terminology.)

Temporal operators   As indicated earlier temporal logics extend classical logics with a set of temporal operators. The following is a typical set of such operators:

$\bigcirc P$ next P, i.e. P holds in the next state of the system.

$\square P$ henceforth P, i.e. P holds in every future state of the system.

$\diamondsuit P$ eventually P, i.e. P holds in at least one future state of the system.

$P \cup Q$ P until Q, i.e. P holds until a state is reached in which Q holds.

Example

Maintaining mutual exclusion between two processes, P1 and P2 that share a resource, may be expressed as:

$\square \neg$ (crit_region_P1∧crit_region_P2)

where crit_region_P1 is a predicate that holds if P1 is in its critical region and crit_region_P2 holds if P2 is in its critical region. Furthermore, freedom from starvation in a solution to the mutual exclusion problem could be expressed as:

$\square$(ready_CR_P1→$\diamondsuit$crit_region_P1)
    ∧$\square$(ready_CR_P2→$\diamondsuit$crit_region_P2)

where ready_CR_P1 holds if P1 is ready to enter its critical region and ready_CR_P2 holds if P2 is ready to enter its critical region. The proposition states that whenever P1 or P2 are ready to enter their critical region they eventually will. The mutual exclusion requirement is an example of a safety property while freedom from starvation is a fairness property (see Appendix A for clarification).

Expressibility and decidability Two of the most important concepts in the choice of a logic are the expressibility and decidability of the logic. It is essential that, when using a logic to specify a system, the logic is sufficiently expressive for the desired application domain. This involves considering many of the issues that we will raise shortly, for example, the linear versus branching view of the underlying semantics, the chosen time domain and permitted operations on time, the need for past-tense operators, etc. Each of these issues has an impact on the expressiveness of the logic, and exactly what is required for the chosen application domain must be decided.

By way of clarification, a logic, or more generally a specification language, is decidable for a particular validation question if there exists a decision procedure, i.e. an algorithm, that will answer the question for all statements in the language. Decidability of logics usually focuses on satisfaction, i.e. it considers the existence of algorithms that check whether or not any statement in the logic is satisfiable. In a very broad sense, a statement is satisfiable if an implementation (also called a model) exists that satisfies the statement. For example, a statement that $x=7$ and $x=9$ at the same time, would not, in general, be satisfiable, as it expresses a contradiction that cannot be implemented.

Typically there is a trade-off between the expressiveness of the logic and its decidability, i.e. very expressive notations are often undecidable.

Categories of temporal logic There are many different classes of temporal logic. The following list considers the main characteristics of these different classes.

- *Propositional temporal logic versus first-order temporal logic* With first order temporal logics, a major consideration is the interaction of temporal operators and quantifiers in the syntax of the logic, for example, whether temporal operators are allowed within the scope of quantifiers. The trade-off against restricting the syntax is decidability: logics in which no syntactic restrictions are imposed tend to be undecidable.

- *Linear time versus branching time* This choice determines the underlying nature of qualitative time in the logic. The linear model of qualitative time takes the view that, at each moment, there is only one possible future moment. With branching time models, time is viewed to have a branching tree-like structure where, at each moment, there may be different possible future moments (see Appendix A for a further discussion of linear and branching time semantic models). There is still much debate concerning which approach is preferable; detailed comparisons of linear time versus branching time can be found in Lamport (1980), Emerson & Halpern (1986) and Pnueli (1985). For example, it has been claimed that branching time logics cannot express certain types of fairness conditions (Lamport 1980). However, this claim was largely refuted in Emerson & Halpern (1986).

  In general, both linear time logics and branching time logics are adequate for the specification and verification of concurrent systems, but the simplicity of linear time is a strong advantage. However, one advantage of branching time logics is that they can be used to prove the existence of an alternative path in a system, i.e. to prove that there is a choice of paths that a system could follow and not just a trivial solution with only one path.

- *Future versus past temporal operators* In most temporal logics, only future-tense operators (such as until and henceforth) are provided. Generally, for the specification of computer systems, this is all that is required since a definite starting point exists from which all logic statements can be based. Past-tense operators, such as once (often denoted $\diamondsuit$) and has-always-been $\boxdot$, can therefore be shown to provide no extra expressive power. However, the use of past-tense operators can simplify formulae and result in more intuitive and easily readable specifications.

Temporal logics do not provide any mechanism to permit the specification of quantitative time. Consequently, many real-time extensions have been proposed. Such extensions are considered in the next section.

5.3.2   Time in specification logics

The main focus of this section will be real-time extensions to temporal logics; these will be discussed in the next subsection. However, we will also discuss an important timed extension to first order logic in the second subsection.

Category of real-time temporal logics
The aim of this subsection is to present some of the distinguishing characteristics of real-time temporal logics. Some of these characteristics will also be considered in the following timed process algebra section and will therefore be discussed only briefly here. For a more detailed survey of different logic-based techniques for the specification of real-time systems, see Alur & Henzinger (1991).

Discrete versus dense time domain Discrete time domains model the passage of time as a sequence of discrete points. Such time domains are typically modelled as the non-negative integer numbers (also called the natural numbers). In contrast, in a dense time domain for any pair of time points, a third point can be found that is between the two points, i.e. time is dense. Such time domains are typically modelled as either rational or real numbers. Most real-time temporal logics use a discrete time domain. This is regarded as being sufficient for reasoning about systems where the granularity of time can be adjusted as required. Additionally, although a dense time domain could be argued to be more realistic, the use of it generally rules out the possibility of obtaining decision procedures. However, an interesting piece of work is presented in Alur et al. (1991) where, by relaxing the notion of punctuality (stating that an event should occur at a precise time), a metric interval temporal logic (MITL) is shown to combine the best of both worlds, that is, realism and decidability.

Bounded operators, freeze quantification or explicit clock variables
There are three main ways of introducing time into the syntax of a temporal logic. The first technique, the bounded operator approach, involves adding time-bounds to temporal operators. For example, the bounded operator $\square_{>2}\, p$ represents "p always holds after time 2". Koymans adopts this technique in MTL (metric temporal logic) (Koymans 1990). One criticism of the bounded operator approach has been that it cannot be used to specify the time between two non-adjacent events, such as, "q happens after p and then r follows q, but within 5 units of time from p". However, as pointed out in Alur & Henzinger (1990), due to the discrete nature of time in MTL, the above property can be expressed as:

$$\square\left(p \rightarrow \bigvee_{t=0}^{5} \Diamond_{=t}\left(q \wedge \Diamond_{\leq 5-t}\, r\right)\right)$$

where the big v notation defines a generalized or, for example,

$$\bigvee_{t=0}^{5} s_t = s_0 \vee s_1 \vee s_2 \vee s_3 \vee s_4 \vee s$$

Thus, the formula states that, after every p, there is a choice of times (between 0 and 5) at which q must occur and then r will occur at a time which is less than or equal to 5 units of time after the occurrence of p. It should be noted, however, that this technique of specifying time over non-adjacent events is inappropriate if, for example, p and r are separated by a large number of other events.

The second main technique, freeze quantification, was introduced by Alur & Henzinger in the timed propositional temporal logic, TPTL (Alur & Henzinger 1989, 1994)). In this technique, the time of a state is accessed through a quantifier that binds (or freezes) a variable to the corresponding time. For example, using freeze quantification, the constraint over non-adjacent events described above can be expressed as:

$$\square x.\left(p \rightarrow \Diamond\left(q \wedge \Diamond y.\left(r \wedge y \leq x+5\right)\right)\right)$$

In this expression, the variable x is bound to the time at which p occurs. At some time in the future, q will occur and following this, at a time denoted by y, r will occur and y should be within the required bound.

The third technique involves the introduction of an explicit clock variable. This variable, usually denoted by T, is set to the current value of a global clock in each state. Referring back to the above example, this could be expressed in an explicit clock logic as:

$$\forall t.\square\left(\left(p \wedge T = t\right) \rightarrow \Diamond\left(q \wedge \Diamond\left(r \wedge T \leq t+5\right)\right)\right)$$

The global (rigid) variable, t, is set to the value of the global clock (T) at the time at which p occurs. When r eventually occurs, the value of the global clock should be within the required bound. The real-time temporal logics XCTL (explicit clock temporal logic) (Harel et al. 1990b) and RTTL (real-time temporal logic) (Ostroff 1992a) are two examples of explicit clock temporal logics.

Operations on time Together with the chosen time domain, the set of allowed operations on time determine the decidability of a real-time propositional temporal logic. There are a number of possibilities for this set of operations, the most primitive of which simply uses the successor operator. This can be extended to enhance both the readability and the succinctness of formulae by allowing addition by constants (i.e. expressions of the form $t+c$, where t is a timing variable and c is an integer constant). Note, however, that this extension does not increase expressibility, since addition by constants can be represented by repeated successor operations. A more general set of operations allows the addition of two (or more) timing variables. This does add extra expressive power since it allows, for example, the specification that events p and q are always separated by a constant time interval.

Non-temporal real-time logics

The section above has considered real-time extensions to temporal logic. However, one real-time logic that is not based on a temporal logic deserves a mention in this survey; this is the logic RTL (real-time logic). RTL is a first-order predicate logic originally defined by Jahanian & Mok (1986). In RTL, systems are assumed to consist of a number of time-consuming actions that may occur in parallel. Events are temporal markers, which, for example, may denote the time at which an action began or ended. Events can be counted, thus making it possible to refer to the ith occurrence of some event. The occurrence function, denoted @, provides a mapping between events, their indices and time. For example, the formula $@(e,i)=t$ states that the ith occurrence of event e occurred at time t. Formulae in RTL are composed of standard arithmetic relations and algebraic expressions over time constants and the occurrence function, first-order logical connectives, equality/inequality predicates and quantifiers (over indices only, quantification over event variables is not allowed). Another feature of RTL is a shorthand notation that allows the specification of an interval during which some property is true. This is known as a state predicate and is denoted by $P[x,y]$ that defines an interval such that P becomes true at time x and subsequently becomes false at time y.

Two particularly interesting pieces of work exist that incorporate the use of RTL. The first of these considers the use of RTL to complement the specification language Z with respect to real-time (Fidge 1992). The second of these considers the use of a variant of RTL (a logic called QL) with the synchronous programming language Esterel (Stefani 1993). The latter of these two pieces of work will be discussed more fully in Section 5.7.

Summary

This section has focused on real-time extensions of temporal logics. Some of the important characteristics displayed by such logics are summarized in Table 5.1.

5.3.3 Analysis

In terms of the requirements that were identified in chapter 4, specification logics (and temporal logics, in particular) are highly applicable to our domain of interest. They are applicable in the following respects:

Table 5.1 Characteristics of various linear real-time temporal logics.

Real-time temporal logics	Reference	Time domain	Can express punctuality?	Time mechanism on time	Permitted operations	Future/ past-tense operators
MTL	Koymans 1990	Discrete	Yes	B.Op	+ constant only	P
TPTL	Alur & Henzinger 1989	Discrete	Yes	FQ	+ constant only	F
XCTL	Harel et al. 1990a	Discrete	Yes	EC	general addition	F
RTTL	Ostroff 1992a	Discrete	Yes	EC	totally general ops	F
MITL	Alur et al. 1991	Dense	No	B.Op	+ constant only	F

Key: B.Op=Bounded operator, FQ=Freeze quantification, EC=Explicit clock, P=includes both future and past-tense operators, F=Future-tense operators only.

- Description of concurrent systems is supported; such systems are the specific target of temporal logics.
- Abstract specification that avoids prescription of particular implementation solutions is supported by temporal logics. Thus, they address the problem of over specification. In particular, they are highly suited to abstract specification of global requirements.
- Specification of real-time constraints is supported by real-time variants of temporal logic. This is a particularly important issue since we are interested in modelling quality of service constraints, which are a specific class of real-time constraint. Furthermore, research on validation with temporal logics has addressed the issue of determining that real-time constraints are satisfied (e.g. model checking (Clarke et al. 1986)).

However, it is also clear that in terms of our requirements, logic based approaches are limited in some important respects. Most significantly, the domain of application of formal specification that we are addressing requires some operational specification of system behaviour. For example, the ODP computational language is a behavioural interaction model, which contains explicit interaction paradigms. These would not be as naturally modelled in temporal logics as in the "algorithmic" specification techniques that we will consider next.

5.4   Process algebras

5.4.1   The basic approach

The process algebra approach was developed within the concurrency theory field through the seminal work of Hoare (1985), Brookes et al. (1984) and Milner (1980, 1983). These workers have sought an elegant mathematical framework for modelling concurrency and their approach has been applied to the formal specification and validation of concurrent systems. The resulting process algebra model offers some key advantages over state transition based approaches such as finite state machines and Petri nets (see Section 5.5 and Section 5.6 respectively):

- An elegant set of operators for developing concurrent systems is central to the process algebra approach. Thus, succinct expressions of communicating concurrent processes can be made. The emphasis on non-determinism in process algebras supports abstract specification of "possible" implementation behaviour.
- A rich and tractable mathematical model of the semantics of process algebras has been developed. This model is based upon concepts of equivalence through observation of the external behaviour of a specification. Such notions of observation seem contradictory to models containing causal relationships (in particular Petri nets) since, in such approaches, the internal behaviour is clearly of significance. For process algebras, concurrency is classically modelled as interleaving.
- Specifications can be built in a compositional manner from the abstract to the concrete in the same notation. These compositional properties enable parts of specifications to be refined and substituted in place.

Thus, many authors (Nicola 1986, Milner 1986) argue for the process algebra approach on grounds of analytical power. However, this argument between the so called intensionalists (who view the internal behaviour of concurrent systems as of central importance to specification, c.f. Petri nets) and extensionalists (who believe the internal behaviour of concurrent systems can be abstracted away from) has not been conclusively resolved.

CCS (Milner 1980) and CSP (Hoare 1985) are the archetypal languages of the process algebra approach. CIRCAL (Milne 1985) and ACP (Bergstra & Klop 1986) are also important early approaches. Characteristics of these languages are the elegant and small set of basic operations used to express communicating concurrent behaviour:

- *Synchronous communication* Synchronous communication (see Appendix A) is employed in process algebras, since it is argued to be the most primitive of communication paradigms (Hoare 1985).
- *Choice* Alternative behaviours can be defined using this construct
- *Non-determinism* Alternative behaviours, the choice of which is beyond the control of the external observer, can be defined using non-determinism.
- *Concurrency* Behaviours can be composed in parallel. The resulting behaviour interleaves the possible actions of the constituent behaviours.
- *Restriction* Information hiding is defined formally in process algebras using restriction. A special action is used to denote internal (hidden) activity.
- *Relabelling* This is a means of avoiding naming conflicts.

All process algebras contain operators to express this set of basic operations although a certain amount of diversity exists between the precise realization of these operations.

In addition to the classic process algebras it is also worth highlighting Milner's more recent work on π-calculus (Milner et al. 1992). Classic process algebras employ a static process structure, thus preventing dynamic reconfiguration of processes and of communication channels between processes. As indicated earlier, this can cause problems in specifying distributed systems where such mobility is important. This problem requires processes to be mobile, both in terms of the creation of processes and in terms of the communication links between process instantiations. The π-calculus addresses this issue of mobility.

The dynamic capabilities of π-calculus are clearly of great interest for specifiers of distributed systems and a number of researchers are applying related techniques in the distributed systems setting (Najm & Stefani 1992). However, a full consideration of process mobility is beyond the scope of this book and thus we take note of the limitations of many process algebras and the promise of π-calculus, but will concentrate on the timing aspects of process algebras in the remainder of the book.

The next section returns to this main concern: timed extensions to process algebras. In particular, we will consider some of the general principles of time in process algebras in preparation for the more in depth discussions to be made in the later chapters of this part.

5.4.2   Time in process algebras

The classic process algebra model concentrates solely on the specification of the relative ordering of events. This deficiency has led to many timed extensions to these techniques being proposed. For example, CELOTOS (van Hulzen et al. 1990), TIC (Quemada et al. 1991), LOTOS-T (Miguel 1991), TLOTOS (Leduc & Léonard 1993), U-LOTOS (Bolognesi & Lucidi 1992) and ET-LOTOS (Léonard & Leduc 1994) are some of the timed extensions to LOTOS, SCCS (Milner 1983); TCCS (Tofts 1988), wCCS and sCCS (Tofts 1990), Timed CCS (Yi 1990), TPL (Regan 1991) and TPCCS (Hansson 1992) are timed extensions to CCS; while Reed & Roscoe (1988) Davies (1993) and de Boer & Hooman (1992) describe timed extensions to CSP. The major characteristics of such approaches are categorized below (note that the most important issues will be discussed in more detail in Ch. 7):

Discrete versus dense time domain
A discrete time domain (e.g. the non-negative integers) can only measure the time at which events occur with finite precision. So, for example, if two or more events were to occur between two adjacent values from the chosen discrete time domain, they could only be distinguished by temporal order-

ing, not by the exact times at which they occurred. In contrast, if a dense time domain (e.g. the non-negative rationals or real numbers) is used, the precise time at which events occur can be measured. The trade-off between the two approaches is that, although a dense time domain can be viewed as being more expressive, the reasoning and proving of properties about time from a dense time domain becomes more complex (Yi 1991). In many application areas this extra complexity is unnecessary, especially if the granularity of time can be adjusted as necessary.

Instantaneous versus time consuming events

In most of the proposed timed process algebras (e.g. TLOTOS, U-LOTOS, Timed CCS and TPL), events are instantaneous, that is, a process is allowed to perform an infinite number of events in a finite time interval. Such processes are often referred to as Zeno-processes. However, a few proposals, notably the Timed CSP of Reed & Roscoe (1988), prevent the expression of such processes by imposing a small delay between events from sequential processes. Although this approach has been argued to be more realistic (in terms of executability), it significantly increases the complexity of the underlying theory. Additionally, when a fixed delay between events is imposed, the abstractness of time is lost since specifications depend on the value of this delay (an implementation decision).

Time deadlock

In an untimed process algebra, deadlock is used to model a process that can no longer perform any event. Most timed process algebras adopt the view that time should always be allowed to proceed, i.e. a deadlocked process should not prevent the passage of time (e.g. LOTOS-T, ET-LOTOS, TPL). An alternative approach, however, permits the existence of timed deadlocks, that is, a state is reached in which time can no longer proceed. U-LOTOS is an example of such an approach. Although time deadlocks may seem counter-intuitive, it is argued in Groote (1990) that they may be useful in detecting certain timing inconsistencies in specifications.

Maximal progress versus action urgency

Maximal progress (also referred to under the names maximal parallelism and minimal delay) ensures that internal events, that is, those events that can no longer be influenced by the environment, occur as soon as possible. Techniques such as LOTOS-T and the Timed CSP of Reed & Roscoe (1988) both impose a maximal progress assumption on processes. In CCS-based techniques, maximal progress is closely related to communication since, in such techniques, a communication yields a τ action (an internal event). Consequently, by applying the maximal progress assumption, if a communication is possible, it will occur before time is allowed to pass. Timed CCS and TPL are examples of CCS-based techniques employing maximal progress.

An alternative approach to maximal progress is provided by the action urgency of U-LOTOS. In this approach, a notion of urgency can be applied to any event, not just to internal events. If a given event is specified as being urgent, a process may block the passage of time until the given event has occurred, i.e. execution of the action must occur before any delay is permitted. Note that if urgency is applied to a particular event and the environment is not willing to participate in this event, time deadlock will occur. The debate between maximal progress and action urgency will be revisited in Chapter 7.

Persistency

This term is used to refer to processes in which the passage of time cannot suppress the ability to perform an action. For example, if a process $P \xrightarrow{\sigma} P'$ and $P \xrightarrow{a}$ then P is persistent if $P' \xrightarrow{a}$ (the notation $P \xrightarrow{x} Q$ means that process P performs an action x and transforms into process Q; σ represents a delay of one unit of time).

Some timed process algebraic techniques enforce the persistency property (e.g. U-LOTOS). However, in process algebras such as ATP, TCCS and TPL, a new operator is introduced into the language to model a choice that is determined by the passage of time. It is argued that the addition of this new operator (in addition to the standard choice operator) makes the language more expressive. To illustrate this, consider a process that can either perform a receive action or, at time 1, can perform a timeout. In a persistent process algebra, this timeout scenario could be expressed as follows (where a dot represents action prefix, + represents choice and σ represents a delay of one unit of time):

receive.RecProc + σ.timeout.TimeoutProc

In this expression, at (and after) time 1, there is a non-deterministic choice between the timeout and the receive action, i.e. the passage of time has not affected the system's ability to perform a receive action. By introducing a new operator to model a choice that is determined by the passage of time, the situation can be specified where, after time 1, the receive action is disabled, regardless of whether a receive event is possible at that, or any future, point in time. For example, the above timeout scenario could be expressed using the ATP operator $\lfloor x \rfloor (y)$ as follows (the operator can be interpreted as "either do x now or, after one unit of time, do y"):

⌊receive.RecProc⌋(timeout.TimeoutProc)

In this example, the timeout event may occur at any time after one unit of time has passed; however, the receive action cannot occur after time 1.

Table 5.2 Characteristics of various asynchronous *timed* process algebras.

Timed techniques	Reference	Discrete/ dense time	Instantaneous/ time consuming events	Time deadlock	Maximal progress/ urgency	Persistency
CELOTOS	van Hulzen et al. 1990	Discrete	Inst	No TDN	None	P
TIC	Quemada et al. 1991	Discrete	Inst	NoTD	None	Not P
LOTOS-T	Miguel 1991	Not Exp Def	Inst	No TD	MP	Not P
TLOTOS	Leduc & Léonard 1993	Discrete	Inst	TD	U	P
U-LOTOS	Bolognesi & Lucidi 1992	Discrete	Inst	TD	U	P
ET-LOTOS	Léonard & Leduc 1994	Not Exp. Def.	Inst	No TD	MP	P
TCCS	Tofts 1988	Discrete	Inst	TD	U	Not P
ATP	Nicollin et al. 1990	Discrete	Inst	TD	U	Not P
Timed CCS	Yi 1990	Not Exp. Def.	Inst	No TD	MP	P
TPL	Regan 1991	Discrete	Inst	No TD	MP	Not P
TPCCS	Hansson 1992	Discrete	Inst	No TD	MP	Not P
Timed CSP	Reed & Roscoe 1988	Dense	TC	No TD	MP	P

Key: Not Exp. Def.= not explicitly defined, Inst=instantaneous, TC=time consuming, TD= time deadlock, MP=maximal progress, U=urgency, P=persistent.

Summary
This section has highlighted the main characteristics of different timed process algebras. Table 5.2 categorizes various techniques with respect to the issues that have been discussed.

5.4.3 Analysis

Process algebras have a number of distinct advantages over many other formal specification techniques: they have an elegant and expressive set of operators, clean semantics, a rich and tractable underlying mathematical model that lends itself to validation and enables specifications to be constructed in a stepwise manner. In addition, a large number of toolkits are now available, particularly for the language LOTOS. There is also a large research community looking at extending the techniques, for example to support dynamic reconfiguration. In addition, they meet many of the requirements that we explicitly identified in Chapter 4.
- Specification of concurrency and interaction in behaviour is a particular objective of process algebras.
- While CCS, CSP and the original theoretically motivated techniques are incomplete as specification notations, LOTOS has a full data part (although, it should be pointed out that there are some technical problems with the LOTOS data language (ISO 1994)).

- Process algebras support abstract specification. This is principally facilitated by allowing non-determinism in specifications.
- Although process algebras such as CCS, CSP or LOTOS are not sufficient to capture the behaviour of real-time systems, considerable ongoing research is trying to extend these techniques to support such a class of specification. Explicit representations of time, either through timestamps or a delay operator, and some form of urgency principle (such as maximal progress), are being incorporated in order to represent real-time behaviour.

For these reasons, process algebras are strong candidates for the specification of distributed multimedia systems.

5.5   Finite state machine based

5.5.1   The basic approach

Finite state machines (FSM) are a well known formalism. They model computation using two classes of behaviour: events, which express instantaneous change, and states, which possess a duration in time. However, in their purest form they are not a rich enough modelling technique to be used as a general purpose formal specification technique. Finite state machines, for only moderately complex problems, become unmanageably large and chaotic and, in addition, only slight extensions to a machine can result in an exponential growth in states (Ostroff 1989). This is attributable to the flat nature of finite state machines and that all states have to be expressed explicitly.

In order to make finite state machine based modelling viable, a number of extended finite state machine (EFSM) paradigms have been proposed (Harel 1987, ISO 1987, CCITT 1988, Ostroff 1989). Although there is a degree of diversity in these extensions, they all tackle the basic limitations of finite state machines in a similar manner. The following types of extension are generally included:

1. *Composition*   A means of composing finite state machines hierarchically from smaller machines is included. Furthermore, since pure finite state machines are totally sequential, a means of composing finite state machines according to a parallel behaviour is needed.
2. *Communication*   Having assumed a parallel composition operator, communication between finite state machines is required. This implies that simple events are not sufficient and events that can model intermachine communication are required.
3. *Data*   A method for representing groups of states that denote numerical information must be defined. Thus, extended finite state machines are not simply a control flow paradigm, but incorporate data in order

to denote different instances of a particular group of states.
These additions typically give extended finite state machines the power of Turing machines.

A further addition that is incorporated in many extended finite state machines is quantitative time. However, not all techniques employ the same timing approach. There is also a significant diversity in communication mechanisms employed: some models are based on synchronous communication, while others employ asynchronous communication, or even broadcast communication.

Extended finite state machines have to some extent moved out of the purely theoretical community and have been used in applied domains. Extended finite state machines have been found to be an expressive and usable tool, in particular, as a means of describing communication protocols (hence, the standardization of Estelle (ISO 1987) and SDL (CCITT 1988)). We will consider three extended finite state machine techniques in this book Estelle, SDL and TTM (Ostroff 1989):

- *Estelle* Estelle is an imperative language for defining extended finite state machines. It was developed within the Open Systems Interconnection (OSI) work as a vehicle for specifying OSI communication protocols.
- *SDL* SDL was developed by CCITT as a language for specifying telecommunications protocols. The language has similarities to Estelle. However, it also boasts a graphical dialect that is commonly used as a design tool.
- *TTM* Ostroff's TTM model has been specifically developed as the algorithmic part of a dual language approach, RTTL/TTM, for formally describing real-time discrete event processes. The TTM extended state machine notation enables algorithm expression, while the real-time temporal logic RTTL enables requirements of the algorithm to be specified.

We will introduce the principles of EFSMs using the latter of these notations. TTM extends basic finite state machine events to comprise a guard followed by an operation. Thus, conditions for executing the event can be defined in the guard, and actions to be performed on execution of the event can be defined in the operation. If there is no condition for executing an event, the guard is dropped. Receipt and sending of communications can be incorporated into operations. The communication paradigm employed is synchronous, specifically, using the CSP communication primitives defined by Hoare (1985). It should be pointed out that the use of synchronous communication contrasts with the use of asynchronous communication in SDL and Estelle.

5.5.2   Time in EFSMs

Quantitative time is typically incorporated into EFSMs using a delay or timeout operator. As an illustration of such an extension we consider the incorporation of quantitative time in TTM. A standard delay, with upper and lower time bounds, can be associated with events (see Section 6.2 and Section 6.3 for discussion of the timing models of SDL and Estelle). This notation has been used by Ostroff (1989) to express a number of algorithms in real-time control systems, such as train/gate and factory systems.

We will demonstrate TTMs with a simple protocol example: the alternating bit protocol. The simplicity of the alternating bit protocol, and the fact that its behaviour is typical of many other protocols, has made it a suitable example with which to test the adequacy of different languages. It was designed to ensure reliable transmission of messages over what may be an unreliable medium. To achieve this, the sending process numbers the messages with alternating bits, 0 and 1. Having sent a message with one of these bits, the sender must wait for an acknowledgement with the same bit before sending any new messages. However, since the medium may be unreliable, a timer is used to limit the amount of time the sender must wait before re-transmitting the message. Therefore, if a message with the same bit arrives before the timeout value, the sender can proceed and send the next message with the alternate bit. On the other hand, if the sender times out, or if an acknowledgement arrives with the wrong bit, the sender re-transmits the message with the original bit and again awaits an acknowledgement. At the opposite end of the medium, the receiving process always acknowledges messages with the same bit as the message just received.

Example
Quantitative time is needed in this example in order to express a simple retransmission timeout. The sender process in the alternating bit protocol is shown in TTM in Figure 5.1a.

We use some notational conventions in this diagram. First, the <x,y> notation means a communication packet of two elements, secondly, i_j is an

Sender

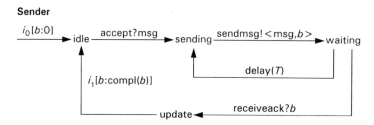

Figure 5.1a   The alternating bit sender in TTM.

92

action internal to a particular TTM process and finally, the notation $[y{:}E]$ assigns the value of the expression E to the variable y.

It should be noticed that none of the actions are dependent upon a pre-condition, i.e. there are no guards in the process. In addition, the timeout is clearly shown as a choice between receiving an acknowledgement or retransmitting if the delay expires after time T. The specification uses the variable b as a sequence number for the messages sent.

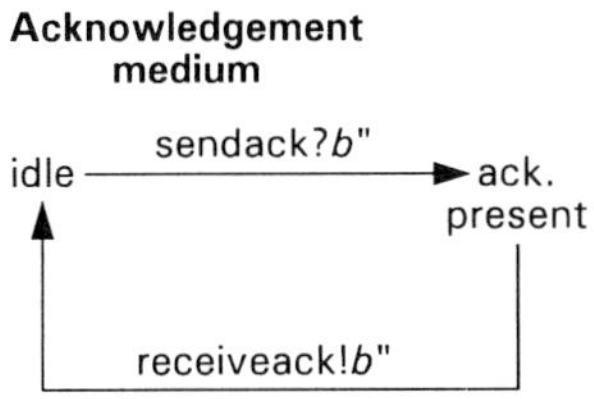

Acknowledgement medium

idle ————sendack?*b*"————▶ ack. present

receiveack!*b*"

Figure 5.1b   The alternating bit acknowledgement medium in TTM.

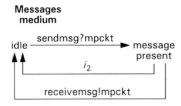

Messages medium

idle ————sendmsg?mpckt————▶ message present

i_2

receivemsg!mpckt

Figure 5.1c   The alternating bit messages medium in TTM.

The medium is defined in TTM in Figures 5.1b and 5.1c. These figures show that there are two mediums: the acknowledgement and messages mediums. The former is assumed to be reliable and the latter is assumed to be unreliable. Thus, in the latter, there is a non-deterministic choice between passing on a message or losing the message (shown as the internal action i_2). These mediums are not buffered; rather they are blocked to further input once a message has been received. This is a standard simplification of a medium's behaviour.

Finally, the receiver process would be defined as shown in Figure 5.1d. Owing to the reliability of the acknowledgement medium this process does not have to include a timeout. The process simply receives messages, delivers them to the environment and sends acknowledgements. The operations fst and scnd access respectively the first and second elements of the message packet (mpckt).

From the published literature, the precise timing semantics of the TTM delay operator is not clear. Specifically, the semantics of the upper delay time bound forces the timeout to complete at time T in the above sender

Receiver

Figure 5.1d The alternating bit receiver in TTM.

process. However, in the absence of a maximal progress rule in the TTM semantics (Ostroff 1992b), time could pass even when a `receiveack` is offered by the acknowledgement medium. Thus, in the present form the above protocol example is not completely correct.

5.5.3 Analysis

Although TTMs are a nice vehicle for introducing extended finite state machines, they are not an appropriate choice for formal specification. In addition to the above mentioned uncertainties over the timing model, TTM is limited in terms of usability. Specifically, TTM is a purely visual notation without a language version, although Ostroff has considered a mapping to an existing real-time language. In addition, there are no graphical tools to support the notation. Thus, although the notation has been found suitable for expressing a certain specific class of real-time problems the language is limited as a more general specification tool.

These limitations, though, are not inherent in the extended finite state machine paradigm itself and are not mirrored in the EFSM notations Estelle and SDL. Both these formal specification techniques support a quantitative timing model, which may fulfil our (real-)time requirements. In addition, both satisfy the more general criteria for formal description, such as expressiveness and existing validation tools, that we set out in Chapter 4. Also, Estelle and SDL clearly satisfy all our concurrency and interaction requirements. Dynamic configuration of processes is also provided in Estelle and the restandardization of SDL, SDL-92, boasts a fully fledged object-oriented structure. Furthermore, Estelle and SDL are standardized and thus satisfy our requirement for interoperability.

5.6 Petri nets

5.6.1 The basic approach

Petri nets are a likely candidate technique, since they fulfil our interaction and concurrency based requirements. They have been developed specifically as a model of concurrency and have been used extensively to model communication protocols (Danthine 1982). Furthermore, quantitative time and probabilistic extensions to Petri nets have been extensively considered, with many of the techniques having been applied to the development of real-time systems (Coolahan & Roussopoulus 1983) (Leveson & Stolzy 1987).

The major characteristic of Petri nets is that they model true concurrency (see Appendix A for clarification of terminology). Advocators of Petri nets argue that linear modelling of concurrent problems implies over-specification.

Petri nets are a bi-partite graph, with the disjoint node sets being called transitions and places respectively. Tokens flow over nets. Although Petri nets have been applied diversely, three particular classes of Petri nets can be highlighted: condition/event nets, place/transition nets and nets with individual tokens. These classes of nets are distinguished by the interpretation that they enforce on the Petri net constituents:

1. *Condition/event nets* Places are interpreted as conditions.
2. *Place/transition nets* More than one token can reside at each place, i.e. there is a notion of quantity.
3. *Nets with individual tokens* Tokens are not restricted to a single type. Tokens of a number of different types can be passed in the net.

A rich theory expressing the mathematical characteristics of Petri nets exists and validation techniques for Petri nets have been developed from this theoretical backbone. A number of comprehensive texts on the topic have been written (Peterson 1981, Reisig 1985).

It is also worth pointing out that Petri nets have been used in the multimedia setting. Specifically, the work of Berra et al. (1990) describes a distributed multimedia database server, using timed place Petri nets in order to express the real-time synchronization relationships between multimedia entities. This application of Petri nets only satisfies a specific part of the requirement for description of distributed multimedia systems. In particular, there is no consideration of the expression of quality of service with Berra's notation and complete system specifications are not considered.

5.6.2 Time in Petri nets

Petri nets were the first formal model of concurrency to which time was added, e.g. Merlin & Farber (1976) was one of the earliest timed Petri net models. Since this early work, various styles of timed Petri nets have been developed, with each model associating a quantitative timing value with a different Petri net entity. Three basic forms can be found in the literature: *timed arc Petri nets* (Walter 1983), *timed transition Petri nets* (Merlin & Farber 1976) and *timed place Petri nets* (Coolahan & Roussopoulus 1983). These approaches have been variously employed to model timed concurrent systems. The debate between the three different classes of timed Petri net seems not to have been concluded, since different models are favoured by different researchers. However, an inherent trade off between expressive power and analytical power in timed Petri nets has been highlighted (Bolognesi et al. 1990). Specifically, timed transition Petri nets are the most expressive; examples of computations which can be expressed in timed transition nets and not in other timed nets have been given. In particular, a classic symmetric timeout, as expressed in the following example with timed transition Petri nets, cannot be expressed in other timed nets.

Example
Figure 5.2 shows the example of a symmetric timeout protocol expressed in a timed transition Petri net notation. The example is adapted from Bolognesi et al. (1990).

Places are denoted as circular nodes, transitions as line segments and tokens as smaller black circles. Tokens reside in places for non-atomic periods of time, while transitions fire instantaneously. A transition fires if all

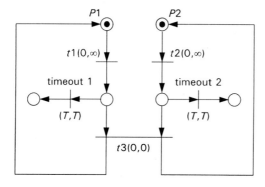

Figure 5.2   A symmetric timeout in timed transition Petri nets.

its input places (i.e. places with arrows to the transition) contain tokens and the timing constraint associated with the transition is satisfied. Timing constraints are expressed as relative time intervals. Times are selected non-deterministically from within the time interval. The selected time defines the instant the transition is taken relative to the instant at which all its input places become occupied.

The Petri net in Figure 5.2 shows two processes, $P1$ and $P2$, which are interacting via a common transition, $t3$. Timeout1 or timeout2 will fire if transition $t3$ is not taken within T time units of one of its input places becoming occupied.

The reason for this discrepancy between timed arc and timed transition Petri nets is that only the latter exhibit "must" timing semantics, i.e. exhibit urgent behaviour (see Appendix A and the discussion in Section 5.4.2). In fact, Bolognesi et al. (1990) have highlighted that only timed transition Petri nets can simulate Turing Machines; the other models are not Turing equivalent, and they are less expressive than untimed Petri nets.

However, a tradeoff exists, since timed transition Petri nets are difficult to analyze. For example, timed transition Petri nets are undecideable in the two important properties of Boundedness (of circulating tokens) and Reachability (of a given marking). In contrast, timed arc Petri nets are decideable in both these properties and timed place Petri nets have been shown to map well to Markov performance models.

5.6.3 Analysis

It seems then that while timed Petri nets are an extensively studied paradigm, conclusive recommendations for which style to employ do not exist. In fact, the trade-off in the theory of timed Petri nets between expressive power and analytical power is a common conflict for formal description in the presence of time. A further issue that is not specific to the Petri net field is the need for an urgency principle in order to force choice to take precedence over time.

However, in spite of the many attractive features, it is clear that Petri nets do not fulfil our requirements. The major reason for this is not specific to the timed version of Petri nets. While Petri nets offer an elegant model of concurrent behaviour, they are not complete in the sense of exhibiting the full expressiveness of a programming language. For example, Petri nets exhibit the following deficiencies in expressiveness:

1. A fully usable data part is not available to pure Petri net models.
2. Petri nets are flat and are thus limited in terms of modularity and compositionality. Specifically they have been criticized in terms of the ability to build large Petri nets from small Petri nets (Milner 1986).
3. The more recent algebraic approaches have advantages in terms of formalized semantics and analytical power. In particular, process algebras offer more tractable mathematical theories of concurrency (Milner 1986). An important reason for this is the observational approach advocated by proponents of the extensionalist view of concurrent systems, which leads to easily analyzed linear models.

Resolution of these problems has been sought in a number of directions, e.g. building programming languages on top of Petri nets and coloured Petri nets (Jensen 1990). However, these approaches are not fully mature and are not widely used outside the Petri net community. Thus, although Petri nets satisfy our requirements fully in terms of expressing concurrency and partially in terms of expressing real-time behaviour, they are limited as a completely usable specification tool for all aspects of development of distributed multimedia systems.

5.7   Synchronous languages

5.7.1   The basic approach

Synchronous languages are a specific class of high-level languages. It is suggested that they are suitable for all stages, including specification, of development of reactive systems (distributed real-time systems are a class of reactive systems). As mentioned earlier, there are four programming notations that can be classed as synchronous languages: the declarative languages Signal (Gautier et al. 1986) and Lustre (Halbwachs et al. 1990); the imperative language Esterel (Berry & Gonthier 1988); and the visual formalism Statecharts (Harel 1987). The first three of these approaches are fully executable programming languages, while the last is a formal design notation.

All synchronous languages adhere to a common principle of computation called the synchrony hypothesis, which states:

  (a) *The internal mechanism of the system*   Every action (computation or internal communication) is instantaneous, i.e. has a zero duration.
  (b) *The communications with the external world*   Communication with the environment is achieved by reacting to input signals (external stimuli) by instantaneously emitting output signals.

The synchrony hypothesis, is argued to be feasible in practice since "zero time" effectively means "less time than the inter-arrival gap between events from the surrounding environment". Synchronous languages are compiled into finite state automata, and as long as these automata are capable of making transitions faster than state changes in the outside environment, the synchrony hypothesis is effectively upheld.

One particularly interesting application of synchronous languages has been made by researchers at CNET. They have used the principles of synchronous languages in order to develop a synchronization model based on the notion of reactive objects. These objects accept events from an outside environment and instantaneously respond by generating new events. Reactive objects are programmed with synchronous languages. The concept of reactive objects has been used as the basis of a computational model for distributed multimedia applications (Stefani et al. 1992). In their approach, applications consist of a set of interacting objects. Some objects in the environment are reactive, while others are not. The reactive objects provide the necessary real-time control required, for example, to implement continuous synchronization across two or more continuous media transmissions. To supplement this model, a quality of service language is provided to constrain the communication between objects. This can be used, for example, to bound the delay on control messages from reactive objects to other objects in the system. An interesting feature of this approach is that timing assumptions are isolated in the quality of service declarations (all other parts of the system are assumed to take zero time). These declarations can therefore be used to determine requirements on the underlying support platform.

5.7.2 Time in synchronous languages

The imposition of the synchrony hypothesis greatly simplifies the modelling of both concurrency and time. It is an abstraction device that transforms real-time modelling into specification of event orderings. Thus, the synchrony hypothesis reduces the real-time specification problem to a standard ordering problem. Furthermore, non-determinism arising from interaction between concurrent entities is not propagated inside systems; rather, the typical partial order of concurrent behaviour is mapped into a total ordering. The nature of synchronous languages will be clarified in the next chapter, when we present an example description in a synchronous language.

5.7.3 Analysis

By employing the synchrony hypothesis, it is argued that synchronous languages succeed in marrying expressiveness with formal characteristics. These languages have a number of attractive features for the specification of real-time systems including:
1. They support reasoning about real-time.
2. They allow any signal to be treated as a clock.
3. They encourage the isolation of real-time assumptions.
4. They reduce real-time specification to specification of event ordering.

Furthermore, synchronous languages do, in general, satisfy the requirements we laid out in Chapter 4. In particular, they offer an attractive and very interesting model of time; they are expressive, in the sense that they support compositional and modular specification development. In addition, a data part can be imported into the language from a host system. It is also claimed that they support formal reasoning and validation (Berry & Gonthier 1988, Benveniste & Guernic 1991).

In addition, researchers at CNET have shown that the features of synchronous languages are applicable to modelling multimedia computations (Stefani et al. 1992). The separation of real-time assumptions is particularly important in deriving the quality of service properties of distributed multimedia applications.

5.8   Other approaches

A considerable amount of research has been directed at developing fully expressive formal specification techniques within the software engineering community. These techniques pay particular attention to the building of large and complex software systems. Major characteristics of these formal specification techniques are:

1. A high level of abstraction is maintained (in order to aid abstract algorithm expression). The languages are generally based upon simple mathematical notation; sets, relations, functions and logic are the major constituents of these notations.
2. A rich model of program development is defined, with particular emphasis placed on the means by which implementations can be developed in a sequence of small (and provable) refinements.
3. Modularization is of central importance in order to aid development of complex systems. Object-oriented techniques are often incorporated for this end.

The two most well known of such techniques are VDM (Jones 1990) and Z (Spivey 1989), although the B approach (Abrial 1996) offers a rich variant of Z that pays particular attention to program refinement. However, for our requirements these techniques are generally limited in their handling of concurrency and distribution. It is argued that some of these techniques can abstract over concurrency and distribution issues. However, for concrete specification of concurrent behaviour as required in the computational and engineering ODP viewpoints, such techniques are fundamentally limited (although, it should be noted that Z based notations are strong candidates for the ODP information viewpoint). For these reasons we will make no further consideration of this class of formal specification techniques.

5.9   Overall analysis

This chapter has presented an assessment of the state of the art in formal specification against the requirements of distributed multimedia computing. Broadly, the state of the art of formal description is somewhere at the level of incorporating quantitative time. Event orderings can be satisfactorily expressed by formal specification techniques and well founded mathematical models for such formal specification techniques have been defined. In particular, branching (concurrent) orders of events can be satisfactorily modelled using such paradigms as labelled transition systems (Keller 1976), extended finite state machines (Danthine 1982) or event structures (Winskel 1989). In addition, validation techniques for these paradigms have been developed, e.g. CÆSAR (Garavel 1990), model checking

(Clarke et al. 1986), EDB (INT 1992b). However, although quantitative time is included in some formal specification techniques (e.g. Estelle) and has been added to a number of others (e.g. LOTOS), the mathematical properties enforced upon these techniques have not been conclusively defined. It is especially the case that validation techniques for timed formal specification techniques have proved difficult to develop.

As emphasized a number of times, there is a definite conflict between what theoreticians can provide in the way of models of concurrency and what users need. Some techniques have been developed from the theoretical side, i.e. with nice mathematical properties as their first concern, and others have been developed from the applied side, i.e. with full expressiveness as the main concern. This distinction is highlighted in Figure 5.3.

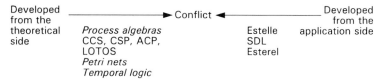

Figure 5.3   The conflict between theory and practice.

Very closely related to this distinction is that between techniques which are more overtly specification oriented and those that are more implementation oriented. The former are designed with the objective of being highly abstract and avoiding definition of specific behaviour, while the latter more closely resemble implementation languages and are also not so easily verified. Figure 5.4 and Table 5.3 highlight this distinction:

It should be noted that Table 5.3 contains general features and is not intended to be hard and fast. In particular, there are many exceptions to these criteria, e.g. π-calculus and Petri nets are both theoretically motivated, although the former employs dynamic reconfiguration and the latter employs a non-interleaved model of concurrency.

More specification oriented   *More implementation oriented*

CCS	LOTOS		Estelle	Esterel
CSP			SDL	
ACP				

Figure 5.4   Specification oriented and implementation oriented approaches.

Table 5.3 Features of specification vs implementation oriented approaches.

Features of specification oriented approaches	Features of implementation oriented approaches
High emphasis on non-determinism	Prioritized choice
Linear time, interleaving models	Non-interleaved models
Synchronous communication	Asynchronous communication
Limited timing models	Rich model of time
Verifiable (or more nearly verifiable)	Rely on validation through simulation
Map to inefficient implementations	Efficient mapping to implementation
Incomplete language with limited data part	Complete language with usable data part
Declarative language styles	Imperative language styles
Static process structure	Dynamic reconfigurability

5.10   Conclusions

We have presented a broad and general survey of formal specification techniques, in which a large number of techniques have been discussed. This survey will be used both as the basis for the comparison of more specific formal techniques to be performed in the next two chapters and in order to inform the development of our new approach in part IV. In particular, a number of the techniques and principles that have been introduced in this survey will prove influential in the development of our approach.

In the next chapter, we will focus directly on the candidate techniques that are most likely to fulfil our requirements for formal specification of distributed multimedia systems. In selecting the techniques to consider further in this part we have rejected two important classes of technique, Petri nets and specification logics.

We reject Petri nets because, while they are an important theoretical technique, they are not a fully usable specification notation. As highlighted in Section 5.6.3 Petri nets do not support data and are limited in terms of compositionality.

From within the specification logics domain, temporal logics, and real-time temporal logics in particular, have many attractive features. However, they are not targeted at specification of the concrete algorithmic behaviour of distributed systems. We will return to temporal logics in Parts IV and V of this book; they will play a central role in the new approach that we propose. Their role in this approach, however, is in addition to a base behavioural specification technique. It is such base techniques that we will focus on in the next two chapters, which will consider three classes of technique: process algebras, EFSMs and synchronous languages.

CHAPTER 6

Assessment of specific formal specification techniques

6.1 Introduction

The conclusions of the previous chapter have centred on the mismatch between the practical (implementation oriented) and the theoretical (specification oriented) in formal description. Unfortunately, formal description of distributed multimedia systems seems to fall firmly at the point of mismatch. In particular, the real-time requirements of multimedia suggest more implementation oriented features are required of formal specification techniques. The benefits of abstract techniques, such as elegance and rigour, and most important the consideration of time and performance, are vital to the realization of both standardization and formal system development for multimedia.

As indicated previously, within this spectrum of techniques it is however clear that certain of the approaches have basic deficiencies that prevent them from satisfying the requirements for formal description of multimedia systems. Consequently, here we focus on just three of the classes of formal specification techniques, namely extended finite state machines, synchronous languages and process algebras, which all seem to be potentially suitable techniques.

Each of the candidate classes of formal description will be illustrated through representative formal notations from within the class. In choosing which notations to focus on we have put particular emphasis on the requirement for open systems solutions. Specifically, from amongst the EFSM techniques we will focus on Estelle and SDL, from the process algebra domain we will consider LOTOS and as a representative synchronous language we will focus on Esterel. The first three of these are all standardized languages, while the fourth, although not standardized, is being extensively employed in the ODP open systems domain. A subset of these techniques have been compared previously in the literature (Turner 1993), but never against multimedia requirements.

Each of the classes of FDT will be considered separately. We will use the multimedia stream example that was introduced in Chapter 4 as a common point of comparison between the techniques. However, in order to simplify presentation, we consider the specification with a reliable medium, i.e. messages are never lost, corrupted or re-ordered. The behaviour of the source and sink processes is relatively easy to model. However, in order to fully express the behaviour of the system, we must enforce a latency delay on the transmission of data between the source and sink and this is less straightforward. Specifically, a channel that simply inputs a frame, enforces a latency delay and then outputs the frame is likely not to be satisfactory, since the evaluation of the latency delay will block the channel from receiving the next frame; it is important that the channel acts as a queue. It should also be noted that placing the input frames into a queue data structure will not resolve the problem, as enforcing the timing delay either before a frame is added to the queue or as it is removed, will cause an unsatisfactory blockage. One way to express the desired behaviour is to evaluate the delay latency in parallel with other frames being input to the channel.

Full specifications of the multimedia stream are included in Appendix B. However, the main text of this chapter will concentrate on the expression of the channel's behaviour in each of the formal specification techniques.

6.2   Estelle

6.2.1   An overview of the language

Estelle is a high level language for defining extended finite state machines. The actual state machine is hidden from the user, although the state machine model is reflected directly in the Estelle syntax. Specifically, the Estelle syntax enables states and transitions (events) between states to be defined directly in the language syntax.

Estelle incorporates all the classical finite state machine extensions. The following list highlights the major aspects of the extensions:

- The data extensions to the finite state machine paradigm are defined using standard Pascal.
- Parallel composition of sub-machines is defined through a module hierarchy structure. Modules on the same level of the hierarchy can execute in parallel according to either asynchronous or synchronous parallel behaviour (see Appendix A for clarification of terminology).

The particular class of parallel behaviour is determined by common parent modules.

- Communication is asynchronous in Estelle, using unbounded FIFO queues. Multi way communication can be defined by target modules sharing the same queue.
- Dynamic reconfiguration of the module structure is offered in Estelle. Specific operators are available to create and release both tasks (the init and release operations) and channels (the connect/disconnect and attach/detach operators).
- Non-determinism between transitions can be defined in two ways, either explicitly using the module hierarchy structure or implicitly as choice between transitions within the same module.
- Priorities can be defined on the choice of transitions.
- Quantitative time is incorporated in Estelle using a delay operator.

The standard tutorial on Estelle is due to Budkowski & Dembinski (1987).

To the user, parallel behaviours in Estelle should be viewed as truly parallel, in contrast to the process algebra approach. However, the semantics of Estelle are defined in terms of interleaving and simulators unravel Estelle specifications in an interleaved fashion. In general, validation tools for Estelle perform such unravelling and step through specifications either interactively or using random search. A number of such validation tools have been developed (examples are EDB (INT 1992b), ESTIM (de Saqui-sannes & Courtiat 1989) and Io (Fernandez et al. 1992)).

Synthesis of implementations has also been found to be viable with Estelle and tools, which generally map to either C or ADA, have been developed (INT 1992a). Furthermore, initial results on comparing the efficiency of code generated from Estelle specifications and written by hand have proved favourable.

Estelle lacks the rich mathematical theory underpinning formal specification techniques with more theoretical origins, such as Petri Nets and process algebras. In particular, mathematical proof is not facilitated with Estelle since proof systems have not been developed and, furthermore, the model of observational equivalence central to process algebra verification has no mirror in Estelle.

However, model checking from temporal logic has been applied to validation of Estelle. XESAR (Richier et al. 1987) takes temporal logic formulae and checks them against the finite state graph generated by CÆSAR from Estelle specifications. Notably, XESAR is designed to work from a non-standard version of Estelle, called Estelle/R, which employs a synchronous rather than asynchronous communication primitive. However, realistic verification of large specifications has proved impossible with this tool due to state space explosion problems.

6.2.2   Modelling the medium

The following module expresses the behaviour of the channel in the multi-media stream example. Unfortunately, it is beyond the scope of this book to give a full presentation of the Estelle syntax; the interested reader is referred to Budkowski & Dembinski (1987). However we will discuss the major features of the specification pertaining to real-time.

```
module cchannel systemprocess;
ip inchan : SourceOut (receiver);   outchan : SinkIn (sender);
{input and output channels}
end;

  body cchannelbody for cchannel;

  {-------------- child process of cchannel ------------}
  module transmitfr process;
  ip chan : intracchannel (transfr); {input and output  channel
                                        for subprocess}
    export done:boolean;
  end;

  body transmitfrbody for transmitfr;
  state WAITING,SENDING;
  var fr_no:integer;
  initialize to WAITING
    begin done:=false end;

  trans
  from WAITING to SENDING
    when chan.requesttrans(frno) {receive a frame from  parent
                                    process (cchannel)}
      name T2 : begin
        fr_no:=frno
      end;

  from SENDING to WAITING
  (*) delay(80,90)   {the latency value imposed on the channel}
      name T3 : begin
        output chan.finishedtrans(fr_no); {output frame to parent
                                            process}
        done:=true                  {indicate process can be
                                      released}
      end;

    end;   {of module transmitfr}

  { Main body of the cchannel module starts here }
```

```
ip subchan : array[1..maxtrans] of intracchannel (cha);
{channels to child processes}

modvar transf:transmitfr;
state TRANSMIT;
var i: integer;
initialize to TRANSMIT
 begin i:=1 end;

trans
from TRANSMIT to same
   when inchan.frame(frno)
    name T4 : begin
      init transf with transmitfrbody; {create a child
                                      (transmitfr) process}
      connect subchan[i] to transf.chan; {connect channels to
                                        child process}
      output subchan[i].requesttrans(frno); {output to child
                                            process}
      all transmitfrbody:transmitfr do {kill child processes
                                       when done}
       if transmitfrbody.done then release transmitfrbody;
       if (i=maxtrans) then i:=1 else i:=i+1;
      end;

from TRANSMIT to same  {this transition passes frames from
                        the child process out of the channel}
  any j:1..maxtrans do
   when subchan[j].finishedtrans(frno)
    name T5 : begin
      output outchan.frame(frno);
      end;

end;    {of module cchannel}
```

The module cchannel uses the dynamic process reconfiguration facilities of Estelle to create instances of the child module transmitfr that transmits a single frame with the required latency delay. Importantly, any number of child modules can be transmitting at the same instant, thus, cchannel does not block.

The timing behaviour in the example is expressed using the Estelle delay operator. Using this operator the offering of a transition can be suspended until a delay has been evaluated. In addition, this delay can be expressed over an interval, enabling non-deterministic timing to be modelled. This is demonstrated in the module transmitfr above, in which the delay clause (marked *) suspends transition *T3* for between 80 and 90 time units, and the time unit is chosen non-deterministically. The timing semantics of Estelle are defined in clauses 7.5.7.4 and 9.6.5 of the Estelle standards document (ISO 1987). The following is an informal description of these semantics.

Assume a transition t with clause delay$(E1,E2)$.

1. Having become newly enabled t cannot be executed until it has remained enabled for at least $E1$ time units.
2. If t has been enabled for E time units, where $E1 \leq E < E2$, then even if t is the only enabled transition within a module, t may or may not be offered for execution. This enables non-determinism of timing properties to be specified, thus leaving specific timing as an implementation issue. In addition, $E2=*$ can be used to indicate no upper bound and that there is no requirement that the transition ever be offered for execution.
3. If t has been enabled for E time units, where $E \geq E2$, then if t is the only transition enabled, t will fire. However, if there are other enabled transitions at this moment, any may fire (notice that priorities can be used to force t to fire at this stage).

Although the informal timing semantics of Estelle are relatively powerful, ambiguities have been located in the standards document. The work of J-P. Courtiat has clarified these formal semantics (Courtiat 1989). Interestingly, this work has used timed transition Petri nets as a base notation to define the Estelle timing semantics.

In contrast to the timing model for TTMs, Estelle does exhibit urgent timing behaviour. First, the mechanism for selecting fireable transitions enforces an urgency to enable communication. Furthermore, the upper delay time bound forces a delay to complete if no other alternative exists. Finally, particular time communication conflicts can be resolved using priorities in Estelle.

Tools that perform validation in the presence of time have also been developed. For example, EDB facilitates the simulation of time parameters by resolving delay values and simulator specified global timing parameters such as the time taken to execute a certain class of transition. It should be noted though that some difficulties in present versions of EDB have been located with the timing aspect of the tool.

Although in general Estelle specifications cannot be said to be succinct, the above specification of the multimedia stream channel is particularly inelegant. This arises because of the complexity of expressing dynamic reconfiguration and from the setting up of associated communication channels.

6.2.3 Assessment

Estelle provides an accepted model of quantitative time. It should be noted in particular that the extensive debate concerning the timing model that should be adopted within the process algebra community has no equivalent for Estelle, see Chapter 7. We tentatively suggest a number of possible reasons why this may be the case:

(a) A major concern for integration of time into process algebras is to maintain compatibility with the semantic model fundamental to the approach. Specifically, time has been found difficult to resolve with the existing observational mathematical model of process algebras. Such mathematical theory does not exist for Estelle and the semantic model of Estelle is presented in a highly mechanistic fashion with which time can be easily reconciled.

(b) Asynchronous communication reduces timing conflicts between communicating processes, i.e. the timing properties of the two processes are independent and do not need to be reconciled at the point of communication. Rather, timing conflicts are smoothed out through buffering between communicating processes.

(c) Priorities can also be used in order to resolve specific conflicts between the passage of time and choice.

In addition to the model of time provided in Estelle, it is a technique that satisfies the more general criteria for formal description that we require, such as usability and existing validation tools. Estelle also clearly satisfies all our concurrency and interaction requirements. In particular, asynchronous communication is central to Estelle. Dynamic configuration of processes is also provided, although a fully fledged object-oriented structure has not been incorporated. Furthermore, Estelle is a standard and thus satisfies our requirement for interoperability.

The limitations of Estelle are inelegance in specifications written with the language and mathematical tractability of the language. The former can be demonstrated by comparing the stream specification in Estelle and in LOTOS, see Section 6.5.2. The latter arises because Estelle lacks the rich mathematical theory underpinning other formal specification techniques, such as Petri nets and process algebras. In particular, mathematical proof is not facilitated with Estelle and, furthermore, the model of observational equivalence central to process algebra verification has no mirror in Estelle.

6.3   SDL

6.3.1   An overview of the language

SDL has very strong similarities to Estelle; it incorporates the standard finite state machine extensions in a similar way and the language also employs asynchronous communication. However, some important differences between the two languages do exist. First, SDL offers a rich graphical model for specification development. Specifically SDL subsumes two distinct, but equivalent, formal notations SDL-PR and SDL-GR. The former is a standard textual formal language, while the latter is a graphical formal description notation. In addition, the data extensions to the finite state machine paradigm are defined using an abstract data typing language. This contrasts with the use of Pascal in Estelle. SDL supports quantitative time through the definition of timers; this construct will be discussed in the next subsection.

It should also be noted that a revised version of SDL was defined in 1992 (Faergemand & Olsen 1992) that incorporates a number of new features, including, most significantly, object-orientation. This has relevance for the definition of ODP object-oriented concepts. SDL is widely used in the telecommunications domain and is well supported with tools, for example, the *sdlvalid* tool (Holzmann 1992).

6.3.2   Modelling the medium

Figure 6.1 contains a specification of the channel for the multimedia stream in SDL-GR. The specification is in three parts. The first is a block diagram that defines the interconnection of processes that make up the channel. Signals into and out of the block are defined with arrows touching the perimeter of the block diagram (signal routes ssourceOut and ssinkIn). This block contains the processes cchannel and transmitfr. The former of these receives frames (the Outframe signal) and then dynamically creates an instance of process transmitfr to impose a latency delay. Thus, the specification has the same form as the solution employed in the Estelle specification, although the frame number to be transmitted by transmitfr is passed as a parameter to the subprocess. In the Estelle specification a communication channel is set up to pass this information. Once again it is not possible to give a complete introduction to SDL; the interested reader is referred to Turner (1993).

Quantitative time can be modelled in SDL using timers. These can be activated during a transition using the set construct, for example, the *T*5 timer in the transmitfr process. Notice that the expression *now* gives the current global time in the interpretation of the specification and that the *any* construct enables the expiry time of *T*5 to be selected non-deterministically

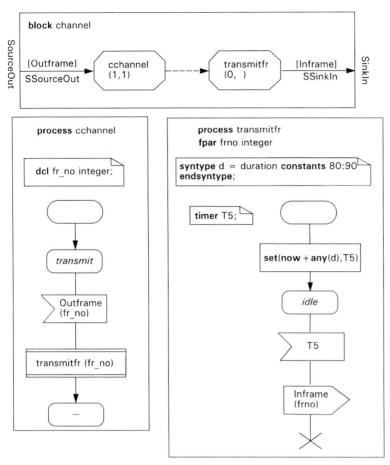

Figure 6.1 SDL Specification of Channel.

from the interval 80:90 (this is an SDL-92 feature). When a timer expires, a signal with the name of the timer (here *T5*) is placed in the input queue of the process.

6.3.3 Assessment

Specifications in SDL seem generally to be more simple than equivalent specifications in Estelle and, in particular, the visual nature of SDL is appealing. However, this aside, SDL exhibits similar benefits and flaws to Estelle. The language is well developed with a rich tool environment, but intractable problems exist in validation of SDL specifications (Holzmann 1992). For example, the unbounded input queues used in SDL prevent finite state exploration.

6.4   Esterel

6.4.1   An overview of the language

The Esterel language comprises standard imperative language constructs
and temporal constructs. The imperative constructs include assignment,
sequencing, conditional selection, parallel composition and traps. The
temporal constructs offer facilities to manipulate signals (these are broadcast communication primitives). There are temporal constructs that send
signals, select conditionally dependent upon the presence of a signal, iter-
ate dependent upon the presence of signals and wait for signals to arrive.

Programs written in the language are intended solely to express reaction
to the stimulus of an external environment. In particular, Esterel does not
offer data typing mechanisms as such (these must be imported from a host
environment).

6.4.2   Modelling the medium

The behaviour of the channel can be expressed as follows in Esterel:

```
module channel:
constant TRUE: boolean, FALSE: boolean;
type elt_type, queue_elem, queue_type;
input CLOCKTICK, SourceOut (elt_type);
output SinkIn (elt_type);

function new_queue (): queue_type;        % These are externally
                                          % defined
function top (queue_type): queue_elem;    % data manipulation
                                          % functions
function add_last (queue_elem, queue_type): queue_type;
function remove_top (queue_type): queue_type;
function empty (queue_type): boolean;
function calc_delay (queue_elem, integer): integer;
function make_pair (elt_type, integer): queue_elem;
function fst (queue_elem): elt_type;

                         % THREAD 1
signal CurrentDate (integer) in [ %This thread issues a signal defining
                                  % the current time according to
  var cur: integer in [           % some external signal CLOCKTICK
    every CLOCKTICK do cur := cur + 1; emit CurrentDate (cur) end
  ] end % var
  ||                              % THREAD 2
  signal UpdateQueue, RemoveTop, % This thread places input frames into
```

```
                                    % the queue
      TopQueue (queue_elem), NextWait (integer) in [
    every SourceOut do emit UpdateQueue end % every
    ||
    var queue: queue_type, NewWait: boolean in [ % THREAD 3
                                    % This thread handles the queue
      queue := new_queue ();        % manipulation and evaluating when
      every UpdateQueue do [        % the next frame should be emitted
        NewWait := FALSE;
        present SourceOut then
          if (empty (queue)) then NewWait := TRUE end; % if
          queue := add_last (make_pair (?SourceOut,
                                        ?CurrentDate),queue);
        end; % present
        present RemoveTop then
          queue := remove_top (queue);
        if (not (empty (queue))) then NewWait := TRUE end; % if
        end; % present
        if (NewWait) then
          emit TopQueue (top (queue));
(*)       emit NextWait (calc_delay (?TopQueue, ?CurrentDate))
        end % if
      ]end % every
    ]end % var
    ||                          % THREAD 4
    var ToBeSent: elt_type in [ % This thread emits frames from the
                                % channel
      loop
        await immediate NextWait;
        ToBeSent := fst (?TopQueue);
        await (?NextWait) CLOCKTICK;
        emit UpdateQueue; emit SinkIn (ToBeSent); emit RemoveTop
      end % loop
    ]end % var
  ]end % signal
]end % signal
```

This example demonstrates the radical manner in which Esterel (and synchronous languages in general) handle time. More precisely, there are no specific timing operators included in the specification (such as the Estelle delay operator). In addition, there is no predefined (and all pervasive) global clock that synchronizes the passage of time through the whole specification. Rather, the clock is defined explicitly (as the externally defined periodic signal CLOCKTICK) and the ticks of the clock have the same attributes as all other signals in the specification. Thus, there is nothing special about clocks; any periodic transmission of a signal can be used to synchronize an Esterel computation (i.e. time is multiform). This also means that there is no quantification of the passing of time. Rather a qualitative ordering of event occurrence can be enforced, as in this example. This is in accordance with the enforcement of the synchrony hypothesis.

The expression of the channel's behaviour is quite different from that in Estelle and SDL. In particular, there is no dynamic instantiation of processes. Rather, a static process structure is maintained. This has the following general form:

THREAD 1	THREAD 2	THREAD 3	THREAD 4
issues data | | [	receives frames | |	manages the	| | transmits]
stamps	from source	queue	frames

In particular, the latency delay is only enforced in thread 4 and this evaluates in parallel with threads 2 and 3, which receive frames and adds them to the queue. Thus, the evaluation of the latency delay in thread 4 cannot block new inputs from being inserted into the queue. This form of solution is possible in Esterel because of the radical handling of time arising out of the imposition of the synchrony hypothesis.

The combination of the synchrony hypothesis and broadcast communication enables a time stamping signal denoting the current time relative to global time to be defined. Importantly, in Esterel any process can either access this signal at the same instant as other processes access the same signal or else ignore it. Thus, the required latency delay to enforce in thread 4 can be determined relative to the amount of time the frame has been queued for in thread 3. Such explicit definition of periodic timing behaviour and flexible handling of clocks is very difficult to express in either the EFSM or process algebra models. The timing mechanism of Esterel also enables timing arithmetic to be performed as shown in statement (*) where the latency delay required is determined relative to the amount of time the frame has been in the queue.

6.4.3   Assessment

Esterel can be seen to offer the following benefits:
1. Esterel seems generally to be a more elegant notation than Estelle, although the dynamic configuration mechanisms offered in Estelle may make the language more powerful.
2. Efficient automata based implementations can be mapped to and from the language.
3. The most significant benefit of the approach is the handling of timing behaviour. There are no separate timing constructs and mechanisms,

as was the case in Estelle. Rather, time and communication in general are handled in a uniform manner.

In terms of satisfying our requirements some weaknesses with the language can be highlighted:

1. The language is generally too implementation orientated and it does not support abstract specification. In particular, non-determinism is not included in the language.

2. Although formal semantics for synchronous languages have been defined (Berry & Gonthier 1988, Benveniste & Guernic 1991), the language is not mathematically tractable, in the sense that, say, the process algebras are. For example, there is no equivalent of the process algebra theory of observational equivalence or of preorder refinement.

In summary, the implementation benefits of synchronous languages are obtained at the expense of specification features. In particular, synchronous languages are completely deterministic and thus, abstract specification is limited in the language. Also, the synchrony hypothesis must be applied with care, since paradoxes such as events disabling their own cause, can arise (Ostroff 1992b).

6.5   LOTOS

6.5.1   An overview of the language

As stated in Chapter 5, a number of different process algebraic techniques exist, notably CCS (Milner 1980), CSP (Hoare 1985) and LOTOS (ISO 1988). While CCS and CSP are both extremely valuable formal specification techniques, we will focus on LOTOS for a number of reasons:

• LOTOS consists of two components: a process algebraic language and an abstract data typing language (CCS has no equivalent data typing language). The ACT-ONE (Ehrig & Mahr 1985) abstract data typing language has been used for this purpose. Note however that the full usability of the ACT-ONE language has been questioned by a number of researchers (Thomas 1993).

• LOTOS has been standardized by ISO and is a recognized formal specification technique within OSI and ODP.

• LOTOS specifications can be written in a wide variety of styles, some of the major ones being identified in Turner (1990) and Vissers et al. (1991). These different styles capture different structures or characteristics of systems and their use can enhance the readability and understanding of a specification.

LOTOS (ISO 1988) has been developed and standardized in parallel with Estelle as a language for specifying OSI protocols. Drayton et al. (1991) contains a straightforward introduction to the language, with more advanced treatment in Bolognesi & Brinksma (1988). Broadly speaking, LOTOS is an application oriented composite of CCS, CSP and CIRCAL (Milne 1985). It builds a more usable specification language upon the mathematically oriented notation of the classic process algebras.

Owing to the standardization of LOTOS and the application oriented nature of the language, a large number of tools have been developed; the Lotosphere project (Bolognesi et al. 1992) is a good example of such work. However, the application of LOTOS is at present limited in terms of complete software development. For example, existing tools have proved unable to produce efficient executable code from LOTOS (Nirschl et al. 1993, Ernberg et al. 1993). This is in contrast to the finite state machine based approaches where relatively efficient executable code can be produced (Andreu et al. 1993).

6.5.2   Modelling the medium

The succinctness of specification in LOTOS can be seen by comparing the LOTOS definition of the multimedia example with the corresponding Estelle, SDL and Esterel specifications (see Appendix B). Furthermore, a major part of the specification presented involves the definition of a queue data type (which is a standard LOTOS structure). Hence, the actual definition of the stream behaviour is very concise. One particular influence on this fact is the declarative nature of LOTOS process instantiation as compared to Estelle's and Esterel's imperative structure.

Notice that although quantitative time cannot be expressed in standard LOTOS the positions at which timing evaluations take place can be shown in the specification. In particular, `timeout1` models the latency error check (95 milliseconds), `timeout2` forces the 50 millisecond gap before the next frame should be transmitted and `timeout3` models the jitter error check (10 milliseconds).

In addition, modelling of the channel using a queue data type is possible since events are not timed, i.e. the latency delay is modelled as an instantaneous event and thus, blocking problems waiting for timers to expire are avoided. The channel can be succinctly expressed as:-

```
process channel[SourceOut,latencydelay,SinkIn] (buf:buffer):noexit:=

  (SourceOut?fr_no:Nat;
   channel[SourceOut,latencydelay,SinkIn] (add(fr_no,buf)) )
  []
   [fst(buf) ne fst(nil)] -> (* where ne is not equal *)
     ( latencydelay!fst(buf);
```

```
      SinkIn!fst(buf);
      channel[SourceOut,latencydelay,SinkIn](rmv(buf)) )
endproc (* channel *)
```

6.5.3   Assessment

Critically, LOTOS does not satisfy our requirement for specification of quantitative time. Thus, in its standardized form the language is not sufficient for formal description of distributed multimedia systems. However, we do believe that the expressiveness and analytical power of the LOTOS approach make it a strong basis for a satisfactory technique. In addition, it should be pointed out that the current standardization of an enhanced LOTOS language is seeking to address this issue by adding real-time to the language.

6.6   Conclusions and overall assessment

As indicated in the previous chapter there is a spectrum of formal specification techniques with clear trade-offs between respective techniques. We will highlight the relative benefits of the four techniques we have focused on in the context of the requirements categories set out in Chapter 4. We will consider distribution, real-time and usability requirements separately.

- *Distribution features*   In terms of distribution features there are significant differences between the four approaches (e.g. LOTOS uses synchronous communication, Estelle and SDL use asynchronous communication and Esterel employs broadcast communication). With respect to the distribution requirements of this book, all the techniques are satisfactory. Specifically, they all offer some form of concurrency and interaction as part of an explicit modelling of system behaviour.

Table 6.1   Real-time support in the various languages.

Language	Syntax of quantitative time	Nature of the passage of time
Estelle	Delay operator	Time passes implicitly (i.e. implicit global clock)
SDL	Timers	Time passes implicity (i.e. implicit global clock)
Esterel	No implicit operator (expressed arithmetically over explicitly defined periodic timing signals)	No implicit passing of time
LOTOS	No quantitative time	No quantitative time

117

- *Real-time*   In a general sense, of the four techniques, it is only standard LOTOS that does not satisfy the requirement to express quantitative time. However, there are significant differences between the
  timing mechanisms of Esterel, Estelle and SDL. These are highlighted
  in Table 6.1.

    Table 6.1 indicates that the handling of time in Esterel is the most
  radical; the language offers a wholly different means of modelling the
  passage of quantitative time. There seem to be benefits in the Esterel
  timing model, e.g. it enables arithmetic on timing signals to be expressed and also, through the synchrony hypothesis, presents an appealing model of timing behaviour.

- *Usability*   It is in this category that the most interesting trade-offs
  between the four techniques can be highlighted. All the techniques
  offer a complete data manipulation component (i.e. Estelle using
  Pascal, SDL using ADTs, Esterel by using data functions defined in
  a host language and LOTOS using ACT-ONE) and generally enable
  compositional development of specifications. However, there are
  significant differences between first, the levels of abstraction supported by the techniques and secondly, the ability to validate or synthe-
  size implementations with the techniques. The trade-offs with respect
  to these issues are highlighted in Figure 6.2.

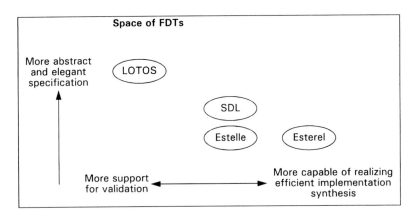

Figure 6.2   Comparison according to usability issues.

In summary then, while all the four techniques satisfy our distribution
requirements and Estelle, SDL and Esterel generally offer facilities to
model real-time, there is significant diversity between the qualities that affect usability of the techniques. Specifically, LOTOS more fully supports
validation and abstract specification, while Estelle, SDL and, to an even

greater extent, Esterel, facilitate realistic implementation synthesis at the expense of specification features.

We will now focus on LOTOS and its timed extensions in the next chapter. We have chosen to focus on the process algebra based approaches because of the elegance, abstractness and general specification oriented nature of the techniques. As stated earlier, amongst the process algebras, we have focused on LOTOS based techniques because of LOTOS' role in standardization activities.

CHAPTER 7

Evaluation of LOTOS based techniques

7.1 Introduction

This chapter initially considers standard LOTOS as defined in ISO (1988). However, as indicated previously there is an ongoing debate within the LOTOS community concerning the lack of quantitative time in LOTOS. This has led to a plethora of timed variants of the language being developed. While many researchers have gone on to develop timed extensions to LOTOS, little has been written on exactly what timing features LOTOS can and cannot provide. The following sections aim to address this point using examples taken from the alternating bit protocol where appropriate.

In addition, in order to complete the comparison of techniques begun in the previous chapter we will conclude this chapter with a more in-depth consideration of a specific, prominent, timed LOTOS, LOTOS-T. In particular, a specification of the multimedia stream will be presented in this language. As in the previous chapter, we focus on the modelling of the medium (the complete specification is given in Appendix B).

7.2 The alternating bit protocol in LOTOS

The simplicity of the alternating bit protocol, and the fact that its behaviour is typical of many other protocols, has made it a suitable example with which to test the adequacy of different languages. Section 5.5.2 describes the basic behaviour of the protocol.

7.2.1   A LOTOS specification of the alternating bit protocol

This section presents a typical LOTOS specification of the alternating bit protocol (for example, as found in Leduc & Léonard (1993)). Figure 7.1 shows the different components of the protocol specification:

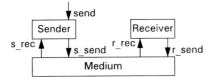

Figure 7.1   Components of the alternating bit protocol specification.

Figure 7.1 shows three components to the alternating bit protocol specification: the sender of messages, the receiver of messages and the medium (channel) over which all messages are transmitted. Since all communication is via the medium, the sender and the receiver behave independently. Messages are transmitted from the sender to the receiver using alternating sequence numbers (0 and 1) to permit the sender to distinguish between the current message and the previous message. Note that the events s_send, s_rec, r_send and r_rec will all be hidden in the LOTOS specification. These events are internal to the behaviour of the protocol, and hence should not be able to be influenced by the protocol's environment. The overall behaviour can be specified as follows:

```
process ABProtocol [ send ] : noexit :=
  send;
    ( hide s_send, s_rec, r_send, r_rec, timeout in
    ( s_send !0; Sender[ s_send, s_rec, timeout ] ( 0 )
      |||
    Receiver[ r_send, r_rec ] )
    |[ s_send, s_rec, r_send, r_rec ]|
    Medium[ s_send, s_rec, r_send, r_rec ]
    )
endproc (* ABProtocol *)
```

The job of the sender process is to wait for a reply from the receiver, thus acknowledging receipt of the message. However, problems may occur at the receiver (e.g. system failure), or during transmission (e.g. message loss or corruption), which cause the message to be either delayed or lost. Consequently, if a reply is not received before a pre-determined time limit, the process should timeout and re-send the previously transmitted message. To model a timeout, a standard LOTOS event has been used, that is, no special semantics have been introduced. To comply with the description of the alternating bit protocol described above, the sender can be specified as follows (where eq is an equality check between natural numbers):

```
process Sender [ s_send, s_rec, timeout ] ( n:nat ) : noexit :=
  s_rec ?m:nat;
    ( [ m eq n ] -> (* reply is from current message, continue and
                       send next message *)
    s_send !compl ( n ); (* send the complement of n *)
    Sender [ s_send, s_rec, timeout ] ( compl ( n ) )
    []
    [ not ( m eq n ) ] -> (* reply is from old message, so re-send
                             current message *)
    s_send !n; (* re-send message *)
    Sender [ s_send, s_rec, timeout ] ( n )
  )
[]
  timeout; (* reply has taken too long, therefore timeout and
              re-send current message *)
    s_send !n; (* re-send message *)
    Sender [ s_send, s_rec, timeout ] ( n )
  endproc (* Sender *)
```

For the sake of simplicity, assume that all that the receiving process does is to receive a message from the sender and return a reply (with the same sequence number that the message just received). In practice it would additionally have to deal with the possibility of duplicate transmissions, but we will ignore this here. This process can be specified as follows:

```
process Receiver [ r_send, r_rec ] : noexit :=
  r_rec ?n:nat; r_send !n; Receiver [ r_send, r_rec ]
endproc (* Receiver *)
```

Modelling an unreliable medium

In order to test the specification of the alternating bit protocol, it is necessary to model a medium over which the messages can be transmitted. Again for simplicity, assume that a one-slot simplex medium is in use, i.e. the medium can only handle one message at any one time and can only transmit messages in one direction at any one time. The medium is also assumed to be unreliable; hence, messages may be lost during transmission. To model this, the internal action, i, is used to represent the loss of a message. Therefore, after a message has been sent, the medium has a non-deterministic choice between delivering the message or performing an internal event (message loss). In either case, the medium is then ready to accept another message for transmission.

```
process Medium[ s_send, s_rec, r_send, r_rec ] : noexit :=
  s_send; (* accept message for transmission from Sender to
           Receiver *)
   ( r_rec; Medium[ s_send, s_rec, r_send, r_rec ]
   []
   i (* message lost *) ; Medium[ s_send, s_rec, r_send, r_rec ]
   )
[]
   r_send; (* accept message for transmission from Receiver to
            Sender *)
   ( s_rec; Medium[ s_send, s_rec, r_send, r_rec ]
   []
   i (* message lost *) ; Medium[ s_send, s_rec, r_send, r_rec ]
   )
endproc (* Medium *)
```

7.2.2   Analysis of the specification

Analysis of this alternating bit protocol specification shows that it is dead-lock-free, that is, no state is reached in which there is no possible future event. Additionally, the use of LOTOS tools (such as Mañas (1992)) can be used to show that the specification is consistent with the description of the alternating bit protocol given at the start of this section.

The specification given above assumes that the medium is unreliable. However, suppose that, at some date in the future, the unreliable medium is upgraded to a completely reliable medium, that is, a medium in which messages will never be lost. The behaviour of the new medium process can be specified as follows:

```
process ReliableMedium[ s_send, s_rec, r_send, r_rec ]
                       :noexit :=
  s_send; (* accept message for transmission from Sender
           to Receiver *)
   r_rec; ReliableMedium[ s_send, s_rec, r_send, r_rec ]
   []
  r_send; (* accept message for transmission from
           Receiver to Sender *)
   s_rec; ReliableMedium[ s_send, s_rec, r_send, r_rec ]
endproc (* ReliableMedium *)
```

Replacing the old unreliable medium with the new reliable medium in the ABProtocol process has an interesting consequence. The new specification is no longer deadlock-free: a state exists in which there is no possible future event. To establish why, consider the following sequence of events:

1. The sender transmits its first message, synchronizing with the (reliable) medium on an s_send event.
2. The medium delivers the message, synchronizing with the receiver on an r_rec event.
3. The receiver replies by synchronizing with the medium on an r_send event.
4. At this point, the sender has the non-deterministic choice between synchronizing with the medium on an s_rec event, or performing a timeout. Suppose it chooses to timeout.
5. The sender can now only offer an s_send event, but it must synchronize with the medium to perform this event. On the other hand, the medium can only offer an s_rec event, and it must synchronize with the sender. Therefore, neither process can proceed. Since no other events in the specification are possible at this point, deadlock exists.

In the original specification, the fact that the unreliable medium could non-deterministically lose messages masked this problem. Having timed out, the unreliable medium has a non-deterministic choice between offering an s_rec event (for which it must synchronize with the sender) and performing an internal action (representing the loss of the message). At this point, the sender is not in a position to synchronize on an s_rec event; therefore, the only option is for the medium to lose its message. This option is not available if a reliable medium is used.

To summarize, although the specification of the alternating bit protocol given above appears to be satisfactory when an unreliable medium is used, problems occur when the unreliable medium is substituted for a reliable medium. Since the alternating bit protocol should work across a reliable medium, as well as an unreliable medium, the specification is clearly not satisfactory.

7.2.3   Correcting the specification

Deadlock occurs in the specification when communication is no longer possible between the sender and the medium; one process is waiting to synchronize on one event, while the other process is waiting to synchronize on a different event. Two possible solutions are presented below.

Modifying the medium's behaviour
One possible solution to the problem of deadlock would be to modify the behaviour of the medium, allowing it to accept a message for transmission to the receiver, while still trying to deliver a message to the sender. For example, a duplex medium could be specified (messages may be transmitted in both directions at any given time) rather than a simplex medium. However, this simply postpones the problem of deadlock. If the sender repeatedly selects the timeout in favour of receiving the incoming message

(as in step 4 above), the medium will eventually fill up and deadlock will again occur. Therefore, to remove deadlock from the specification by modifying the medium, it is necessary to use a duplex medium with unbounded buffers, i.e. permit the medium to hold a potentially infinite number of messages in both directions at any one time.

Unbounded buffers, as used in (pure) asynchronous communication, are a perfectly valid abstract model of a medium, and are frequently used in specifications. However, in this specification, the behaviour of the protocol should be correct regardless of the type of medium used, whether that be reliable or unreliable, bounded or infinite. Consequently, although deadlock has been removed from the specification, for the purpose of this chapter, simply remodelling the medium is not viewed as a satisfactory solution.

Modifying the sender's behaviour

Another, more satisfactory, solution exists if the specification of the sender is considered. After the sender has timed out, it is committed to re-sending its message. At this point, if the sender is permitted to receive a message, even if it is ignored (since it arrived after the timeout), the medium can be unblocked so that it is ready to accept another message for transmission. This new behaviour can be specified as follows:

```
process NewSender [ s_send, s_rec, timeout ] ( n:nat )
                    : no exit :=
  s_rec ?m:nat;
    ( [ m eq n ] -> (* reply is from current message, continue and
                       send next message *)
    s_send !compl ( n ); (* send the complement of n *)
    NewSender [ s_send, s_rec, timeout ] ( compl ( n ) )
    []
      [ not ( m eq n ) ] -> (* reply is from old message, so re-send
                             current message *)
      s_send !n; (* re-send current message *)
      NewSender [ s_send, s_rec, timeout ] ( n )
    )
  []
  timeout; (* reply has taken too long, therefore timeout and
             re-send message *)
    ( s_send !n; (* re-send current message *)
    NewSender [ s_send, s_rec, timeout ] ( n )
    []
    s_rec ?m:nat; (* allow message to be received to unblock
                     medium, but ignore *)
    s_send !n; (* re-send current message *)
```

```
    NewSender [ s_send, s_rec, timeout ] ( n )
    )
endproc (* NewSender *)
```

Although both of the solutions presented above result in correct deadlock-free behaviour, the latter solution may be used regardless of the type of medium used to test the protocol.

7.2.4   Summary

A LOTOS specification has been given of the alternating bit protocol and has been written in a format typical of many simple protocol specifications in the literature. This specification adequately models the intended behaviour of the alternating bit protocol when an unreliable medium is used. However, an interesting consequence of upgrading the unreliable medium with a reliable medium is that the new (upgraded) specification is no longer deadlock-free. Two solutions have been proposed involving modifications to the medium and the sender respectively. The latter of these provides a more general solution, since it can be used regardless of the type of medium, whether reliable or unreliable, bounded or infinite.

Consequently, it has been shown that a correct specification of the alternating bit protocol can be achieved using standard LOTOS. The abstract notion of time needed in such protocols (e.g. simple timeouts) can be specified without the need for any extension to LOTOS.

7.3   Simulating quantitative time in standard LOTOS

Protocols such as the one described above need only an abstract notion of time. LOTOS has been shown to be an adequate specification language for this very simple class of time. However, for systems such as multimedia systems, it is often necessary to measure the passage of time, that is, it must be possible to specify quantitative time.

It is the lack of an explicit representation of quantitative time in LOTOS that has drawn criticisms from a number of researchers and which has led to the vast number of timed LOTOS extensions being developed. Before evaluating such extensions, it is first interesting to consider "simulating" quantitative time in LOTOS, i.e. using standard LOTOS syntax and semantics to model quantitative time. In this way, it can be demonstrated why, if at all, timed extensions are necessary. The alternating bit protocol is again used as an example to compare different possible approaches. One particularly relevant paper to this discussion is van Hulzen et al. (1990), in which the authors consider two ways to simulate clocks in standard LOTOS (referred to as "clocks using processes" and "clocks using data"). Their conclusions are consistent with those presented below and are referenced where appropriate.

7.3.1 Synchronized delay events

Suppose that the alternating bit protocol has access to a clock process that supplies a (global) notion of time to any process needing it. This clock process can be initialized to zero every time a message is sent and can be used to count the time that has elapsed since its transmission. Consider the case where all processes must synchronize for a delay event to occur; that is, time cannot pass in one process without passing in all other processes. Note that a LOTOS event, delay, is used to represent the passage of one unit of time and the event, query_clock, is used to allow the sender process to read the current value of the clock counter. The overall behaviour of this new timed protocol can be specified as follows:

```
process TimedABProtocol [ send ] : noexit :=
  send;
   ( hide s_send, s_rec, r_send, r_rec, timeout, delay,
         query_clock in
    s_send ?n:nat; Clock[ s_send, delay, query_clock ] ( 0 )
    | [ s_send, delay, query_clock ] |
    ( (s_send !0; TimedSender [ s_send, s_rec, timeout, delay,
                        query_clock ] ( 0 )
      | [ delay ] |
      TimedReceiver [ r_send, r_rec, delay ] )
    | [ s_send, s_rec, r_send, r_rec, delay ] |
    TimedMedium [ s_send, s_rec, r_send, r_rec, delay ]
  ) )
endproc (* TimedABProtocol *)
```

As the clock process counts the elapsed time since the last message was sent, the counter must be reset to zero whenever a message is transmitted (i.e. whenever an s_send event occurs) and, if a delay occurs, the value of this counter should be incremented by one. The only other possible behaviour of the clock is the query_clock event. By synchronizing on this event, the sender process can query (read) the value of the clock:

```
process Clock [ s_send, delay, query_clock ]
                ( current_time:nat ) : noexit :=
s_send ?n:nat; (* another message being transmitted, there -
                fore reset counter *)
  Clock [ s_send, delay, query_clock ] ( 0 )
  []
  delay; Clock [ s_send, delay, query_clock ( succ (current_time) )
```

```
[]
query_clock !current_time; (* return the current value of the
                          counter *)
Clock[ s_send, delay, query_clock ] ( current_time )
endproc (* Clock *)
```

Suppose that a value of 5 units of time is placed on the timeout in the sender process. The sender should wait for a period of 5 units of time for a reply from the receiver, and, if no reply arrives in this time, the sender should timeout and re-send its message. Therefore, before the sender performs any event, it must query the value of the clock. Note that delays are only permitted up to the timeout value; once this time has been reached, the only possible behaviour is the timeout. Similarly, it is only possible to receive a message up to the timeout value. Note also that the sender process includes the extra behaviour from process NewSender (described in Section 7.2.3 above) to ensure that the specification is free from deadlock (we use the following relations on natural numbers: le for less than, eq for equals and gt for greater than):

```
process TimedSender[ s_send, s_rec, timeout, delay,
                     query_clock ] ( n:nat ) : noexit :=
  query_clock ?time:nat; (* read the current value of the clock
                         counter *)
  [ time le 5 ] ->
    s_rec ?m:nat;
    ( [ m eq n ] -> (* reply is from current message, continue
                    and send next message *)
    s_send !compl( n ); (* send the complement of n *)
    TimedSender[ s_send, s_rec, timeout, delay, query_clock ]
               ( compl( n ) )
    []
    [ not ( m eq n ) ] -> (* reply is from old message, so re-send
                          current message *)
    s_send !n; (* re-send current message *)
    TimedSender[ s_send, s_rec, timeout, delay, query_clock ]
               ( n )
    )
  []
  [ time le 5 ] -> (* allow the process to delay up to the timeout
                   time *)
    delay; TimedSender[ s_send, s_rec, timeout, delay,
                       query_clock ] ( n )
  []
  [ time gt 5 ] ->
```

```
        timeout; (* reply has taken too long, therefore timeout
                    and re-send current message *)
        ( s_send !n; (* re-send current message *)
        TimedSender[ s_send, s_rec, timeout, delay, query_clock ]
                    ( n )
        []
        s_rec ?m:nat; (* allow message to be received to unblock
                        medium, but ignore *)
          s_send !n; (* re-send current message *)
            TimedSender[ s_send, s_rec, timeout, delay, query_clock]
                    ( n )
        )
endproc (* TimedSender *)
```

The behaviour of the receiver and the medium remain unchanged, apart
from the introduction of possible delay events. The specification of the new
(timed) medium is given below (note that an unreliable one-slot simplex
medium is used):

```
process TimedMedium[ s_send, s_rec, r_send, r_rec, delay ]
                    : noexit :=
  s_send; (* accept message for transmission from Sender to
            Receiver *)
    TimedMedium1[ s_send, s_rec, r_send, r_rec, delay ]
                (* instantiate subprocess *)
  []
  r_send; (* accept message for transmission from Receiver to
            Sender *)
    TimedMedium2[ s_send, s_rec, r_send, r_rec, delay ]
  []
  delay; TimedMedium[ s_send, s_rec, r_send, r_rec, delay ]
where
  process TimedMedium1[ s_send, s_rec, r_send, r_rec, delay ]
                    : noexit :=
  r_rec; TimedMedium[ s_send, s_rec, r_send, r_rec, delay ]
  []
  i (* message lost *);
    TimedMedium[ s_send, s_rec, r_send, r_rec, delay ]
  []
  delay;
    TimedMedium1[ s_send, s_rec, r_send, r_rec, delay ]
    (* stay in subproc. *)
endproc (* TimedMedium1 *)

process TimedMedium2[ s_send, s_rec, r_send, r_rec, delay ]
                    : noexit :=
```

```
  s_rec; TimedMedium[ s_send, s_rec, r_send, r_rec, delay ]
  []
  i (* message lost *);
    TimedMedium[ s_send, s_rec, r_send, r_rec, delay ]
  []
  delay;
    TimedMedium2[ s_send, s_rec, r_send, r_rec, delay ]
    (* stay in subproc. *)
 endproc (* TimedMedium2 *)
endproc (* TimedMedium *)
```

The new (timed) receiver can be specified similarly. As can be seen from the new specification, it is possible to use standard LOTOS events to model the passage of time, and it guards to ensure that events are only offered at the intended times. This approach is comparable to the "clocks in LOTOS using data" approach presented in van Hulzen et al. (1990). However, for the above example, the extra processes significantly complicate the specification and they obscure the original structure. As a result, the specification is longer and less readable.

The cause of this problem lies with the delay events: in order to avoid blocking the clock, delays must be offered as alternatives to most events. Additionally, after a delay, the process should be able to offer all the events that were possible before the delay (subject to any guards still being satisfied). In the receiver and the medium, this results in a particular specification style being imposed on the specifier where each behaviour consists of a single event followed by a process instantiation. Therefore, if a process contains several (sequential) events, these must be split up through the use of extra processes. In van Hulzen et al. (1990), the authors claim that "the amount of extra processes is demanding for the specifier and masks the architecture of the specification". They continue that "furthermore, the structure resulting from this approach imposes a particular specification style" and hence "the possibility to select an appropriate specification style is lost". Comparisons can be drawn between this imposed style of behaviour and the behaviour of a state machine (from a given state, there is a choice of possible actions, each of which leads to another state). Consequently, this style is known as a state-oriented specification style.

7.3.2 Interleaved delay events

An alternative approach to the one presented above can be found in Clark (1992), where an object-oriented specification style is used to specify clock objects. This approach is also comparable with the "clocks in LOTOS using processes" approach of van Hulzen et al. (1990). As with the approach described above, the current value of the clock can be queried by other processes. However, instead of delay events appearing in all processes and being synchronized throughout the specification, delays appear only in the clock process and are interleaved with all other events:

```
process AltTimedABProtocol [ send ] : noexit :=
 send;
 ( hide s_send, s_rec, r_send, r_rec, timeout, delay,
        query_clock in
   s_send ?n:nat; Clock[ s_send, delay, query_clock ] ( 0 )
   | [ s_send, query_clock ] | (* note: not synchronizing on
                                   delay *)
   ( ( s_send !0; AltTimedSender [ s_send, s_rec, timeout,
                                    query_clock ] ( 0 )
     |||
     Receiver [ r_send, r_rec ]
     )
   | [ s_send, s_rec, r_send, r_rec ] |
   Medium [ s_send, s_rec, r_send, r_rec ]
   )
 )
endproc (* AltTimedABProtocol *)
```

In this specification, the clock process is identical to the clock in the previous specification (`TimedABProtocol`). The new sender process is also very similar to process `TimedSender`, the difference being that there are no delay events in the new process and consequently the middle (guarded) choice from process `TimedSender` disappears. The main advantage of this specification is in the description of the `Receiver` and `Medium`. These processes need not, and do not, refer to the clock or the passage of time.

This approach avoids the need for extra processes and does not impose any specific style on the specifier. However, since the clock's delay events are interleaved with all other events in the system, events cannot be guaranteed to happen at the intended time. For example, consider the situation where the sender reads the value of the clock in order to determine whether or not it should perform an s_rec or a timeout event. Suppose the clock query results in an s_rec event being offered. The clock process may then perform a (potentially infinite) number of delays, before the sender actually performs the event. Therefore, this approach does not provide a true measure of the time at which events occur; it simply ensures that they do not occur *before* a given time (number of delays).

7.3.3 Summary

The following points summarize this section so far:
- LOTOS is an adequate technique for the specification of simple (abstract) timeouts, not involving the specification of quantitative time.

- It is also possible to "simulate" quantitative time in LOTOS, for example, by modelling clocks. This may be achieved as follows:
  - Clocks can be modelled by using a standard LOTOS event in the specification to model the passage of time. This delay event can either be synchronized with delay events in other processes or appear solely in the clock and be interleaved with all other events in the specification.
  - If delays are synchronized and appear in all other time-related processes (to ensure that time cannot pass in one process without passing in all others), the specification is significantly complicated. A state-oriented specification style is imposed on the specifier; the need for extra processes with this style generally obscures the structure of the specification and results in longer, less-readable specifications.
  - If a delay event appears solely in the clock, and is interleaved with all other events in the specification, the clock cannot measure the exact time at which an event occurs; it can only ensure that a particular event does not occur before a specified time.

Therefore, it can be concluded that, in addition to being suitable for the specification of abstract timing constraints, LOTOS can also be used to specify that events occur after a given (quantitative) time. However, this does not provide a true (complete) measure of the time at which events occur and cannot, therefore, be considered as a completely satisfactory specification technique for the modelling of quantitative time.

7.4 Extending LOTOS with quantitative time

In this section, various extensions to LOTOS are considered that permit the specification of quantitative time. The first extension considered is that of a clock extended LOTOS (van Hulzen et al. 1990). This section then progresses to look at other, more typical, timed extensions to LOTOS based on delays and timestamps.

7.4.1 A clock extension to LOTOS

Having reached similar conclusions to those drawn in Section 7.3, van Hulzen et al. proceed by developing a clock extension to LOTOS that is based on modelling various possible clock operations, such as starting, reading and resetting clocks (van Hulzen et al. 1990). The new language, Clock Extended LOTOS (or CELOTOS, for short), introduces two (predefined) data types to model clock identifiers and durations, and extends the concept of an event to permit a clock to be started within an event. Consequently, a clock is started simultaneously with the occurrence of an event, i.e. no time can pass between the clock being started and the event occurring or vice-versa. Clocks can also be easily read using this language, as shown in the example below:

```
process CELOTOSprotocol [ send ] : noexit :=
  send;
  ( hide s_send, s_rec, r_send, r_rec, timeout in
   ( s_send !0 <| start ( C, 0 ) |>; (* start clock C with initial
                                         duration value zero *)
     Sender [ s_send, s_rec, timeout ] ( 0 )
     |||
     Receiver [ r_send, r_rec ]
   )
   |[ s_send, s_rec, r_send, r_rec ]|
   Medium [ s_send, s_rec, r_send, r_rec ]
  )
where
  process Sender [ s_send, s_rec, timeout ] ( n:nat ) : noexit :=
    s_rec ?m:nat [ ( read( clock( C ) ) le 5 ]; (* test duration
                                                   value of clock C *)
    ( [ m eq n ] -> (* current message *)
      . . .
      []
      [ not ( m eq n ) ] -> (* old message *)
      . . .
    )
    []
    timeout [ ( read( clock( C ) ) gt 5 ];
      s_send !n; (* re-send message *)
      . . .
  endproc (* Sender *)

  (* process definitions for Receiver and Medium (no time
     involved) *)
  . . .
endproc (* CELOTOSprotocol *)
```

In CELOTOS, time passes through all processes (and clocks) in the system at the same rate, the rate being dictated by a global clock. It is the ticking of this global clock (ticks appearing at the semantic level only) that causes the value of all clocks currently in use to be incremented. Time can always pass in the specification, regardless of what other events are possible. Consequently, there is no way to force the occurrence of a particular event or to ensure that it will occur before a given time. This issue will be discussed in more depth below.

One nice characteristic of this approach is that it is possible to measure the duration of time between ordered, but not necessarily consecutive, events. As will be shown below, few approaches allow this to be done directly and/or elegantly. However, one of the drawbacks of the approach is that, while involving few syntactic extensions to LOTOS, it considerably increases the complexity of the semantics. It has also been characterized as an implementation-oriented enhancement of LOTOS (Bolognesi & Lucidi 1992) due to its explicit manipulation of timers (clocks) .

7.4.2 Delay operator and timestamp extensions to LOTOS

The treatment of time in CELOTOS is not typical of timed extensions to LOTOS. Most techniques introduce quantitative time into the language either through the use of new delay operators or through timestamps attached to events.

Approaches such as Temporal LOTOS (Regan 1993) and the language $\rho 1$ (Bolognesi & Lucidi 1991) introduce a special delay event into the language (into both the syntax and the semantics), representing the passage of one unit of time. For example, in Temporal LOTOS, the behaviour "σ; a; ..." means that there should be a delay of one unit of time (event σ) before performing event a. It is indicated in Regan (1993) that this delay operator can, in fact, be derived from the "then" operator $\lfloor...\rfloor(...)$, introduced in the timed language ATP (Nicollin et al. 1990). This operator represents a choice that is determined by the passage of time; it specifies that either the first parameter is executed now, or else, after a (unit) delay, the second parameter is to be executed. The behaviour "σ; P" is hence equivalent to the behaviour $\lfloor \text{stop} \rfloor (P)$.

An alternative approach is to allow timestamps to be attached to events, stating the time at which that event should occur (usually, with respect to the time of the previous event). One of the first examples of a timestamp-based approach was provided by the language TIC (Quemada et al. 1991). In TIC, the behaviour "a; b {t}; ..." means that the event b should occur t units of time after the occurrence of event a. Note that the use of timestamps in the syntax of a language does not preclude the use of some other representation of the passage of time (e.g. delays) in the semantics of the language.

A number of timed process algebraic techniques have been developed based on both delays and timestamps. The following section considers the relative expressiveness and elegance of these time constructs for the specification of a selection of real-time properties.

7.4.3 Comparing delays and timestamps

To allow the comparison of these two approaches, four simple classes of time constraint are considered:

- Minimum time constraints – an event should not occur before a given time.

- Maximum time constraints – an event should not occur after a given time.
- Bounded time intervals – an event should occur within a given interval (i.e. a minimum and a maximum time bound should be imposed).
- Specific time instances – an event should occur at one specific time. Note that this is a particular case of a time interval where the upper bound is the same as the lower bound.

Examples of each of these constraints will be given using both Temporal LOTOS (which uses delay operators) and TIC (which uses timestamps). The timing of non-adjacent events will also be considered.

Minimum time constraints

As an example of a minimum time constraint, suppose that some event, b, should not happen within 3 time units of the occurrence of another event, a. After the occurrence of b, process P is instantiated. In Temporal LOTOS, this can be specified as:

$a; \sigma^3; b; P$

This represents the occurrence of event a followed by three sigma events (delays) followed by the occurrence of event b. It is noted in Regan (1993) that parameterizing sigma actions is actually incorrect syntax. However, since it is easy to prove that parameterized sigmas can be defined in terms of a parameterized "then" operator[1], this abbreviated notation will be used here. According to the Temporal LOTOS semantics, after the three delays, b can delay further. Therefore, event b occurs at some time after 3 time units (not necessarily at time 3); hence, the property of a minimum time bound has been specified. Note that, for reasons that will become clear in the next section, it is assumed that b is not an internal (hidden) event. For comparison, consider the specification of the same example in TIC:

$a; b \{3..no\_limit\}; P$

In this behaviour, there is a choice of time instants at which event b can occur. This style of timed specification gives more indication that event b can happen after 3 time units than the delay equivalent, although both provide short, succinct expressions of the same property.

---

1. Two definitions are given in (Regan 1993). The first is that $\sigma;Q$ can be defined as $\lfloor stop \rfloor(Q)$ and the second defines a parameterized "then" operator:
$\lfloor P \rfloor^{n+1}(Q) = \lfloor P \rfloor(\lfloor P \rfloor^n(Q))$ and $\lfloor P \rfloor^0(Q) = \lfloor P \rfloor(Q)$
From these definitions, it can be seen immediately that $\sigma;Q \equiv \lfloor stop \rfloor^0(Q)$. The conjecture is that $\sigma^n;Q \equiv \lfloor stop \rfloor^{n-1}(Q)$. Assume this result is true for $n=k$, and try to prove (by induction) for $n=k+1$, i.e. prove that $\sigma^{k+1};Q \equiv \lfloor stop \rfloor^k(Q)$
$\lfloor stop \rfloor^k(Q) = \lfloor stop \rfloor(\lfloor stop \rfloor^{k-1}(Q)) \equiv \lfloor stop \rfloor(\sigma^k;Q) \equiv \sigma;\sigma^k;Q = \sigma^{k+1};Q$
Therefore, the conjecture is true by induction.

Maximum time constraints

Suppose now that event b should not happen later than 3 time units after the occurrence of event a. This can be specified in Temporal LOTOS as:

$a; \lfloor b; P \rfloor^3(\text{stop})$

In this behaviour, event b can either occur immediately after event a, or up to 3 units of time after a. If 3 units of time expire without the occurrence of b, b can no longer occur. In TIC, this example can be written as:

$a; b \{0..3\}; P$

This latter expression is more succinct than the first, since no alternative behaviour is specified for the case when b does not occur within the given time bound (explicitly given as stop in the Temporal LOTOS expression). However, many examples may actually need this alternative behaviour to be specified (e.g. receive message or timeout scenarios). Therefore, there is no significant advantage in using one approach in favour of the other for the specification of maximum time bounds.

Bounded time intervals

The specification of bounded time intervals simply involves the combination of the above two types of time constraint, i.e. imposing a minimum bound and a maximum bound on the occurrence of an event. However, in the delay-based notation, different operators have been used for each type of constraint. Suppose that event b should happen between 4 and 10 units of time after event a. This results in the following Temporal LOTOS specification:

$a; \sigma^4; \lfloor b; P \rfloor^6(\text{stop})$

As with the minimum time bound, provided b is not an internal event, b can be delayed further after the four explicit delays. Hence, it is possible for b to occur up to the maximum time bound. After this time, b can no longer occur. This is not a particularly elegant solution, since it is necessary to calculate the difference in time between the upper and lower time bounds of the time interval (as the parameter to the "then" operator). In contrast, the equivalent behaviour in a timestamp notation can be expressed as:

$a; b \{4..10\}; P$

In this approach there is no need to calculate the difference between the upper and lower time bounds. It is also not necessary to specify an alternative behaviour (in case b does not happen within the required behaviour).

Therefore, for this class of time constraint (bounded time intervals), the timestamp-based notation provides a more elegant specification than the delay-based notation.

Specific time instances
Suppose that event *b* should occur 5 units of time after event *a*. This can be expressed in Temporal LOTOS as:

$a; \sigma^5; \lfloor b; P \rfloor (\text{ stop })$

The same behaviour can be written in TIC as:

$a; b \{5\}; P$

As mentioned above, a specific time instance is simply a special case of a bounded time interval where the upper bound is the same as the lower bound. Therefore, as expected, the timestamp-based notation provides a more elegant expression of specific time instances than the delay-based notation.

Timing non-adjacent events
One important observation is that neither delays nor timestamps allow a particularly elegant specification of time constraints applied over non-adjacent events. For example, consider specifying that some event, *c*, occurs 10 units of time after another event, *a*. Suppose that another event, *b*, separates the occurrence of events *a* and *c*, but it is not known at exactly what time *b* will occur. One way to specify such constraints is to time intermediate events, as in:

$a; \text{choice } t\text{:nat } [] \ [0 \le t \le 10] \rightarrow (b \{t\}; c \{10-t\}; \dots)$

This notation follows that defined for LOTOS-T (Miguel 1991) in which, after event *a*, there is a choice of times (between 0 and 10) at which *b* should occur. Providing this event occurs within the required time bound, event *c* can be offered such that it occurs 10 units of time after *a*. However, this approach is inappropriate if *a* and *c* are separated by several events.

A second way to specify time constraints over non-adjacent events is to introduce new synchronizing behaviour and use a constraint-oriented style of specification, e.g.

$a; b; c; \dots$
$|[a, c]|$
$a; c \{10\}; \text{stop}$

This overcomes the problem of the first method when events *a* and *c* are separated by several events. The second approach does, however, introduce extra detail into the specification which significantly complicates the structure.

While this example has used a timestamp-based notation, it can be seen that an equivalent specification based on delays would be no more elegant.

7.4.4 Summary

From this comparison of delays and timestamps it can be concluded that, for the time constraints considered, timestamps provide a more elegant notation than the more primitive delays. However, it is important to note that neither approach provides a particularly satisfactory solution to modelling time constraints over non-adjacent events.

7.5 Extending LOTOS with maximal progress/urgency

The concepts of maximal progress and urgency were introduced in Section 5.4.2. They represent two possible mechanisms by which some priority of event occurrence can be imposed over the passage of time. The alternating bit protocol provides a good example of why this may be required. At the point where the sender is waiting for a reply to be delivered, the process has a non-deterministic choice between timing out or receiving the reply. Clearly, if a message has been lost at some stage of transmission, the sender needs to timeout and re-send the message. However, the medium may be waiting to deliver the message to the sender; even at this stage, the sender may still choose to timeout. To prevent this, it may be desirable to impose a priority on the s_rec event over the timeout event. Given a choice, the sender must then receive the message (rather than timing out), thus saving unnecessary re-transmissions. There is no way in standard LOTOS to give the passage of time a lower priority than the occurrence of other events. For this reason, many timed extensions to LOTOS also include the concept of maximal progress or action urgency. These two concepts are discussed below.

7.5.1 Maximal progress

Applying a maximal progress assumption ensures that internal events, occur "as soon as possible" (i.e. before the passage of time). To interpret the "as soon as possible" phrase, it is necessary that there is some representation of the passage of time in the semantics of the language. The maximal progress assumption can then ensure that internal (or hidden) events that are possible, occur before the passage of time (i.e. their execution is not unnecessarily delayed).

There are a number of extensions to LOTOS which incorporate a maximal progress assumption. The delay based technique, Temporal LOTOS, introduced in the previous section is one such extension. TIC, on the other hand, does not incorporate maximal progress. However, a similar, but more recent, timestamp-based technique, LOTOS-T, does incorporate a maximal progress assumption (Miguel 1991).

139

7.5.2 Action urgency

An alternative approach to maximal progress is provided by the concept of action urgency. There are at least two distinct ways in which urgency can be applied to a specification. The first of these is detailed in Leduc & Léonard (1993). In this approach, all actions (except those that explicitly permit time to pass) must occur before the next delay action. Consequently, as for maximal progress, there must be some representation of the passage of time in the semantics of the language. A second approach, presented in Bolognesi & Lucidi (1991), allows a more flexible specification of urgent actions. A new operator called urgency, denoted by $\rho(U)$ (where U is a list of event gates), is introduced to express the fact that each of the given actions (or interactions) in U is to be performed urgently, as soon as all the involved partners are ready. This language is called $\rho1$.

7.5.3 Comparing maximal progress and urgency

The languages LOTOS-T and $\rho1$ will be used in this section to illustrate and compare the use of maximal progress and action urgency (respectively). Consider first the minimum time constraint described above. The LOTOS-T specification of such a constraint is identical[2] to the TIC specification given above, namely:

$a; b \{3..no\_limit\}; P$

It was stated that, provided b is not an internal event, b can occur at any time once 3 time units have passed since the occurrence of event a. Now consider this behaviour if b is an internal event:

hide b in $(a; b \{3..no\_limit\}; P)$

In LOTOS-T, the maximal progress assumption is applied to internal events; hence, b must occur as soon as possible. Since there is nothing to delay the occurrence of b (such as synchronizing with another process), b will occur exactly 3 units of time after event a. The same minimum time constraint can be expressed in $\rho1$ as follows (note that $\rho1$ uses a dot for an action prefix and uses the prefix (n). to denote a delay of n time units):

$\rho(b) (a. (3). b. P)$

After event a, there is a delay of three units of time after which b occurs

---

2. Note that the notation used for the expression of time intervals (i.e. {3..no_limit}) is a syntactic shorthand not defined in the LOTOS-T original paper. However, such shorthands can easily be defined by combining standard LOTOS operators such as the general choice operator with the new time-related operators.

urgently. In this example, as in the LOTOS-T example, this means that b will occur immediately, since nothing can delay its occurrence.

7.5.4   Summary

This section has shown that both LOTOS-T (using maximal progress) and ρ1 (using action urgency) can give priority to the occurrence of an event over the passage of time. However, it is important to note that action urgency can be applied to both internal and observable events. Hence, strictly speaking, it is a more expressive concept than maximal progress. On the other hand, proposers of the maximal progress approach take the view that observable events can always be influenced (e.g. delayed) by the environment; consequently, their occurrence should not be forced (Regan 1991).

7.6   Other characteristics of timed LOTOS extensions

In this section, two other possible characteristics of timed extensions to LOTOS are discussed, namely the concepts of persistency and time deadlocks.

7.6.1   Persistency

A persistent process is one in which the passage of time cannot resolve choice (Nicollin & Sifakis 1991), see the definition in Section 5.4.2. Temporal LOTOS, for example, permits non-persistent behaviour. In Temporal LOTOS, there are two choice operators: the standard choice operator, [], and the "then" operator, $\lfloor ... \rfloor(...)$. Consider the behaviour of the first of these operators (assume that neither event a nor event b are internal events):

$a; P \; [] \; \sigma; b; Q$

This expression can perform event a now (and then instantiate process P) or delay by one unit of time and then offer either event a (followed by P) or event b (followed by Q). At this point, the expression may also delay further before performing either a or b. In other words, the passage of time does not resolve the choice. However, Temporal LOTOS includes a second choice operator to model a choice which is determined by the passage of time, as in the following example:

$\lfloor a; P \rfloor(b; Q)$

In this expression, either event a occurs now (followed by P) or, after one unit of time, b occurs (followed by Q). First, note that event a cannot occur after one unit of time and secondly that, providing b is not an internal event, its occurrence may be further delayed.

It is important to note that this last example can be modelled in a timestamp-based notation such as TIC or LOTOS-T as follows:

$a\{0\};P \; [] \; b\{1..no\_limit\};Q$

This explicitly states that event a can only occur at time zero (now) and is therefore disabled after the passage of one unit of time.

To summarize, in a delay-based notation, such as Temporal LOTOS, the additional choice operator gives the language extra expressiveness by permitting the expression of scenarios in which the passage of time disables the possibility of an event occurring. However, this can be modelled in timestamp-based notation such as TIC or LOTOS-T without the need for an extra operator. Therefore, the need for an explicit non-persistency operator depends on the way in which time is introduced into the language.

7.6.2   Time deadlocks

The final characteristic that will be considered is that of time deadlocks, that is, processes in which any action or time delay is impossible. From the languages mentioned in this chapter, only $\rho1$ supports time deadlocks. Consider the following example (in $\rho1$):

$(\rho(b) \, b.P \,) \; |[\, b \,]| \; (\, (1).b.Q \,)$

The urgency of b in the left hand expression means that this event must occur immediately (i.e. it cannot delay). However, the right-hand expression enforces a delay before the occurrence of event b. This is a time deadlock, since any further action or time delay in the specification is impossible.

It has been argued (Groote 1990) that time deadlocks can be useful in detecting inconsistencies in a specification, for example, when a behaviour must synchronize on a given event at times when another parallel behaviour is unable to offer that event. However, it is rather counter-intuitive for a deadlocked process to prevent the passage of time in the rest of the system. For example, given a protocol specification, a time deadlock in the sender would block the passage of time in the receiver, even though the processes are meant to be independent.

7.7   The stream example revisited

In order to complete the comparison of techniques made in the previous chapter this section considers specification in timed LOTOS in the terms of the previous chapter. We will consider one of the most prominent of the timed LOTOS's and give a specification of the multimedia stream channel in the language. This will then allow us to make a comparison between timed LOTOS approaches and the approaches considered in Chapter 6: Estelle, SDL, Esterel and LOTOS.

7.7.1 An overview of the language

LOTOS-T (Miguel et al. 1993) is one of the most prominent timed exten-sions to LOTOS. It is targeted at the expression of communication protocols, for which it was developed in the OSI95 5431 ESPRIT project "High performance OSI protocols with Multimedia support on HSLAN's and B-ISDN". As indicated earlier LOTOS-T supports maximal progress and employs a timed action prefix notation. The language is upward com-patible with standard LOTOS. Expressive timing operations can be con-structed by combining the timed action prefix with standard LOTOS operators, especially the generalized choice operator.

The LOTOS ACT-ONE abstract data type language is used to define a discrete time domain (although, dense (but not continuous) time can also be modelled) for the timing behaviour. The use of ACT-ONE enables per-formance properties to be determined. In addition, a further extension, LOTOS-P, is being developed for expression of probabilities.

7.7.2 Modelling the medium

The incorporation of quantitative time into the LOTOS-T specification pre-vents the queue data type solution presented in Section 6.5.2 from being suitable. However, a succinct expression of the required channel behaviour can be made:

```
process channel [SourceOut, SinkIn] : noexit : =
  SourceOut?fr_no:Nat;
    ( ( choice t:Nat [] [79<t< 91] -> i {t}; SinkIn!fr_no; stop )
    |||
    channel [SourceOut, SinkIn]    )
endproc (* channel *)
```

The | | | interleaved parallel composition operator is used in order to prevent the channel from blocking. Specifically, the recursive call to chan-nel enables a new frame to be input into the process (through gate SourceOut) at any point during the evaluation of the latency delay (event $i \{t\}$). However, this solution only works in the presence of time, as the imposition of timing constraints prevents the channel from reordering frames, i.e. all frames have to stay in the channel for at least 80 time units before they can be output (through gate `SinkIn`). Thus, a frame cannot be jumped.[3]

7.7.3 Assessment

The benefits of LOTOS-T are that it incorporates a realistic model of time into the process algebra approach, which can be argued for on grounds of elegance and abstraction. The approach broadly fulfils all our requirements, to support distribution, real-time and usability. The most striking point of comparison between the technique and the other techniques highlighted in Chapter 6 is the simplicity of the channel specification. This simplicity arises because of the power of the standard LOTOS operators and of the simple timed action prefix notation. This comparison gives a strong justification for preferring the process algebraic approaches over either of the other candidate techniques. It is also important to point out that similar concise specifications of the channel's behaviour could be made in any of the major time extended LOTOS proposals.

The limitations of the approach are really immaturity; it is new and a complete tool set has not at present been provided. This limitation is true of all the timed process algebras that have been developed to date and in a general sense the process of evaluating these timed extensions and assessing them is still underway. Thus, although we have chosen to consider LOTOS-T in this chapter (because it is a high profile technique amongst the timed process algebras) we are not at this stage particularly advocating the language over other timed process algebras.

7.8 Summary

This chapter has initially considered the use of standard (untimed) LOTOS for the modelling of abstract time constraints (such as simple timeouts) and quantitative time constraints. It has been shown that, in general, standard LOTOS is not sufficient for the latter class of time constraints. A number of timed extensions to LOTOS have therefore been considered. Characteristics of these approaches have been discussed, namely the choice between delays or timestamps, the choice between maximal progress or action urgency and the concepts of persistency and time deadlocks. The main conclusions are that timestamp-based notations generally provide a more elegant expression of time constraints than delay-based notations and that action urgency can be applied to observable events

---

3. This is not entirely true, since the time interval $79<t<91$ would enable two frames received straight after one another to be reordered, but this is prevented in our example by the sink process transmitting every 50 time units.

Table 7.1 Characteristics of some timed extensions to LOTOS

Language	Reference	Timestamp*	Delay*	Maximal progress	Urgency	Time deadlock	Persistency
CELOTOS	van Hulzen et al. 1990	×	×	×	×	×	✓
TIC	Quemada et al. 1991	✓	×	×	×	×	×
LOTOS-T	Miguel et al. 1993	✓	×	✓	×	×	×
Temporal LOTOS	Regan 1993	×	✓	✓	×	×	×
ρ1	Bolognesi & Lucidi 1991	×	✓	×	✓	✓	✓

* Note that the columns marked timestamp and delay refer to the way in which quantitative time has been introduced into the syntax of the language; they say nothing about how the passage of time is modelled in the semantics.

whereas maximal progress can only be applied to internal events.

Table 7.1 summarizes the techniques mentioned in this chapter and categorizes them according to the characteristics that have been discussed.

We have also shown that a major timed extensions to LOTOS, LOTOS-T, can be compared very favourably with the other techniques discussed in Chapter 5, Estelle, SDL, Esterel and standard LOTOS.

7.9 Discussion – abstraction and urgency

There are a number of interesting debates within the formal methods research community concerning issues highlighted in this chapter. One of these debates involves the need for a concept such as maximal progress or urgency in a specification language. Many authors believe that the concept of having some form of priority of event occurrence over the passage of time is essential in a timed model. To quote from Leduc & Léonard (1993):

> . . . a timed model cannot be useful if it does not allow the expression that a given synchronization must occur urgently, i.e. as soon as possible; ... This requirement is closely related to the ability to model timers: without urgent actions, there is no way to specify the necessity for an action to occur at (or before) a specific time instant, or to occur as soon as possible.

However, an opposing view is that by constraining non-determinism, one moves away from an important goal of specification, namely, abstraction. This view is taken in Quemada et al. (1991), where the authors state that the maximum parallelism hypothesis is

> ... a very implementation oriented hypothesis which tries to make use of the computing resource, such that when something is done and the processor is free, then the processor shall not stay idle and do it.

They proceed by saying that their approach (TIC) is specification orientated and attempts to be implementation independent, as they claim any formal description technique should be.

This argument can be taken even further and applied to timed formal specification in general. One of the central goals of specification is abstraction; specifications should be abstract and should not impose specific implementation solutions. Time can be seen as compromising this abstraction, resulting in implementation dependent specifications. On the other hand, time is necessary for the realistic specification of real-time systems and is essential for the verification of real-time properties. The following part of this book proposes a new approach to specification to address this conflict.

PART IV

A new approach

This part describes a new approach to formal description of distributed systems that is specifically developed to support multimedia systems. The part consists of three chapters. Chapter 8 presents the motivation for the development of a new, LOTOS based, approach to timed formal description. This new approach has been developed in direct response to the perceived state of the art of timed formal description (as presented in Pt III of this book). Chapter 9 then describes the real-time temporal logic QTL that is at the heart of the new formal specification technique. Finally, Chapter 10 presents an approach to the verification of LOTOS/QTL specifications.

CHAPTER 8

Introducing the new approach

8.1   Introduction

This chapter presents a new approach to the formal specification and verification of distributed multimedia computing. In the previous chapter, it
was shown that the process algebra LOTOS is suitable for the specification
of an abstract notion of time, for example where it is sufficient to specify
that a timeout event occurs. However, problems arise with LOTOS when it
becomes necessary to specify quantitative time, such as placing a value on
the time at which a timeout occurs. Various categories of timed extensions
to LOTOS have been considered and it has been shown that, with these
extensions, quantitative time constraints can be specified. While such an
approach could be used, we believe there are strong motivations to adopt
an alternative approach. Section 8.2 examines these motivations in some
depth. Section 8.3 then presents the principle behind the new approach,
i.e. maintaining a separation of concerns. Section 8.4 presents the new
approach with an evaluation of this approach given in Section 8.5. Following this, Section 8.6 presents some related work and Section 8.7 summarizes the chapter.

8.2   Motivation for the new approach

The need to incorporate quantitative time in formal descriptions has been
emphasized throughout this book. We have also indicated that there is
a need for formal descriptions to be abstract. This is required in order
that specifications do not rule out valid implementations. Thus, over-
specification must be prevented by avoiding implementation decisions
during specification. However, it is our tenet that the *need to incorporate*

time into specifications is in conflict with the *desire to obtain abstraction in specifications* (Bowman et al. 1994). For classical system development, time and performance are implementation issues while, for time-critical systems, time and performance are the concern of every stage of system development. This presents a conflict: the highest level of abstraction (abstract specification) must be reconciled against the lowest level (time and performance). To date, most research has been directed at the mechanics of timed formal description (e.g. developing valid and elegant semantic models for timed formal notations), while less consideration has been made of the more subjective issue of which technique produces the most abstract and elegant specifications.

Specifications developed with single language based approaches typically embed precise timing values into the specification of behaviour. Such grounding of behaviour in time leads to specification that is not abstract and is inherently constrictive for system development. This leads to two main problems:

- *Implementation specific*   In single language approaches, timing characteristics specific to a particular implementation are often embedded directly into formal descriptions of real-time systems. Such implementation specific formal description, first, affects the portability of specifications and, secondly, prevents specifications of real-time components from being fully general.
- *Position of existing standards*   A further issue that arises is the position of existing standards; these clearly become obsolete with the advent of new timed formal description techniques (FDTs). Moreover, many of the tools and techniques that have been developed for untimed FDTs are also obsolete with respect to the new FDTs.

We will present two illustrative examples of the constraining effect of time on behaviour. The language LOTOS-T is used for these examples.

Illustration A

It is our belief that over-specification is common in timed formal description. In fact, in a very general sense, time can be seen always to constrain the possible behaviour of a specification.

Consider the LOTOS behaviour:

(a; stop | | | b; stop) | | | c; stop

The possible transitions of this system are shown in Figure 8.1a. However, when we enforce timing values on the firing of events in this behaviour, such as in the LOTOS-T behaviour:

($a\{5\}$; stop | | | $b\{3\}$; stop) | | | $c\{4\}$; stop

the set of possible evolutions of the behaviour are constrained (see Fig. 8.1b).

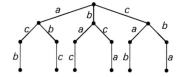

Figure 8.1a Possible transitions.

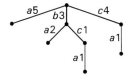

Figure 8.1b Constraining non-determinism.

Fundamentally, the abstract offering of possible behaviours inherent in LOTOS specifications is constrained by the addition of time. This aspect is exacerbated by the enforcement of the maximal progress assumption as found in a range of timed extensions to LOTOS, including LOTOS-T (see Ch. 6).

Hiding b and c in the previous LOTOS-T behaviour, i.e.

hide b,c in (($a\{5\}$; stop ||| $b\{3\}$; stop) ||| $c\{4\}$; stop)

results in the following possible evolutions (Fig. 8.1c):

Figure 8.1c Introducing maximal progress.

The argument here is not that this is an incorrect expression of timed behaviour (it may be exactly the behaviour that a system developer wishes to express), but that it is not abstract specification. The allowable evolutions of the system have been constrained to such a degree that we cannot be said to be expressing possible behaviours, as is required of specification. This form of timed formal description seems to be more suitable for the design phase of system development, but, for specification in the presence of time, we believe that special abstraction paradigms must be used.

151

Illustration B
If we return to the LOTOS-T specification of the multimedia stream example in Chapter 7, we see that it represents a satisfactory description of the
stream's behaviour, yet it again represents an over-specification in that precise timing values have been embedded into the behaviour. The specification is not an expression of possible behaviours, but rather it describes a
definite sequence of events ordered in quantitative time.

Non-determinism does arise in timed behaviour, as shown in the specification of the channel in LOTOS-T (taken from Ch. 7),

```
process channel[SourceOut,SinkIn]:noexit:=
 SourceOut;

   ( ( choice t:Nat  [79<t<91] -> i {t}; SinkIn; stop )
     |||
     channel[SourceOut,SinkIn]   )
endproc (* channel *)
```

enabling a number of possible timing behaviours to be modelled. This adds
to the level of abstraction in the behaviour by introducing a style of non-
determinism over quantitative time.

However, we believe that, although such means of obtaining abstraction
are helpful, they do not tackle the root of the conflict between abstraction
and time. Fundamentally, abstract specification in the presence of time
requires more than the standard abstraction devices of untimed formal
description. If we look more closely at the multimedia stream example, we
see that time arises in a number of different ways in the formal description.
Specifically, we can distinguish between real-time requirements and real-
time assumptions, i.e.
- *Real-time requirements*   These express the desired real-time properties
  of the system being specified. For example, the following requirements can be identified on a stream:
    RR_1.   The sink should receive frames at the same rate as they are
    transmitted (e.g. 20 frames per second) although a degradation to
    15 frames per second is acceptable.
    RR_2.   Each frame should be delivered with a latency between
    100 ms and 120 ms.
  These correspond directly to (real-time) QoS requirements, i.e. RR_1 is
  throughput, and RR_2 captures both latency and jitter.
- *Real-time assumptions*   These properties state the timing constraints
  enforced by the implementation, rather than the timing characteristics
  that are desired of the developed system. For example, the following
  assumptions can be identified on a stream:
    RA_1.   The source process transmits the first frame at time 0 (the full
    stream specification in Appendix B makes the correctness of this
    property apparent).

RA$_2$.   Then the source transmits one frame every 50 ms.

RA$_3$.   The medium enforces a latency delay of between 80 ms and 90 ms on transmission.

Again, real-time assumptions correspond directly to (real-time) QoS capabilities as discussed in Chapter 4.

These two classes encompass all the timing properties in the multimedia stream example. The only remaining properties to express are purely (abstract) behavioural relationships:

- *Abstract behaviour*   This is the standard temporal ordering of a specification. The abstract behaviour of the stream is captured below:

    AB$_1$.   The data source makes a regular transmission of frames.

    AB$_2$.   The sink receives frames and, if the QoS requirements are met, plays the frame, otherwise an error is raised.

Abstract behaviour often refers to time, but is not grounded in time, e.g. a timeout may be included in the abstract behaviour without being associated with a specific execution timing.

It is our tenet that the problem with single language based timed formal description is that the above three aspects are entwined and confused. In addition, single language based techniques do not faciliatate the natural expression of QoS requirements and capabilities. We believe that the three should be treated separately, i.e. a separation of concerns should be maintained.

8.3   A separation of concerns

8.3.1   The principle

The principle behind the proposed new approach is that of maintaining a *separation of concerns*. A separation is drawn between the specification of the *behaviour* of a system and the specification of *requirements*. Their purposes are clearly distinct; the former describes the *actual* behaviour of a system, while the latter reflects the *desired* properties of a system (for example, that the specification is deadlock-free). It should be noted that this separation of concerns is typical of many existing dual language specification techniques (for example, TTMs/RTTL (Ostroff 1992a) and TPCCS/ TPCTL (Hansson 1991)). Importantly, however, a further separation of concerns can be drawn when time is considered. Time can occur in various forms in a specification, as illustrated in Figure 8.2.

The first important distinction shown in Figure 8.2 is between *behavioural time* and *real-time*. Behavioural time refers to an event that is associated with time passing in an algorithm, but which does not relate this event to real-time. These events can be viewed as *placeholders* in a specification (e.g. the occurrence of a timeout event or an event representing the tick of a

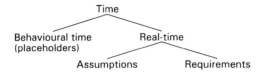

Figure 8.2   Different types of time in a specification.

clock). Intuitively, such events are associated with the passing of time, but formally they are no different from any other event. In contrast, real-time associates behaviour with *real world clocks* (e.g. a timeout happens after 250 milliseconds, or a clock tick corresponds to the passage of one second).

The second distinction in Figure 8.2 refers back to the separation of concerns between the specification of the behaviour of a system and the specification of requirements. When time is considered, a distinction can be drawn between the real-time assumptions *in* a specification and the desired real-time requirements *across* a specification. Real-time assumptions effectively *ground* behavioural time in real-time. For example, a timeout event may occur in a specification (behavioural time). This event can be grounded in real-time through the real-time assumptions by associating the timeout event with a specific time instant. Furthermore, real-time assumptions can be used to state the *assumed capabilities* of components in a specification (e.g. a communication channel imposes a minimum latency of 80 milliseconds on each transmission, or the processing of data by a given component takes 5 milliseconds). In contrast, real-time requirements generally apply timing constraints *across* a specification, that is, they provide an *end-to-end* measure of time. For example, a protocol must provide an end-to-end throughput of 20 Kbits/second or an end-to-end latency of 100 milliseconds. Quality of service (QoS) statements such as bounded jitter, latency and throughput are all typical examples of real-time multimedia requirements. It is important to note, however, that real-time requirements are only a subset of the set of all requirements, i.e. requirements need not refer to real-time. For example, it is possible to state that the specification is deadlock-free or, to use another QoS example, that the error rate of transmission never drops below a specified bound. A similar relationship exists between QoS capabilities and real-time assumptions.

To summarize, the proposed approach ensures that a separation of concerns is maintained between

- the specification of behaviour and the specification of requirements, and
- the different types of time appearing in a specification.

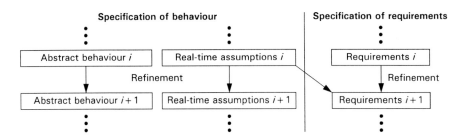

Figure 8.3   An overview of system development using the new framework.

8.3.2   Applying this principle

A language independent framework

Importantly, no mention has yet been made of specific languages in the section above. Instead, a language-independent *framework* has been provided that could be realized using one or more different languages. (One such realization will be described in Section 8.4.) An overview of system development using this framework is illustrated in Figure 8.3.

This figure shows a separation of concerns between the specification of behaviour and the specification of requirements. The former consists of a specification of abstract behaviour together with a set of real-time assumptions which ground the abstract behaviour in real-time. The latter consists of a set of requirements that state the desired properties of the system. Importantly, these different components can be refined independently throughout the early stages of system development. It is only during the final stages, when an implementation is derived, that it becomes necessary to integrate the abstract behaviour and the real-time assumptions.

The refinement of requirements deserves further mention. First, it is important to note that, as mentioned in Chapter 4, requirements may change through system development as a clearer understanding of the system is gained. Therefore, the refinement process may involve a sequence of iterations in which the requirements are modified. Secondly, as illustrated in Figure 8.3, requirements at one level of refinement may be derived from real-time assumptions at the previous level of refinement. For example, consider a latency requirement across a protocol. Suppose that the real-time assumptions for this protocol break this requirement down into the processing times of the sender and receiver and the latency of the communication channel. One possible refinement would be to incorporate compression into the system, thus allowing a lower bandwidth channel to be used. This may be achieved by refining the original channel into three processes: a compression process, a new (lower bandwidth) channel and a decompression process. The real-time assumption governing the latency of the original channel now becomes a requirement for the new channel.

155

New real-time assumptions can be written to state the performance of the new processes. Importantly, having refined a specification in this way, both the old requirement and the new requirement (derived from the real-time assumption) should hold simultaneously. In this example, this means that the end-to-end latency requirement must hold at the same time as the new latency requirement over the refined lower bandwidth channel. This example will be revisited in more detail in Chapter 11.

The verification of requirements against a specification will be considered in Section 8.5.2 below and then in further detail in Chapter 10.

Mapping to the ODP computational language

A number of different formal specification techniques can be used to populate this architecture. However, there is an assumption that the chosen language for expressing abstract behaviour can be written in an object-oriented style to facilitate mapping to the computational language. More specifically, it is assumed that the components in the computational language (objects, interfaces, signals, operations, flows, interface types and bindings) can be represented and identified in the chosen specification technique.

Research in ODP has identified several languages that can be used to represent computational components. The appropriate mappings are currently being defined for LOTOS, Z, SDL and Estelle in ISO/ITU-T X.904 (1995). In particular, this reference contains some templates for the considered FDTs that help build specifications that are compliant with the rules of the ODP computational language. Further discussion on the use of LOTOS in this context can be found in Najm & Stefani (1992) and Vogel (1994). This list is also not exhaustive. Other languages could equally well be used assuming that the appropriate mappings can be defined.

Note that it is not necessary to adopt an object-oriented style in the early stages of specification and refinement. This only becomes essential as refinement proceeds towards realization with respect to the computational model. The specifier will start off with a set of requirements and an initial (abstract) statement of behaviour and associated real-time assumptions. This will then gradually be refined, introducing an object-oriented style until a full set of objects and their required real-time behaviour is identified. In the latter stages of this process, it is also important to identify the mapping to object classes supported by the computational model (i.e. synchronous objects, non-synchronous objects and bindings) and to define interface types and associated quality of service annotations for these classes.

Further discussion of the mapping to the ODP Computational Model can be found in Blair et al. (1995, 1996).

8.4 An approach based on LOTOS and a real-time temporal logic (QTL)

This section considers how LOTOS and a real-time temporal logic (denoted QTL for quality of service temporal logic) can be used within the framework outlined above. The abstract behaviour of the specification will initially be considered, followed by the requirements and the real-time assumptions.

8.4.1 Specifying abstract behaviour

The studies in Chapters 6 and 7 have shown that the specification language LOTOS, and more generally the category of process algebraic techniques, are suitable for the specification of abstract behaviour. Although other languages could be used (e.g. finite state machine based languages), a number of advantages can be gained through the use of a process algebra such as LOTOS. Process algebraic techniques generally feature an elegant set of operators for developing concurrent systems. Thus, succinct expressions of communicating concurrent processes can be made. Similarly, the emphasis on non-determinism in process algebraic techniques facilitates abstract specification, hiding implementation details. Furthermore, rich and tractable mathematical models of the semantics of process algebras have been developed. In LOTOS, this model is based on the concept of equivalences derived from the seminal work of Robin Milner (1989). In addition, owing to the standardization of LOTOS and the application-oriented nature of the language, a number of support tools have been developed (e.g. Lite (Mañas 1992)). Finally, as mentioned above, the use of LOTOS to represent the ODP Computational Model has been investigated in depth (ISO/ITU-T X.903 1995, Najm & Stefani 1992, Vogel 1994).

8.4.2 Specifying requirements

The survey in Chapter 5 highlighted mathematical logics as being particularly suited to the specification of requirements since they state *what* global properties a system should exhibit, but say nothing about *how* the system should achieve these properties. Hansson (1991) justifies the use of a logic to specify requirements as follows:

> The advantage of using a logic to formulate individual properties lies in the separation of concerns, i.e. each relevant requirement can independently be expressed in a separate formula and the total requirements are simply the conjunction of the separate formulas. Also, the individual properties can be proved separately.

157

For the domain of distributed multimedia systems, the chosen logic must be able to specify real-time properties, but, even given this restriction, there still remains a vast number of different techniques to choose from. This choice can be reduced by the decision to use a temporal logic (to allow the expression of liveness properties as well as safety properties (Pnueli 1977)). This issue will be returned to in Chapter 9 where the choice of a logic will be dealt with in greater detail.

8.4.3 Specifying real-time assumptions

This component of the specification has been left until last as it is not obvious which category of specification techniques provides the best notation for specifying real-time assumptions. Clearly, a notation must be used that permits the expression of real-time constraints. Moreover, whichever language is chosen, it is essential that the assumptions can be changed easily and freely during system development. Many assumptions (certainly those used very early in system development) will be estimates and, as the development progresses, they will need to be refined.

Given the decisions above to use a process algebraic technique to specify abstract behaviour and a real-time temporal logic to specify requirements, these two categories are considered for the specification of real-time assumptions. Considering process algebraic techniques first, it is clear that a technique permitting the specification of real-time constraints is necessary. While this rules out the use of LOTOS, one of the many timed extensions to LOTOS (or equally another process algebra) could be used. However, real-time assumptions are intended simply to ground events described in the abstract specification in real-time. Consequently, the power of process algebraic techniques, with respect to their ability to specify features such as concurrent processes, communication and non-determinism, is not necessary.

On the other hand, logics are highly suited to stating *what* a system should perform and not *how* it should perform. Consequently, the approach taken in this book is to specify real-time assumptions in a real-time temporal logic.

A further justification for the use of a real-time temporal logic is that, given that behavioural time is separated from real-time in a specification, benefits can be obtained by using the same language for the real-time assumptions and requirements. For example, one benefit is that only two languages need to be learned instead of three. An additional benefit arises with the verification procedure, through the ability to use existing methods to check the satisfiability of a formula. This will be discussed in more detail in Chapter 10. Consequently, the same logic will be used to specify the real-time assumptions as that used for expressing requirements.

8.5   Analysis of the LOTOS/QTL approach

The aim of this section is to provide an objective analysis of the new proposed approach, considering both its benefits and its drawbacks. In particular, the suitability of the new approach for the specification and
verification of distributed multimedia systems will be considered. Initially,
some benefits that are achieved by maintaining a separation of concerns
will be considered; some drawbacks of this approach will also be highlighted. The proposed approach will then be analyzed with respect to the
requirements for distributed multimedia systems identified in Chapter 4.

8.5.1   Discussion on maintaining a separation of concerns

As explained earlier, the key characteristic of the new approach lies in the
principle of maintaining a separation of concerns, both between the specification of behaviour and requirements and between the different types of
time in a specification. While the first separation is typical of many dual-
language approaches, few approaches exhibit the second separation.

There are a number of benefits to isolating the real-time assumptions
from the algorithmic behaviour of the system. The specification of behaviour remains totally abstract, that is, performance and implementation
considerations are not embedded into this part of the specification. As
mentioned above, an immediate consequence of this is that the timing
information, because it is kept logically distinct, is immediately identifiable and can be easily changed, for example if the timing information of the
underlying network changes. This results in more portable system specifications and also facilitates the expression of *what-if* scenarios (for example,
to consider the effect of changing certain real-time characteristics of the
system or underlying network).

Another benefit of the proposed approach is that different specification
techniques can be used as and where they are most appropriate (a *horses-
for-courses* analogy). Specifically, the process algebra LOTOS is suitable for
the specification of abstract behaviour while (real-time) temporal logics are
particularly suited to the specification of (real-time) requirements.

Furthermore, although LOTOS was originally developed for the specification of OSI protocols, its importance within ODP is clear, particularly
with respect to avoiding the ambiguous expression of system behaviour
that hinders the openness and inter-operability of systems. By using extensions to LOTOS, such as those that incorporate a notion of quantitative
time in the language, the benefits of the standardization of LOTOS are lost
(unless a *standard* timed LOTOS is developed). In addition, a large number
of tools have now been developed for LOTOS (e.g. Lite (Mañas 1992)). By
using standard LOTOS, these tools can still be used with the proposed
approach. Although not covering the whole of the verification procedure

necessary for the new approach, it does mean that it is possible to simulate and verify the specification of abstract behaviour.

There are, however, certain drawbacks to the proposed approach. Perhaps the most significant of these is that the verification procedure becomes more complex than for a traditional single language approach. The implications for verification with the new approach are considered in Section 8.5.2 below and then in more detail in Chapter 10. Additionally, no tool support exists for the entire procedure. However, existing tools can be used on the individual components of a specification to achieve some level of automated verification. A further drawback with a dual-language approach is that it becomes necessary for the specifier to learn two languages, rather than just one; the integration of these two languages (how to use them together) is particularly important and must also be fully understood.

8.5.2 Implications for verification

As mentioned above, one drawback of the new approach is the impact it has on verification. Typically, for specifications written using a single language approach, verification involves some well established techniques to prove that a *refined* specification meets (or satisfies) a previous specification. This is true both for the process algebra LOTOS and for logics. For example, techniques such as equivalence checking and correctness preserving transformations have been developed for LOTOS specifications, while theorem provers exist for logic specifications.

However, such an approach is not sufficient for the verification of specifications exhibiting a separation of concerns (for example, as shown in Fig. 8.3). Not only must a refined specification of behaviour satisfy the previous specification of behaviour, it must also satisfy the requirements. This procedure is further complicated because of the separation between the abstract behaviour and the real-time assumptions. Consequently, two important aspects of verification exist, as shown by Figure 8.4.

The first aspect of verification involves verifying that a refined specification meets a previous specification; this aspect will be referred to as *vertical*

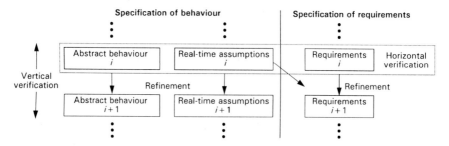

Figure 8.4 Two aspects of verification.

verification. Since each of the components of a specification (abstract behaviour, real-time assumptions and real-time requirements) can be refined independently, existing well-developed verification techniques such as those mentioned above can be used. Consequently, this aspect of verification will not be considered further in this book. The second aspect of verification involves proving that, at a given stage in the system development, each requirement is satisfied by the specification of behaviour; this will be referred to as *horizontal verification.* Techniques such as model-checking have been developed that allow requirements written using logics to be verified against a specification of behaviour that has been written using a different technique. However, with the approach proposed in this book, the specification of behaviour is split into two components: the abstract specification and the real-time assumptions. Consequently, a specialized verification procedure is required. Such a procedure will be developed in Chapter 10.

8.5.3 Meeting the requirements

Any new approach targeted at the specification of distributed multimedia systems must clearly aim to meet (at least the majority of) the requirements identified in Chapter 4. These requirements will be reconsidered below and it will be shown how the new proposed approach addresses each requirement in turn.

- *Usability and naturalness*   In terms of usability, LOTOS is a mature technique supporting abstract data types. The current version of the language has several recognized limitations. For example, it is accepted that the abstract data type component is not optimal. However, these limitations are currently being addressed in the revised LOTOS standard (ELOTOS). The use of a dual language approach enhances naturalness by enabling the most appropriate language to be used for abstract behaviour and real-time concerns. In addition, the separation of concerns between the abstract behaviour and the real-time assumptions means that the abstract behaviour is simpler than if real-time information were embedded in it. This enhances the readability of this component of the specification and means that it is easier to specify. A similar argument also applies to the real-time assumptions.
- *Concurrency*   The parallel composition operators defined in LOTOS provide an appropriate way to specify concurrent (abstract) behaviour between distributed nodes.
- *Interaction*   As above, interactions will be specified in the abstract behaviour. By using LOTOS, synchronous communication can be modelled directly. However, LOTOS can also be used to specify queues or buffers that provide a model of asynchronous communication.

Also, non-deterministic choice can be used in LOTOS to specify unpredictable behaviour.

- *Openness and inter-operability* LOTOS is a standardized formal description technique and has been promoted within ISO. In particular, there has been considerable research using LOTOS as a specification technique within ODP. Consequently, the use of LOTOS to specify distributed systems (or components) goes some way to achieving the goals of openness and inter-operability.

- *Implementation independence* In the new approach, LOTOS is used to specify the abstract behaviour of the system. Consequently, this component of the specification contains no mention of real-time or performance assumptions, thus making the specification more implementation independent.

- *Object-based techniques* Various object-based and object-oriented LOTOS techniques have been developed that can be used to facilitate the specification of distributed systems. For example, Clark (1992) and Najm & Stefani (1992) provide explanations of how an object-based *style* can be employed in a (standard) LOTOS specification. This style allows the modelling of concepts such as data abstraction and information hiding. The papers of Mayr (1989) and Rudkin (1992) consider how LOTOS can be used to model full object-oriented concepts such as classes and inheritance.

- *Dynamic reconfiguration* Although LOTOS does not support full dynamic reconfiguration, several studies have been carried out into how the altering of communication paths and the dynamic creation of objects can be modelled in LOTOS. For example, Fredlund & Orava (1992) describe how dynamically changing communication structures can be specified using LOTOS data values. A further example is provided by Najm & Stefani (1992) in which a simple (formal) object-based language is considered that permits, amongst other things, the explicit creation of objects. By presenting a translation from this language to LOTOS, it is shown that LOTOS can be used to model the dynamic reconfiguration features exhibited in object-based languages. An extension to LOTOS that supports full dynamic reconfiguration (including the dynamic creation and deletion of interfaces), is presented in Koch et al. (1994). However, note that the use of an extended LOTOS would mean that benefits relating to the standardization of LOTOS are lost.

- *Co-existence of different languages for different ODP viewpoints* The co-existence of different languages for different viewpoints and the problem this raises with maintaining consistency across the viewpoints is not addressed in this book.

- *Specification of real-time constraints* A real-time temporal logic (denoted QTL) will be developed in Chapter 9 for the expression of real-time constraints over events occurring in the abstract LOTOS specification. This logic will be shown (in Chs 11 and 12) to be suitable for the specification of quality of service parameters and real-time synchronization scenarios.

- *Specification of probabilistic constraints*   It was highlighted in Chapter 4 that quality of service parameters may include probabilistic, as well as real-time, constraints. However, this book focuses on the specification of real-time constraints and does not address the requirement for probabilities.
- *Easy to identify and change real-time constraints*   By applying the principle of maintaining a separation of concerns, the abstract behaviour is separated from the real-time assumptions and the requirements. This means that all real-time constraints are isolated and are hence immediately identifiable and can easily be modified, if required.
- *Validation, including validation of real-time constraints*   A verification procedure will be presented for the new approach (in Ch. 10) which will permit the formal validation of real-time constraints (as well as other properties).

A number of these points will be analyzed further in the remainder of the book; the requirements are then revisited in the concluding chapter (Ch. 13).

8.6   Related work

In this section, some work that is closely related to the approach proposed in this book will be discussed. In particular, dual language approaches to specification will be considered. There has been a significant amount of research on the use of logic-based approaches to the specification of system requirements, while a different notation is used to specify the behaviour of the system. Several techniques based on this approach are discussed below. One additional technique, however, which does not use a logic-based approach, is also discussed. This work is particularly relevant since it is based on the principle of maintaining a separation of concerns between the abstract behaviour, specified in LOTOS, and the real-time behaviour of a system.

8.6.1   CCS and the process logic $\mathcal{PL}$

One of the most important pieces of work on relating logics to process algebraic specifications was presented by Milner in his book on communication and concurrency (Milner 1989), in which he presents a simple process logic known as $\mathcal{PL}$ (briefly described in Ch. 5). This logic can express the *possibility* and *necessity* of certain events that occur in a CCS specification. A satisfaction relation is defined between the labelled transition system of a CCS process and a $\mathcal{PL}$ formula, thus allowing the proof of whether a $\mathcal{PL}$ formula *satisfies* a given CCS process.

While the link between a logic and a process algebra is relevant to the approach proposed in this book, there are two drawbacks with the work. First, Milner's work does not consider the specification of real-time properties that are necessary for the specification and verification of distributed multimedia systems. Secondly, to quote Milner, "$\mathcal{PL}$ is a logic which only expresses safety properties, not liveness properties" (1989).

8.6.2 CCS and the timed probabilistic logic TPCTL

A piece of work that deals with both of the above problems is provided by Hansson in his thesis (1991). In this work, CCS is extended with a probabilistic choice operator and a special timeout operator, resulting in a new timed probabilistic CCS (TPCCS). A discrete model of time is used that is based on a minimal delay assumption, i.e. communications must occur as soon as they are possible. A logic is then defined and interpreted over processes specified in TPCCS. This logic is based on the branching time logic CTL (Clarke et al. 1986) and, like CCS, is extended with time and probabilities (resulting in a logic called TPCTL). A model checking algorithm is then presented that establishes if a TPCTL formula satisfies a given TPCCS process.

This piece of work results in a very powerful specification technique that permits the specification of both timed and probabilistic behaviours. However, to achieve this, the process algebra CCS has been extended (TPCCS). Consequently, there is no longer an abstract specification of system behaviour: both time and probabilities are embedded firmly into the specification. In contrast, the approach proposed in this book aims to develop a technique that does maintain an abstract specification of system behaviour, while still permitting the specification of real-time constraints.

8.6.3 TTMs and the real-time temporal logic RTTL

Timed Transition Models (TTMs) were developed specifically as the algorithmic component of the dual-language approach, TTM/RTTL (Ostroff 1992a). TTMs were first introduced in Chapter 5. The second component of the dual-language approach is the real-time temporal logic RTTL. RTTL is based on standard Manna & Pnueli linear time logic (Manna & Pnueli 1992), but is extended to permit two distinguished variables, a time variable t (the current clock time) and a next transition variable n (enabling events to be referenced), to be included in propositions. While the TTM component is used to express the algorithmic behaviour, RTTL is used to express the requirements of the system. Although RTTL is a very expressive logic, one drawback is that it has been shown to be undecidable. In addition, as with the TPCCS/TPCTL approach described above, time is directly embedded into the language used to describe the behaviour of the system.

8.6.4 Esterel and the Real-Time Logic QL

This dual-language technique, proposed by researchers at CNET (Centre National d'Etudes des Télécommunications), is particularly interesting since it addresses issues relating to distributed multimedia systems. The technique is described in Stefani (1993) and is based on the use of the synchronous programming language Esterel and a real-time first-order logic named QL. The approach was introduced in Chapter 5. Briefly, systems are considered to be composed of a set of interacting objects, some of which are *reactive*, while others are not. *Reactive* objects behave according to the synchrony hypothesis (see Appendix A) and are written in Esterel. Any communications *inside* reactive objects are instantaneous (synchronous), while communications *between* objects (whether reactive or not) require some non-zero amount of time (asynchronous). To constrain this asynchronous behaviour, a quality of service logic QL (based on the real-time logic RTL) is defined to constrain communications between objects. This can be used, for example, to bound the delay on messages between objects in the system.

An interesting feature of this approach is that all timing assumptions are isolated in the quality of service declarations. This is because, although Esterel incorporates a notion of time into the language, there is no guarantee on the relationship between clock signals and the actual real-time at which they are meant to occur. The lack of this guarantee is known as the problem of *anchoring* (or grounding) clock signals in absolute time (Stefani et al. 1992). In the Esterel/QL approach, the logic QL is used to anchor clock signals in real-time. This is similar to the approach proposed in this book where LOTOS is used to specify abstract timing behaviour and the logic QTL is used to ground abstract timing events in real-time (the real-time assumptions). Consequently, the Esterel/QL approach can be viewed as maintaining a separation of timing concerns.

8.6.5 LOTOS and a new Time-Constrained LOTOS

As with the Esterel/QL approach, the final approach to be considered in this section also provides, to some degree, a separation of concerns. This approach, presented in Schot (1992), is based on the use of LOTOS and a new LOTOS-like language that constrains the time interval elapsing between successive events. Since no name is given to this new language, it will be referred to as time-constrained LOTOS.

The approach described in Schot (1992) is proposed for the formal design of distributed systems. Standard LOTOS is used to specify all aspects of a system that do not involve real-time, while any remaining real-time aspects are specified in the new time-constrained LOTOS. The LOTOS specification can be seen to be constrained, and thus reduced, by the timing specification.

Importantly, the separation between the timed and untimed components of the specification is maintained throughout system development until the implementation phase. Transformations are used to progress between different stages of system development. For the LOTOS component of the specification, formal concepts such as correctness preserving transformations and equivalence relations can be used to determine the validity of a transformed LOTOS specification with respect to the previous specification. However, the new time-constrained LOTOS notation has no formal syntax or semantics. Consequently, the validity of the real-time constraints over a transformed LOTOS specification can only be checked in an informal way.

8.6.6   Summary of related work

A number of pieces of related work have been considered above. The main differences between these approaches to specification and the approach proposed in this book lies in the principle of maintaining a separation of concerns. The first separation is between the specification of behaviour and the specification of requirements. As illustrated above, this separation is typical of many dual-language approaches, where some style of logic is often used to express requirements. However, in addition, a separation is drawn between the different types of time appearing in a specification, specifically between (abstract) behavioural time and the real-time assumptions. Although the last two pieces of related work also exhibit this separation, the Esterel/QL approach does not consider the specification of requirements while the LOTOS/time-constrained LOTOS approach does not use a formal language for the expression of real-time constraints.

8.7   Summary

This chapter has proposed a new approach for the formal specification and verification of distributed multimedia systems. This approach is based on the principle of maintaining a separation of concerns. It has been shown how the process algebra LOTOS and a real-time temporal logic (QTL) can be used in this approach and how this approach differs from a number of pieces of related work. Some benefits and drawbacks of the new approach have also been discussed in this section. To summarize, the main benefits are that:

- the specification of behaviour is abstract in that no performance or implementation considerations are embedded into this component of the specification;

- all timing information is immediately identifiable and can be easily changed;
- as a result of the above point, system specifications are more portable and can express *what-if* scenarios;
- different specification techniques can be used as and where they are most appropriate;
- requirements are formally specified (using a temporal logic);·
- changes are not necessary to the LOTOS standard; hence, existing tools can be used as part of the verification procedure.

However, with the new approach, the specifier must learn two languages and understand how they are integrated. A further drawback is that the verification procedure is more complex than for a single language approach.

CHAPTER 9

The design of the Logic QTL

9.1   Introduction

The previous chapter has outlined a new approach to specification based on the principle of maintaining a separation of concerns. Two languages were proposed for the formal specification of different aspects of a system, the first being the process algebra LOTOS and the second being a real-time temporal logic. A vast number of different styles of real-time temporal logic exist; therefore, it is necessary to decide precisely which style will be used. The following Section (9.2) considers this point, concentrating mainly on the concepts of expressibility and decidability. Having decided which style is most appropriate for the specification (and verification) of distributed multimedia systems, a new logic is developed. This logic, named QTL (for quality of service temporal logic), is based closely on the metric temporal logic MTL presented in Koymans (1990). However, it includes extensions to permit the logic to be used in conjunction with LOTOS. Sections 9.3 and 9.4 describe the syntax and semantics of this new logic respectively. Section 9.5 then presents a note on the use of additional data variables and Section 9.6 summarizes the chapter.

9.2   The choice of a logic

The survey in Chapter 5 of this book has provided an introduction to some of the logics that exist, the field of temporal logic being particularly relevant. This style of logic has been widely applied to computer science since the pioneering work of Amir Pnueli in the 1970s. Temporal logic is simply classical propositional logic that has been extended with a number of temporal operators, typically represented by the symbols: $\Diamond$ for *eventually*,

□ for *henceforth*, ○ for *next* and ∪ for *until*. As reported in Chapter 5, Pnueli justifies the need for a temporal logic (over a first-order logic) because of its ability to express liveness properties, i.e. that something desirable will eventually happen (Pnueli 1977). This will be seen to be necessary in the examples of Chapters 11 and 12.

Perhaps the most significant impact on the choice of a logic arises because of the need to express real-time properties of systems (see Ch. 4), for example stating that a given response is obtained within a certain time. Even given this requirement, there are still a vast number of different logics that could be chosen. To help categorize these logics, two concepts are of particular importance, namely *expressibility* and *decidability*. First, it is important that the chosen logic is sufficiently expressive to permit the specification of required properties from the application domain. Secondly, it is important that, once the properties have been specified, their correct-ness can be verified, i.e. it must be possible to decide algorithmically whether or not a formula is *satisfiable* and whether or not it is *valid* over a given model. To further categorize different logics, it is helpful to consider the following questions:

- Should the underlying nature of time be linear or branching?
- How is real-time to be introduced into the logic?
- Are past temporal operators needed in addition to future temporal operators?
- Is propositional temporal logic sufficient, or is a first-order variant (employing predicates and some form of quantification) necessary?
- Is a discrete or a dense time domain necessary?
- What operations are necessary on timing variables (e.g. is addition by a constant sufficient)?

The following sections outline some important results that have been established in the literature regarding the concepts of expressibility and decidability, and relate these results to the questions posed above. As will be seen, in general, many more results exist for linear-time logics than for branching-time logics.

9.2.1 Expressibility

Results for Linear-time Logics

The three main ways of introducing real-time into a linear-time temporal logic are through the use of *bounded operators*, *freeze quantification* and *explicit clocks*. The techniques MTL (Koymans 1990), TPTL (Alur & Henzinger 1994) and XCTL (Harel et al. 1990b) are representative of these three approaches (respectively). Since the survey in Chapter 5 has already out-lined the main characteristics of each approach, these will not be repeated here. Several results have been established regarding the expressibility of each of these techniques; these results are summarized below.

It is shown in Alur & Henzinger (1990) that MTL and TPTL have the same expressive power. This assumes that a discrete time domain is used. With a discrete time domain, formulae that impose time bounds on non-adjacent events can be expressed in MTL (as shown in Ch. 5), although TPTL does, in general, provide a more succinct expression of the formulae. However, if the time domain is not discrete, such formulae cannot be expressed in MTL (but can be expressed in TPTL). A further point is that the syntax of MTL includes past temporal operators whereas TPTL includes only future temporal operators. Consequently, the expression of properties referring to past states can be expressed more succinctly in MTL than in TPTL.

With respect to the logic XCTL, it is shown in Harel et al. (1990b) that XCTL and TPTL are incomparable with respect to expressibility since there is a property expressible in one logic that is not expressible in the other. The trade-off is between: (a) allowing only one (outermost) level of universal quantification, and permitting general addition between timing variables (as in XCTL): and, (b) allowing the arbitrary nesting of (freeze) quantifiers, but restricting addition to addition by constant only (as in TPTL). The following two examples illustrating the difference between XCTL and TPTL are based on examples provided in Harel et al. (1990b). In XCTL, it is possible to specify that the difference between two events is always smaller than the difference between two other events. For example,

$$\Box(p \wedge (x=T) \rightarrow \Box(q \wedge (y=T) \rightarrow \Box(r \wedge (z=T) \rightarrow (z-y < y-x))))$$

In this XCTL example, p, q, and r are events, x, y and z are timing variables and T is the special variable referring to the current value of the (global) clock. This property cannot be expressed in TPTL since the operations on timing variables are restricted to addition by constant only. The second example illustrates that, in TPTL, it is possible to specify that, if the difference between two events is bounded by some constant, then the difference between two other events will be bounded by a (different) constant. For example,

$$\Box x.(p \rightarrow \Diamond y.(q \wedge (y \leq x+2))) \rightarrow \Box z.(r \rightarrow t.(s \wedge (t \leq z+10)))$$

In this TPTL example, the timing variables x, y, z and t are bound to the times at which events p, q, r and s occur respectively. This property cannot be expressed in XCTL since it is not possible to reduce the formula to one outermost level of universal quantification. Since both of these formulae are perfectly acceptable real-time properties, XCTL and TPTL are viewed as being incomparable with respect to expressibility (Harel et al. 1990b).

The effect of different logics on expressibility

Linear time vs. Branching time Much has been written regarding the relative expressiveness of linear time versus branching time logics in the untimed case (e.g. (Emerson & Halpern 1986; Emerson 1990)). Since these arguments do not change when real-time is introduced into the respective notations, the main issues for *untimed* logics will be summarized here. (Ch. 5 discussed untimed linear versus branching time logics in greater detail.) Emerson & Halpern (1986) conclude that, in general, both linear and branching time logics are adequate for the specification and verification of concurrent systems, but consider that the simplicity of linear time logics gives these logics an advantage over branching time logics. However, an advantage of branching time logics over linear time logics is that branching time logics can be used to prove the existence of an alternative path in a system.

Past operators   Most temporal logics include only future-tense operators in their syntax. For the specification of computer systems, it can be shown that the inclusion of past-tense operators adds no extra expressive power. However, the use of past-tense operators can simplify formulae and lead to substantially more succinct and intuitive specifications of certain properties. It should be noted that the linear-time logic MTL includes past-tense operators, while TPTL and XCTL only include future-tense operators.

Propositional vs. First-order logics   A first-order logic is more expressive than an equivalent propositional version of the logic, since a first-order logic permits predicates and quantification over variables. However, as will be seen below, the extra expressiveness of a first-order logic has a serious consequence in terms of decidability.

The time domain and the permitted operations on time   A discrete time domain is generally regarded as sufficiently expressive for reasoning about most types of computer system since the granularity of time can be adjusted as required (although some researchers argue that dense time logics (Alur et al. 1991) are required to facilitate arbitrary refinement or to describe hybrid analogue-digital systems). It is the permitted operations on time that have a greater impact on expressibility. A basic set of operations contains only the successor operator. Addition by constant can be represented by applying repeated successor operations and hence has no impact on expressiveness (although it does enhance the readability and succinctness of formulae). However, a more general set of operations permits the addition of two (or more) timing variables. This does provide extra expressiveness since it allows the specification of properties such as the time interval between two events always being constant (for example, the time interval from p to q equals the time interval from q to p for every occurrence of events p and q).

9.2.2   Decidability

Complexity terminology
Before considering whether or not decision procedures exist for various
logics, it is first necessary to present some of the terminology used in
describing the complexity of these procedures. A more complete description of terminology can be found in Johnson (1990).

Most terms used in complexity analysis are defined with reference to
Turing machines, specifically deterministic Turing machines (DTMs) and
non-deterministic Turing machines (NDTMs). Many terms also reference
the *time* of a (Turing machine) computation (the number of steps before the
machine halts) and the *space* of a computation (the number of cells of the
tape visited by the machine head during the computation). In the following
text, an algorithm for a formula of length n will be said to run in *polynomial
time/space* if there exists a constant k such that the computation time/space
is $O(n^k)$ (i.e. of order n^k) and in *exponential time/space* if there exists a constant k such that the computation time/space is $O(2^{p(n)})$ where $p(n)=n^k$.

One of the most important complexity classes is the class "P" of decision
procedures; these are procedures that are solvable by DTMs in polynomial
time (the class "NP" refers to those procedures solvable by NDTMs in
polynomial time). The term PSPACE is used to denote the set of procedures
that are solvable by polynomial-space bounded deterministic Turing
machines.

Importantly, however, it has not yet been proved (or disproved) whether
P=PSPACE. If this equality were to be proved true, *all* procedures in
PSPACE would be solvable in polynomial time. Examples such as the
decision procedure for XCTL (described in the following section) highlight
the current gap between the largest known lower time bounds for procedures (in this case, polynomial time) and the time bounds of the best
known algorithms: the satisfiability problem has been proved to belong to
PSPACE, but the decision procedure presented runs in exponential time.

The set of all decision procedures that are solvable in exponential time
are denoted by the term EXPTIME, while EXPSPACE refers to those procedures that require exponential space. Some of the procedures discussed
below are described as taking doubly exponential time, i.e. they operate in
a time bounded by $2^{2^{p(n)}}$ for some polynomial $p(n)$. The class of decision
procedures that operate in this time is often denoted by 2-EXPTIME. The
classes 3-EXPTIME, ..., k-EXPTIME (where k represents the number of levels of exponentiation) can be similarly defined. The term *elementary* refers
to those procedures that are solvable in the union of the classes k-EXPTIME
for $k>1$. A procedure is said to be *non-elementary* if it is decidable, but not
elementary.

Finally, to conclude this section on terminology, the term *complete* is used
to refer to a set of the "hardest" problems in a given complexity class; for

example, the class of NP-complete problems consists of the "hardest" problems in NP. If a problem in this class can be solved in, for example, polynomial time, then all other problems in the set can be solved in polynomial time. Conversely, if any problem in the set is proved to be intractable (no polynomial time algorithm exists) then all the other problems in the set will be intractable. A comprehensive guide to completeness, particularly NP-completeness, can be found in Garey & Johnson (1979).

Results for linear-time logics

Before considering the impact of different logics on decidability, some results regarding decision procedures for the logics XCTL, TPTL and MTL are first discussed.

A singly exponential (time) decision procedure for checking the satisfiability of XCTL formulae is presented in Harel et al. (1990b) (based on the tableau method). The satisfiability problem for XCTL is shown to be PSPACE-complete, i.e. there exists a polynomial space bounded deterministic algorithm that decides satisfiability.

Also presented in Harel et al. (1990b) is an algorithm for checking the validity of XCTL formulae over finite state programs (based on model checking). The algorithm is doubly exponential in the size of the formula and singly exponential in the size of the program. However, it is pointed out that XCTL is not closed under implications (or negation) and hence the model checking problem (does a formula ϕ_s hold over all computations of a given finite state program?) cannot be reduced into the validity problem of the formula $\phi_p \rightarrow \phi_s$, where ϕ_p describes the semantics of the program. Most model checking algorithms for linear temporal logics (e.g. for TPTL) are based on such a reduction. Such an approach is unsuitable for XCTL and hence the model checking algorithm in Harel et al. (1990b) is based on a different, specially developed, procedure.

Alur & Henzinger (1990) show that the satisfiability problem for both TPTL and MTL is EXPSPACE-complete and present (tableau-based) decision procedures that are doubly exponential in the length of timing constraints and singly exponential in the number of temporal and Boolean operators. However, the procedure for MTL depends exponentially on the value of the largest time constant involved, while the procedure for TPTL depends exponentially on the value of the product of all time constants. Consequently, the (worst-case) running time for the MTL procedure will be faster than for the TPTL procedure.

The effect of different logics on decidability

Linear time vs. branching time   In the case of linear logics, the model checking problem is as difficult as the problem of checking satisfiability. That is, both procedures are EXPSPACE-complete for MTL and TPTL, and a special procedure allows both problems to be checked in PSPACE for

XCTL. Fewer results exist for the decidability of branching real-time temporal logics. However, as reported in Ostroff (1992b), the validity problem for untimed branching logics is EXPTIME-complete, while a special algorithm can be employed for model checking branching time logics that is in PTIME.

Two known results relating to branching real-time logics are that the satisfiability problem for the logic RTCTL is EXPSPACE-complete (in doubly exponential time) (Emerson et al. 1991) and that the model checking algorithm for TCTL is PSPACE-complete (Alur et al. 1990).

Past operators MTL includes past operators and has an elementary (although doubly exponential) decision procedure. However, Alur & Henzinger (1990, 1994) show that the inclusion of past operators in TPTL renders the satisfiability problem non-elementary. Harel et al. (1990b) does not consider the effect of past operators on the decidability of XCTL.

Propositional vs. first-order logics Alur & Henzinger state that only propositional versions of temporal logics are decidable (Alur & Henzinger 1991), i.e. first-order logics are undecidable. However, real-time logics have been developed that employ a restricted form of quantification over *timing* variables and include predicates (over timing variables), and yet are decidable. For example, the logic XCTL permits predicates and quantification over timing variables, but restricts the level of quantification to one (outermost) level of universal quantification (which therefore need not be explicitly displayed). As has been stated above, the decidability problem for XCTL is PSPACE-complete.

The time domain and the permitted operations on time These two parameters, namely the domain of time and the permitted operations on time, determine the decidability of a real-time propositional temporal logic. In general, admitting a dense time domain rules out the possibility of obtaining decision procedures. However, an exception to this rule is presented in Alur et al. (1991) where, by relaxing the notion of punctuality, a decidable metric interval temporal logic (MITL) is developed that is interpreted over a dense time domain.

A basic set of time operations contains only the successor operation. More complicated timing constraints can be specified by using a set containing the plus operation. Providing the logic is closed under all Boolean operations and can express punctuality (i.e. one event is followed by another event in precisely n time units), then the satisfiability problem is undecidable for both the dense time domain with just the basic successor operation, and for the discrete time domain when the set of time operations includes plus (Alur & Henzinger 1991). This last result is interesting since the satisfiability problem for XCTL (where the time operations include plus) is decidable. This illustrates that the rule does not generalize for logics that are not closed under Boolean operations (XCTL is not closed under implication or negation). It is also interesting to note that, for the branching time logic TCTL, model checking is possible (in PSPACE) even though the logic employs a dense time domain (and a basic set of timing operations) (Alur et al. 1990).

9.2.3   A logic for distributed multimedia systems

The main impacts of this application domain on the choice of a logic have already been considered, that is, the need for a temporal logic and the need for some representation of real-time. However, as has been shown, this still leaves a vast number of options. The concepts of expressibility and decidability are clearly important in making a choice, hence the results presented above. Two additional relevant concepts that were also highlighted in the requirements of Chapter 4 were *usability* and *naturalness*: how easy is it to specify the required properties and how easy is it to read them once they have been specified?

The choice between using linear-time versus branching-time logics is perhaps the least clear cut of the options that must be considered. While branching time logics have, in general, simpler model-checking algorithms than linear-time logics, it can be argued that linear-time logics provide greater usability and naturalness. The extra expressiveness of branching-time operators (regarding the ability to specify the existence of a particular path) is of no significance for the chosen application domain. Similarly, there appears to be no need to use a dense time domain in preference to a discrete time domain, since the granularity of time can be adjusted as required. Again considering usability and naturalness, there is a strong case for the inclusion of past-tense operators. This somewhat narrows the choice of which style of logic to use. If TPTL is extended with past-tense operators, the decision procedure becomes non-elementary. On the other hand, elementary decision procedures exist for MTL (which includes past-tense operators) although these are more expensive than equivalent procedures for XCTL (EXPSPACE-complete compared with PSPACE-complete). However, it is not known whether the addition of past-tense operators to XCTL renders the decision procedures non-elementary, as is true of TPTL. Taking all these results into consideration, MTL has been chosen to form the basis for a real-time temporal logic for the intended application domain.

To summarize the features of MTL, the logic employs a linear view of the underlying semantics of time, it incorporates past-tense operators as well as the usual future-tense operators, it uses a bounded operator notation for introducing real-time into the logic, no quantification is permitted, it is based on a discrete time domain and uses a basic set of operations (addition by constant only). Finally, the decidability problem for MTL is EXPSPACE complete, the running time being doubly exponential in the value of the largest time constant involved.

The logic MTL was not designed to be used in conjunction with LOTOS. A few changes will therefore be necessary. For example, LOTOS events should be permitted as propositions within the logic, facilities will be necessary to handle data in the logic (for example, data occurring in LOTOS events), and the underlying model will need to be adjusted to reflect the use of LOTOS. The remainder of this chapter concentrates on the definition of such a logic, defining both the syntax and semantics. The logic is denoted QTL, for quality of service temporal logic.

9.3 Syntax of QTL

In the subsequent text, the symbols ϕ, ϕ_1 and ϕ_2 will be used to denote arbitrary QTL formulae. Additionally, assume that the function $\eta(a)$ is defined to take as its parameter a LOTOS event and return the name of the associated event gate (for example, $\eta(a!3)=a$, $\eta(b!2!1)=b$ and $\eta(c)=c$).

The temporal operators in the logic are denoted as follows: $\bigcirc$ denotes the temporal future operator *next*, U denotes the temporal future operator *until*, $\ominus$ denotes the temporal past operator *previous*, S denotes the temporal past operator *since* and $\rightarrow$ denotes the Boolean operator *implies*. A full description of these (and other) logic operators can be found in Manna & Pnueli (1992). The syntax for the real-time temporal logic QTL can be defined as shown below.

9.3.1 Abstract syntax

QTL has the following syntax (where ϕ is an arbitrary QTL formula and $\eta(a)$ denotes the gate name of the LOTOS event a):

$\phi ::= \text{false} \mid \phi_1 \rightarrow \phi_2 \mid \bigcirc_{\sim c} \phi \mid \phi_1 U_{\sim c} \phi_2 \mid \ominus_{\sim c} \phi \mid \phi_1 S_{\sim c} \phi_2 \mid a \mid \pi_1 \sim \pi_2$
$\sim ::= < \mid = \mid >$
$\pi ::= x \mid c \mid x+c$ (* addition by constant only *)

where, $c \in N^0$ (the set of positive natural numbers, including zero), $x \in \text{Var}$ (the set of data variables), $\eta(a) \in \text{Act}$ (the set of LOTOS events) and event a has either the simple form g or the form $g!v_1!v_2...!v_n$ or $g?v_1:\text{nat}?$ $v_2:\text{nat}...?v_m:\text{nat}$ (or any combination of ! and ?) where each $v_i \in N^0$.

Note that although LOTOS events can be specified as QTL propositions, the syntax for these events is restricted slightly from the syntax of standard LOTOS in that the data range is restricted to natural numbers. This avoids the need to consider a many-sorted algebra. A further restriction is that all variables should range over a *finite set* of natural numbers; the reason for this is discussed in Chapter 10.

9.3.2 Derived operators

Additional propositional, existential and temporal operators can be derived from the ones given above. Their derivations are given below:

not:	$\neg\,\phi \equiv \phi \rightarrow \text{false}$
true:	$\text{true} \equiv \neg\text{false}$
or:	$\phi_1 \vee \phi_2 \equiv (\neg\phi_1) \rightarrow \phi_2$
and:	$\phi_1 \wedge \phi_2 \equiv \neg(\neg\phi_1 \vee \neg\phi_2)$
eventually:	$\Diamond_{\sim c}\,\phi \equiv \text{true}\ U_{\sim c}\,\phi$
henceforth:	$\Box_{\sim c}\,\phi \equiv \neg\Diamond_{\sim c}\,\neg\phi$
once:	$\Diamondblack_{\sim c}\,\phi \equiv \text{true}\ S_{\sim c}\,\phi$
has-always-been:	$\boxminus_{\sim c}\,\phi \equiv \neg\Diamondblack_{\sim c}\,\neg\phi$

A number of abbreviations will also be adopted when QTL is used in various examples. These simply provide a shorthand notation and serve to make the logic statements more concise. Examples of some abbreviations that will be adopted are given below:

$$\Diamond_{\geq c}\,\phi \equiv \Diamond_{>c}\,\phi \vee \Diamond_{=c}\,\phi$$
$$O\phi \equiv O_{\geq 0}\,\phi \qquad\qquad\qquad (\text{* unbounded operators *})$$
$$\boxdot\phi \equiv \boxdot_{\geq 0}\,\phi$$
$$V_{t=c}^{c'}\,\phi_{=t} \equiv \phi_{=c} \vee \phi_{=c+1} \vee \dots \vee \phi_{=c'} \qquad (\text{* choice (disjunction) shorthand *})$$

where most notation is as above. Additionally, though, t is a (timing) variable, $c,c' \in N^0$ (such that $c \leq c'$) and $\phi_{=t}$ is a formula including the variable t. In the expansion of the disjunction shorthand, all occurrences of variable t in ϕ are replaced by a constant from the range $[c,c']$. For example, $V_{t=35}^{45}\,\Diamond_{=t}p$ is shorthand for $\Diamond_{=35}p \vee \Diamond_{=36}p \vee \dots \vee \Diamond_{=45}p$.

9.4 Semantics of QTL

Most linear real-time temporal logics are interpreted over *timed state sequences*, that is, sequences of states where each state is associated with a (discrete) time (e.g. TPTL (Alur & Henzinger 1990) and XCTL (Harel et al. 1990b)). QTL formulae are interpreted similarly. Importantly, since QTL will be used with LOTOS, it is necessary to incorporate the occurrence of LOTOS events into the sequences. The notion of timed state sequences, as used by QTL, is defined below.

9.4.1 Timed state sequences

A *state sequence*, σ, is an infinite sequence of states. As above, let $\eta(a)$ take as its parameter a LOTOS event and return the name of the event gate associated with that event. The form of a state sequence can now be described as follows:

$\sigma = \sigma_0\sigma_1\sigma_2 \ldots$ where $\sigma_i \subseteq$ Prop (the set of QTL propositions) for $i \geq 0$ and, $\forall i \geq 0, \exists$ exactly one $x \in \sigma_i$ s.t. $\eta(x) \in$ Act

In QTL's state sequences, each state must include *exactly one* element that is a LOTOS event. A state may also (optionally) include one or more statements of the form $\pi_1 \sim \pi_2$ (following the notation defined above). An example of a possible state is (send !2, $x=0$, $y>5$). Consequently, propositions in QTL are either LOTOS events or equations (inequalities) of the form $\pi_1 \sim \pi_2$. The notation $\sigma_i[\pi]$ will be used to denote the value of π in state σ_i of the state sequence σ.

A (discrete) *time sequence*, τ, is an infinite sequence of discrete times that takes the form:

$\tau = \tau_0\tau_1\tau_2 \ldots$ where $\tau_i \in N^0$, $i \geq 0$.

A *timed state sequence*, ρ, is a pair (σ, τ) where σ is a state sequence and τ is a time sequence. The time sequence of ρ associates a time with every state, and consequently every event, in the state sequence of ρ such that for $i \geq 0$, σ_i occurs at time τ_i.

Every time sequence must be *monotonic*, that is, time cannot decrease throughout a sequence (or, more formally, $\forall i \geq 0$. $\tau_i \leq \tau_{i+1}$). However, unlike Alur & Henzinger (1989), time need not progress from one state to another. The motivation for this comes from the use of LOTOS. In LOTOS, events occur instantaneously, that is, their execution takes no time. Therefore, there is no limit on the number of events that may occur at the same time. This corresponds to micro time in Henzinger et al. (1990), where events are only distinguished by event ordering.

An additional note about the timed state sequences used for QTL is that *time gaps* are permitted in time sequences, that is, there can exist a $t \in N^0$ such that $\neg\exists i \geq 0$ s.t. $\tau_i = t$. A motivation for this is that a LOTOS specification may not offer an event at every time instant.

9.4.2   Satisfiability

For a timed state sequence $\rho = (\sigma, \tau)$, let (ρ, i) represent the timed state sequence starting at action σ_i and time τ_i, denoted (σ_i, τ_i). In particular, $(\rho, 0)$ denotes the timed state sequence starting at action σ_0 and time τ_0. ρ is said to be a model of some formula ϕ iff $(\rho, 0)$ satisfies ϕ (or $(\rho, 0) \models \phi$). The satisfaction relation $\models$ can be defined for QTL as follows (where $\rho = (\sigma, \tau)$):

$(\rho, i) \not\models$ false

$(\rho, i) \models \phi_1 \rightarrow \phi_2$ iff $(\rho, i) \models \phi_1$ implies $(\rho, i) \models \phi_2$

$(\rho, i) \models O_{\sim c}\, \phi$ iff $(\rho, i+1) \models \phi$ and $\tau_{i+1} \sim \tau_i + c$

$(\rho, i) \models \phi_1\, U_{\sim c}\, \phi_2$ iff $\exists j \geq i. (\rho, j) \models \phi_2$ and $\forall k, i \leq k < j. (\rho, k) \models \phi_1$ and $\tau_j \sim \tau_i + c$

$(\rho, i) \models \ominus_{\sim c}\, \phi$ iff $(i > 0)$ and $(\rho, i-1) \models \phi$ and $\tau_i \sim \tau_{i-1} + c$

$(\rho, i) \models \phi_1\, S_{\sim c}\, \phi_2$ iff $\exists j, 0 \leq j \leq i. (\rho, j) \models \phi_2$ and $\forall k, j < k \leq i. (\rho, k) \models \phi_1$ and $\tau_i \sim \tau_j + c$

$(\rho,i) \models a$ iff $\exists x \in \sigma_i$ s.t. $\eta(x) \in$ Act and $a \equiv x$

$(\rho,i) \models \pi_1 \sim \pi_2$ iff $\sigma_i[\pi_1] \sim \sigma_i[\pi_2]$

Note that the penultimate rule governs the satisfiability of a proposition that is a LOTOS event. This rule ensures that, for a LOTOS event a, either $a \in \sigma_i$ or (if $a \notin \sigma_i$) then there exists a LOTOS event in σ_i that is "equivalent to" a. Such equivalent events are determined by the standard LOTOS synchronization rules, e.g. $g!5$ is equivalent to $g!3+2$ (under the usual rules for addition), while $g!0$ is not equivalent to the events $g!1$ or $h!0$.

9.5   A note on data variables

QTL has been defined to be suitable for use in conjunction with LOTOS. However, as will be seen in Chapters 11 and 12, as well as referring to LOTOS events, there is also a need to refer to data variables in QTL formulae. These *data variables* are necessary in order to store additional numerical information such as the number of occurrences of a particular LOTOS event (e.g. the number of timeouts in the example of Ch. 11, Section 11.2) or, more generally, arbitrary functions over event occurrences and their timings (e.g. the video drift variable in the example of Ch. 12). It could be argued that such variables could be defined as part of the abstract behaviour (i.e. in LOTOS). However, this would lead to considerable over-specification. In addition, the variables are more logically associated with the QTL formulae that describe the real-time assumptions and the requirements.

The inclusion of data variable declarations in the verification procedure will be considered in Chapter 10 and their specification will be considered in Chapter 11 (Section 11.2).

9.6   Summary

To summarize, this chapter initially considered the choice of a logic: given the requirements imposed by distributed multimedia applications, what features should the logic possess? Many different variants were considered, but it was decided to focus on a linear real-time temporal logic employing past-tense operators in addition to the usual future-tense operators, a discrete time domain and a basic set of operations (addition by constant only).

The syntax for such a logic (named QTL) was presented and the semantics defined in terms of timed state sequences. Clearly, the decision to combine LOTOS and QTL in specifications complicates any verification procedure. A verification procedure suitable for the LOTOS/QTL approach is developed in the following chapter.

CHAPTER 10

Verification with the LOTOS/QTL approach

10.1   Introduction

Verification of properties of a system will clearly be more complex for a multi-language specification (such as the LOTOS/QTL approach) than for a single language specification. The separation of concerns between the specification of abstract behaviour and the specification of real-time assumptions with the LOTOS/QTL approach further complicates the verification procedure. As introduced in Chapter 8, there are two aspects of verification for such approaches, referred to as *vertical* and *horizontal* verification. This chapter will address only horizontal verification (proving that each requirement is satisfied by the specification of behaviour at each stage of the development process) since existing well-developed verification techniques can be applied to achieve vertical verification. However, the separation of the specification of abstract behaviour from real-time assumptions means that a specialized procedure is needed to achieve horizontal verification. The purpose of this chapter is to develop such a procedure that is specifically designed to be used with the proposed LOTOS/QTL approach. Although the main concern of the chapter is in the development of a suitable verification procedure, issues relating to the complexity of the procedure will be briefly discussed.

In the following Section (10.2), an overview of a verification procedure that can be used with the LOTOS/QTL approach is presented. This overview highlights different stages of the verification procedure, the most important of which will be discussed in more detail in the remaining sections of the chapter. In particular, Section 10.3 develops a tableau-based decision procedure for checking requirements against real-time assumptions and Section 10.4 develops a model checking algorithm for checking requirements against the specified system (represented as an extended finite state machine). Both of these sections use a subset of QTL, denoted QTL⁻. In Section 10.5, extensions that are needed to handle full QTL formulae are explained. Tool support for the verification procedure is discussed in Section 10.6. Section 10.7 discusses alternative approaches to specification. Finally, Section 10.8 summarizes the main characteristics of the verification procedure.

10.2 An overview of the verification procedure

In this section, different stages of the verification procedure are described. First, recall that the various components of a specification written using the proposed approach are:
- the *abstract behaviour* of the system, written in LOTOS;
- the *real-time assumptions* (RTAs), written in QTL (i.e. the real-time behaviour of the system);
- the *requirements*, written in QTL (i.e. the desired behaviour of the system).

In addition, there may also be a set of *data variable declarations*. These will be used to augment the finite state machine derived from the LOTOS specification, thus providing a model over which the truth of QTL formulae can be determined.

Figure 10.1 illustrates how each of these components is incorporated into the verification procedure. Each of the stages will be briefly described below.

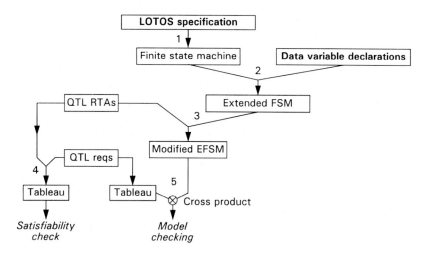

Figure 10.1 An overview of the stages involved in the verification procedure.

10.2.1   Generating a finite state machine (stage 1)

As can be seen from the diagram, the LOTOS specification is initially trans-
lated into a finite state machine (FSM). This process can be achieved
through the use of a tool such as CÆSAR/ALDÉBARAN (Garavel 1990,
Fernandez & Mournier 1990) that generates a finite state machine from a
LOTOS specification providing certain conditions are adhered to. Examples of these conditions are that, in the LOTOS specification, no recursion is
permitted on the left-hand side of a disable operator or on either side of a
parallel operator. Care must also be taken when using infinite data types
(such as natural numbers), so as to avoid a state machine with an infinite
number of states. For example, generating sequence numbers incremen-
tally from an infinite set (to distinguish different transmitted messages)
will not generate a finite state machine. One possible solution to this problem is to use sequence numbers from a finite set, wrapping back to the start
of the set once all numbers have been used. A complete description of the
restrictions imposed by the CÆSAR/ALDÉBARAN tool can be found in
Garavel (1990).

10.2.2   Integrating the data variable declarations to give an extended FSM (stage 2)

The second stage of the verification procedure involves augmenting the
finite state machine with the information provided in the data variable declarations, thus giving an extended state machine (ESM). If the data variables are permitted to range over an infinite domain, this stage will give
rise to a potentially infinite state ESM. Ostroff (1989) points out that, for
arbitrary infinite state ESMs, there is no general decision procedure to
check whether or not the system satisfies a given temporal logic specification. Instead, it is necessary to look for a proof in a deductive proof system
(consisting of axioms and inference rules) for the chosen temporal logic.
One problem with such proof systems is that, to quote Clarke et al. (1986),
"the task of proof construction is in general quite tedious, and a good deal
of ingenuity may be required to organise the proof in a manageable fashion." He adds that, "mechanical theorem provers have failed to be of much
help due to the inherent complexity of testing validity for even the simplest
logics". Although rather dated, this quotation still applies to a large extent
today, at least for non-trivial logics.

   Consequently, in this book, all data variables will be restricted to range
over only a *finite* domain, thus ensuring this stage of the verification procedure results in an extended finite state machine (EFSM).

10.2.3 Modifying the EFSM with respect to the real-time assumptions (Stage 3)

It is possible that certain statements may exist in the real-time assumptions that affect the set of valid paths through the finite state machine. For example, consider the specification of a protocol that contains a possible path to an error event. Consider also a set of real-time assumptions for this protocol that actually prevent this path from occurring (perhaps because time constraints imposed on certain events prevent its occurrence). Suppose that one of the requirements now asked whether or not the error existed in the specification. If only the LOTOS specification is considered, then clearly the answer should be yes, the error does occur. However, if the timing information contained in the real-time assumptions prevents the error event and this information is taken into account, then the answer should be no, the error does not occur. This latter answer would be expected if the real-time assumptions and abstract behaviour had been integrated into a single specification language; similarly, this answer should be expected with LOTOS/QTL specifications. It is therefore necessary to remove paths that exist in the (extended) FSM but which are prevented by the real-time assumptions.

To achieve this, it is first necessary to check if the set of real-time assumptions ϕ_A ($=\phi_{A1} \wedge \phi_{A2} \wedge ... \wedge \phi_{An}$) are *valid* with respect to the EFSM. This involves determining if, for each model ρ derived from the EFSM, ρ *satisfies* ϕ_A, i.e. $(\rho,0) \models \phi_A$. This is the problem of model checking the real-time assumptions against the EFSM, the procedure for which will be described in more detail in Section 10.4. If the real-time assumption is valid, no further action needs to be taken. However, if the real-time assumption is not valid, the EFSM should be modified by removing the invalid behaviour.

One possible way in which this may be achieved is through a slight modification to the model checking algorithm. Briefly, the algorithm involves negating the formula ϕ_A, constructing the cross product of a tableau (derived from $\neg\phi_A$) and the EFSM, and then proving that no "initialised ϕ-path" exists (see Section 10.4). Intuitively, such a path is one that both satisfies the formula and is a legal computation of the EFSM. If an initialized ϕ-path is found, this means that $\neg\phi_A$ is satisfiable, i.e. ϕ_A is not valid. The computation of the EFSM giving rise to the invalid behaviour can be derived directly from the initialized ϕ-path and should be tagged as invalid. In all subsequent model checking procedures, after finding an initialized ϕ-path, the path should be checked to see if this represents invalid behaviour. If so, an alternative initialized ϕ-path should be found.

10.2.4 Checking the requirements against the real-time assumptions (stage 4)

The fourth stage of the verification procedure involves taking one require-ment at a time and checking whether the information in this requirement is consistent with the information in the set of real-time assumptions. For example, consider a system with two real-time assumptions that ensure that event b always follows event a in exactly 2 ms (milliseconds) and that event c always follows event b in 5 ms. A requirement stating that event c should follow event a within 10 ms will always be satisfiable with respect to the above real-time assumptions. However, any requirement that c fol-lows a within a time less than 7 ms will not be satisfiable.

Therefore, an algorithm must be developed that checks if there exists a model such that all real-time assumptions and the requirement are satis-fied. More formally, for a set of real-time assumptions ϕ_A ($=\phi_{A1} \wedge \phi_{A2} \wedge ... \wedge \phi_{An}$) and a requirement ϕ_R, it is necessary to check that there exists a model ρ such that $(\rho, 0) \vDash (\phi_A \wedge \phi_R)$. This aspect of the verification procedure will be considered in greater detail in Section 10.3 below.

10.2.5 Model checking the requirements against the modified EFSM (stage 5)

The final stage illustrated in Figure 10.1 concerns model checking the requirements against the modified EFSM. Similarities exist between this stage in the verification procedure and stage 3. As in stage 3, it is necessary to check if each requirement ϕ_R is *valid* with respect to the (modified) EFSM. More formally, it is necessary to determine if, for each model ρ derived from the EFSM, $(\rho, 0) \vDash \phi_R$. In stage 3, a negative result to this question meant that the EFSM should be modified. In stage 5, however, a negative result to this question simply means that the requirement does not hold over the given EFSM. This aspect of the verification procedure will be con-sidered in greater detail in Section 10.4 below.

10.2.6 Returning to the overall verification procedure

To summarize this overview, it is important to remember that the original aim of verification was to prove whether or not a particular requirement was true for a given specification, the specification being composed of a LOTOS description of abstract behaviour and a set of QTL statements describing the real-time assumptions.

As has been explained above, there are various different stages that must be undertaken as part of the verification procedure. The two most sig-nificant of these stages are those marked 4 and 5, namely:

size of the closure set is at most $1+N(3+2C)$. As C and N grow large, the term $3+2C$ tends to $2C$ and hence the whole expression tends to $2CN$. Consequently, the maximum size of the closure set $Cl(\phi)$ is said to be of order $2CN$ (denoted $O(2CN)$).

Introducing time into the tableau

Consider a model (timed state sequence) $\rho=(\sigma,\tau)$ where the time sequence τ associates a time τ_i with every state σ_i in the state sequence σ. In order to determine the satisfiability of a QTL formula, it is sufficient to consider only those models in which the difference between consecutive times is bounded by C, i.e. $\forall i \geq 0$: $\tau_{i+1}-\tau_i \leq C$.

To illustrate this, consider the examples: $\phi_1=O_{<3}a$, $\phi_2=O_{=3}a$ and $\phi_3=O_{>3}a$ (where a is a LOTOS event). Timed state sequences for which the first example is satisfiable are of the form:

$\rho=((x,0), (a,0), ...)$ or $\rho=((x,0), (a,1), ...)$ or $\rho=((x,0), (a,2), ...)$

where x denotes any event and each pair represents the state σ_i and the associated time τ_i. The sequences for which the second formula is satisfiable are of the form:

$\rho=((x,0), (a,3), ...)$

and those for which the third formula are satisfiable are of the form:

$\rho=((x,0), (a,4), ...)$ or $\rho=((x,0), (a,5), ...)$ or $\rho=((x,0), (a,6), ...)$, etc.

Recall that, to prove the satisfiability of a formula, it is simply necessary to prove the existence of *one* model that satisfies the formula. Clearly for the first two examples, it is only necessary to consider those models where the difference between consecutive times is ≤ 3. Any of the listed models satisfy the formula. For the third example, models with such time differences do not satisfy the formula. However, by considering a time difference of 4, the model does satisfy the formula. The existence of this model means that the formula is satisfiable; time differences greater than 4 need not be considered. It is therefore sufficient to consider only those models in which the difference between consecutive times is bounded by C (where C is the value of the largest constant plus one).

Time is introduced into the tableau method through two sets, one representing the set of possible time differences from the current state to the next state and the other set representing the set of possible time differences between the current state and the previous state. These two sets are denoted $Tdiff = \{Tdiff_t \mid 0 \leq t \leq C\}$ and $Tdiff' = \{Tdiff_t' \mid 0 \leq t \leq C\}$ respectively. In the following section, the notation $Cl^*(\phi)$ will be used to denote the set $Cl(\phi) \cup Tdiff \cup Tdiff'$.

Generating consistent subsets of $Cl^*(\phi)$

The next stage of the tableau method is to find all possible vertices for the tableau (directed graph) associated with formula ϕ. The vertices will be all of the subsets of $Cl^*(\phi)$ that satisfy the rules presented below. These subsets are known as consistent subsets. An intuitive justification for these rules will be given at the end of this section.

A subset Φ of $Cl^*(\phi)$ (i.e. an element of the power set of $Cl^*(\phi)$) is said to be consistent if and only if it satisfies the following rules:

$\text{Tdiff}_t \in \Phi$ for exactly one $0 \leq t \leq C$; denote this t as $\text{nextdiff}(\Phi)$
$\text{Tdiff}_t' \in \Phi$ for exactly one $0 \leq t \leq C$; denote this t as $\text{lastdiff}(\Phi)$

let LE denote the set of all LOTOS events (e) in $Cl^*(\phi)$,
$e \in \Phi$ for exactly one $e \in LE$

$\text{false} \notin \Phi$
for every $\varphi_1 \rightarrow \varphi_2 \in Cl(\phi)$,
$\varphi_1 \rightarrow \varphi_2 \in \Phi \quad \Leftrightarrow \quad \varphi_1 \notin \Phi \vee \varphi_2 \in \Phi$

for every $\varphi_1 U_{=c} \varphi_2 \in Cl(\phi)$,
$\varphi_1 U_{=c} \varphi_2 \in \Phi \quad \Leftrightarrow \quad (c=0 \wedge \varphi_2 \in \Phi) \vee$
$(\varphi_1 \in \Phi \wedge ((\text{nextdiff}(\Phi)=0 \wedge O_{=0}(\varphi_1 U_{=c} \varphi_2) \in \Phi) \vee$
$(0<\text{nextdiff}(\Phi) \leq c \wedge O_{>0}(\varphi_1 U_{=c-\text{nextdiff}(\Phi)} \varphi_2) \in \Phi)))$

for every $\varphi_1 U_{<c} \varphi_2 \in Cl(\phi)$,

$\varphi_1 U_{<c} \varphi_2 \in \Phi \quad \Leftrightarrow \quad (c>0 \wedge \varphi_2 \in \Phi) \vee$
$(\varphi_1 \in \Phi \wedge ((\text{nextdiff}(\Phi)=0 \wedge O_{=0}(\varphi_1 U_{<c} \varphi_2) \in \Phi) \vee$
$(0<\text{nextdiff}(\Phi) \leq c \wedge O_{>0}(\varphi_1 U_{<c-\text{nextdiff}(\Phi)} \varphi_2) \in \Phi)))$

for every $\varphi_1 U_{>c} \varphi_2 \in Cl(\phi)$,
$\varphi_1 U_{>c} \varphi_2 \in \Phi \quad \Leftrightarrow \quad \varphi_1 \in \Phi \wedge ((\text{nextdiff}(\Phi)=0 \wedge O_{=0}(\varphi_1 U_{>c} \varphi_2) \in \Phi) \vee$
$(0<\text{nextdiff}(\Phi) \leq c \wedge O_{>0}(\varphi_1 U_{>c-\text{nextdiff}(\Phi)} \varphi_2) \in \Phi) \vee$
$(c<\text{nextdiff}(\Phi) \leq C \wedge (O_{>0}(\varphi_1 U_{>0} \varphi_2) \in \Phi \vee$
$O_{>0}(\varphi_1 U_{=0} \varphi_2) \in \Phi)))$

Note that the third rule ensures that exactly one LOTOS event occurs in each consistent subset (reflecting the fact that exactly one LOTOS event occurs per state in a state sequence).

The rules for the consistency of *since* formulae are similar to those presented above for *until* formulae, except that the nextdiff integer is replaced by lastdiff. It is interesting to note that the rules for *until* and *since* formulae are significantly more complex than the rules presented in Alur & Henzinger (1990). This is solely because the tool implementing this tableau method strictly adheres to the basic QTL syntax (i.e. no shorthand notations are permitted). The formulae have thus been presented as they have been implemented.

An intuitive justification for the format of the above rules is given below for the two formulae $\varphi_1 \to \varphi_2$ and $\varphi_1 U_{<c} \varphi_2$. The other rules can be similarly justified.

$\varphi_1 \to \varphi_2$: this formula can be equivalently written as $\neg \varphi_1 \vee \varphi_2$. Therefore, if it is known that $\varphi_1 \to \varphi_2$ is true in Φ, then, for the formula to be satisfiable, either $\neg \varphi_1$ must be true in Φ or else φ_2 must be true, i.e. $\varphi_1 \notin \Phi$ or $\varphi_2 \in \Phi$. Similarly, if there exists a $\varphi_2 \in \Phi$ such that, for some φ_1 that is not in Φ, $\varphi_1 \to \varphi_2 \in Cl(\Phi)$ then the formula $\varphi_1 \to \varphi_2$ can be derived and must also be in Φ. Hence the use of the if and only if condition in the rule.

$\varphi_1 U_{<c} \varphi_2$: this formula intuitively means that φ_1 is true until some time ($<c$) at which φ_2 will be true. One valid interpretation of this formula occurs when φ_2 is currently true (i.e. there is no need to consider the value of φ_1). The formula states that φ_2 must be true before time c. Hence, for a formula $\varphi_1 U_{<c} \varphi_2 \in \Phi$, if $c>0$ (the formula cannot be true at a time less than 0) and $\varphi_2 \in \Phi$ then the formula is said to be consistent. If φ_2 is not currently true then φ_1 must be true. However, it must also be established that φ_2 will be true in some future state. If nextdiff (the time to the next state) is zero, then time will not progress between the current state and the next state and, in the next state, the same until formula must still hold, i.e. if $\varphi_1 \in \Phi$ and nextdiff=0 then $O_{=0}(\varphi_1 U_{<c} \varphi_2) \in \Phi$. If nextdiff is greater than zero, then time will progress between the current state and the next state and the time bound on the until operator in the next state must be adjusted to reflect this. Consequently, the condition can be expressed as: if $\varphi_1 \in \Phi$ and nextdiff>0 then $O_{>0}(\varphi_1 U_{<c-\text{nextdiff}(\Phi)} \varphi_2) \in \Phi$. Similar arguments can be employed to justify the backward implication.

Generating the tableau (directed graph) $T(\phi)$

The above section has detailed how to find all possible vertices for the tableau. It is now necessary to describe which vertices (consistent subsets of $Cl^*(\phi)$) can be connected. There exists an edge from vertex Φ to vertex Ψ if and only if the following rules for Φ and Ψ hold:

nextdiff(Φ) = lastdiff(Ψ)

for every $O_{\sim c} \varphi \in Cl(\phi)$,
$O_{\sim c} \varphi \in \Phi \qquad \Leftrightarrow \qquad \varphi \in \Psi \wedge \text{nextdiff}(\Phi) \sim c$

for every $\Theta_{\sim c} \varphi \in Cl(\phi)$,
$\Theta_{\sim c} \varphi \in \Psi \qquad \Leftrightarrow \qquad \varphi \in \Phi \wedge \text{nextdiff}(\Phi) \sim c$

These rules ensure that there is a valid progression of time through connected vertices of the directed graph. They also ensure that if a next formula $O_{\sim c} \varphi$ is in vertex Φ then, for Φ to be connected to Ψ, φ must be in Ψ. Conversely, if a formula φ is in Ψ and $O_{\sim c} \varphi$ is in the closure set then $O_{\sim c} \varphi$ must be in Φ. The rule for previous formulae is interpreted similarly.

Determining the satisfiability of ϕ from $T(\phi)$

A QTL⁻ formula ϕ is satisfiable if and only if the tableau $T(\phi)$ contains an infinite path $\Phi = \Phi_0 \Phi_1 \Phi_2 ...$ such that:

$\phi \in \Phi_0$,

Φ_0 contains no $\ominus$ formulae, and

for all $i \geq 0$,

$\varphi_1 U_{\sim c} \varphi_2 \in \Phi_i \iff \exists j \geq i$ such that $\varphi_2 \in \Phi_j \wedge \Sigma_{i \leq k < j}$nextdiff$(\Phi_k) \sim c$

Such a path is referred to as a *fulfilling path for ϕ* in Harel et al. (1990b) and as a *ϕ-path* in Alur & Henziger (1994). The term fulfilling path will be used in this book. Proofs that the formula ϕ is satisfiable iff a fulfilling path for ϕ exists in the tableau are presented in Harel et al. (1990b) for XCTL and in Alur & Henziger (1994) for TPTL. The following proof for QTL⁻ follows similar arguments to those presented in Alur & Henziger (1994) with the two exceptions that time is handled differently in QTL to TPTL and that no proof is given for *until* formulae in TPTL (the simpler case of henceforth formulae is considered in Alur & Henziger (1994) instead).

Theorem: the formula ϕ is satisfiable iff a fulfilling path for ϕ exists in $T(\phi)$.

Proof:

The following proof is constructed in two halves: the first half (1) proves the forward part of the implication while the second half (2) proves the backward part of the implication.

1. Suppose initially that the formula ϕ is satisfiable and that $\rho = (\sigma, \tau)$ is a model for ϕ. For every state $i \geq 0$ of the model ρ, let

   - $\Phi_i = \{q \in Cl(\phi) \mid (\rho, i) \vDash q\}$;
   - nextdiff$(\Phi_i) = \tau_{i+1} - \tau_i$;
   - lastdiff$(\Phi_i) = \tau_i - \tau_{i-1}$ (for $i > 0$).

   Clearly, each Φ_i will be a vertex in $T(\phi)$ since vertices of the tableau are all consistent elements of the power set of $Cl^*(\phi)$. Additionally, there will be an edge from Φ_i to Φ_{i+1} in $T(\phi)$ since

   i. nextdiff(Φ_i) = lastdiff$(\Phi_{i+1}) = \tau_{i+1} - \tau_i$;

   ii. ($\Rightarrow$) if $O_{\sim c} \varphi \in \Phi_i$, then $\varphi \in \Phi_{i+1}$ since $(\rho, i) \vDash O_{\sim c} \varphi \iff (\rho, i+1) \vDash \varphi$ and (nextdiff$(\Phi_i) = \tau_{i+1} - \tau_i) \sim c$ (from the semantics of QTL);

   ($\Leftarrow$) if $\varphi \in \Phi_{i+1}$ and nextdiff$(\Phi_i) \sim c$, then $O_{\sim c} \varphi \in \Phi_i$ since $(\rho, i+1) \vDash \varphi \iff (\rho, i) \vDash O_{\sim c} \varphi$;

   iii. the third condition regarding edges between vertices containing previous formulae can be similarly proved.

   Therefore, $\Phi = \Phi_0 \Phi_1 \Phi_2 ...$ is an infinite path through $T(\Phi)$. It remains to show that Φ is a fulfilling path for ϕ:

   i. since ϕ is satisfiable, $(\rho, 0) \vDash \phi$; therefore $\phi \in \Phi_0$;

   ii. $\Phi_0 = \{q \in Cl(\phi) \mid (\rho, 0) \vDash q\}$ and $(\rho, i) \vDash \ominus_{\sim c} \Phi \iff i > 0$; therefore Φ_0 contains no $\ominus$ formulae;

   iii. if $\varphi_1 U_{\sim c} \varphi_2 \in \Phi_i$, then $(\rho, i) \vDash \varphi_1 U_{\sim c} \varphi_2 \iff \exists j \geq i$ such that $(\rho, j) \vDash \varphi_2$. Hence $\varphi_2 \in \Phi_j$.

Furthermore, $\tau_j - \tau_i \sim c$ and $\tau_j - \tau_i = \tau_j - \tau_{j-1} + \tau_{j-1} - \dots - \tau_{i+1} + \tau_{i+1} - \tau_i =$ nextdiff(Φ_{j-1})+nextdiff(Φ_{j-2})+...+nextdiff(Φ_i) as required.

Consequently, Φ is a fulfilling path for ϕ (or ϕ-path). This has shown that if the formula ϕ is satisfiable then there exists a fulfilling path for ϕ in $T(\phi)$. It now remains to prove that if a fulfilling path for ϕ exists in $T(\phi)$ then ϕ is satisfiable.

2. Suppose that $\Phi = \Phi_0 \Phi_1 \Phi_2 \dots$ is a fulfilling path for ϕ; it must be shown that there exists a model ρ such that $(\rho, 0) \models \phi$. Let $\rho = (\sigma, \tau)$ such that for every state $i \geq 0$ of ρ:

- $q \in \sigma_i \Leftrightarrow q \in \Phi_i$ and, as above,
- nextdiff$(\Phi_i) = \tau_{i+1} - \tau_i$ and
- lastdiff$(\Phi_i) = \tau_i - \tau_{i-1}$ (for $i > 0$).

It must be shown for all $i \geq 0$ and $\varphi \in Cl^*(\phi)$ that $\varphi \in \Phi_i \Leftrightarrow (\rho, i) \models \varphi$. Providing this is true, it is known that $\phi \in \Phi_0$ and therefore that $(\rho, 0) \models \phi$. Consequently, ρ is a model for ϕ and hence ϕ is satisfiable. The if and only if condition will be proved by considering the structure of formula φ.

i. Suppose initially that a proposition $a \in Cl^*(\phi)$. Since this proof is for QTL⁻, propositions will be basic LOTOS events (i.e. no event offers or constraints involving data variables are permitted). From the definition of ρ, $a \in \sigma_i \Leftrightarrow a \in \Phi_i$ and from the semantics of QTL, a basic LOTOS event $a \in \sigma_i \Leftrightarrow (\rho, i) \models a$, hence $a \in \Phi_i \Leftrightarrow (\rho, i) \models a$.

ii. Suppose next that $\varphi_1 \rightarrow \varphi_2 \in Cl^*(\phi)$. Using the consistency rules for Φ_i, $\varphi_1 \rightarrow \varphi_2 \in \Phi_i \Leftrightarrow \varphi_1 \notin \Phi_i$ or $\varphi_2 \in \Phi_i$. From the definition of ρ and the semantics of QTL it can be seen that either $(\rho, i) \not\models \varphi_1$ or $(\rho, i) \models \varphi_2$, i.e. $(\rho, i) \models \varphi_1 \rightarrow \varphi_2$.

iii. Considering now the temporal operators of QTL⁻, suppose that $O_{\sim c} \varphi \in Cl^*(\phi)$. From the definition of ρ, nextdiff$(\Phi_i) = \tau_{i+1} - \tau_i$ and from the rules for connecting vertices of the tableau, $O_{\sim c} \varphi \in \Phi_i \Leftrightarrow \varphi \in \Phi_{i+1}$ and nextdiff$(\Phi_i) \sim c$. Since $\varphi \in \Phi_{i+1} \Leftrightarrow \varphi \in \sigma_{i+1}$, $(\rho, i+1) \models \varphi$. Additionally, (nextdiff$(\Phi_i) = \tau_{i+1} - \tau_i) \sim c$, hence $(\rho, i) \models O_{\sim c} \varphi$.

iv. Next, suppose that $\varphi_1 U_{\sim c} \varphi_2 \in Cl^*(\phi)$; the proof for this case is significantly more complex than those above. The consistency rules for *until* formulae consider the three cases where $\sim$ is $=$, $<$ and $>$ separately. Only one of these cases will be proved here, namely that $\varphi_1 U_{=c} \varphi_2 \in \Phi_i \Leftrightarrow (\rho, i) \models \varphi_1 U_{=c} \varphi_2$; the other two cases can be proved similarly. From the consistency rules, $\varphi_1 U_{=c} \varphi_2 \in \Phi_i \Leftrightarrow$ one of the two following conditions holds. It will now be shown that either of these two conditions leads to the required result (i.e. that $(\rho, i) \models \varphi_1 U_{=c} \varphi_2$).

First condition: $c = 0 \wedge \varphi_2 \in \Phi_i$. Since $c = 0$, $\tau_{i+1} = \tau_i$ and since $\varphi_2 \in \Phi_i \Leftrightarrow \varphi_2 \in \sigma_i$, $(\rho, i) \models \varphi_2$. Consequently, $(\rho, i) \models \varphi_1 U_{=0} \varphi_2$.

Second condition: $\varphi_1 \in \Phi_i \wedge O_{\sim 0}(\varphi_1 U_{=c\text{-nextdiff}(\Phi i)} \varphi_2) \in \Phi_i$ where $\sim$ is $=$ if nextdiff$(\Phi_i) = 0$ and $\sim$ is $>$ if $0 < \text{nextdiff}(\Phi_i) \leq c$. Since $\varphi_1 \in \Phi_i \Leftrightarrow \varphi_1 \in \sigma_i$, $(\rho, i) \models \varphi_1$. Additionally, (nextdiff$(\Phi_i) = \tau_{i+1} - \tau_i) \sim 0$. Let $c' = c - \text{nextdiff}(\Phi_i)$. From the rules for connecting vertices of the tableau, $O_{\sim 0}(\varphi_1 U_{=c'} \varphi_2) \in \Phi_i \Leftrightarrow$

$\varphi_1 U_{=c'}\varphi_2 \in \Phi_{i+1}$. The next stage involves proving that $\varphi_1 U_{=c'}\varphi_2 \in \Phi_{i+1} \Leftrightarrow \exists j \geq i+1$ s.t. $\varphi_2 \in \sigma_j$ (hence $(\rho,j) \models \varphi_2$) and $\forall k, i+1 \leq k < j$ $\varphi_1 \in \sigma_k$ (hence $(\rho,k) \models \varphi_1$). This will be proved in two parts in the paragraphs labelled ($\Rightarrow$) and ($\Leftarrow$) below. Once this has been proved, the semantics of QTL can be applied to give $(\rho, i+1)$ $\models \varphi_1 U_{=c'}\varphi_2$. Consequently, since $(\rho,i) \models \varphi_1$ and $c'=c$-nextdiff(Φ_i), (ρ,i) $\models \varphi_1 U_{=c}\varphi_2$ as required.

It remains to show that $\varphi_1 U_{=c'}\varphi_2 \in \Phi_{i+1} \Leftrightarrow \exists j \geq i+1$ such that $\varphi_2 \in \sigma_j$ and $\forall k, i+1 \leq k < j$ such that $\varphi_1 \in \sigma_k$.

($\Rightarrow$) Φ is a ϕ-path, therefore $\exists j \geq i+1$ s.t. $\varphi_2 \in \sigma_j$ (hence $\varphi_2 \in \Phi_j$) and $\Sigma_{i \leq k < j}$nextdiff(Φ_k)=c'. Without loss of generality, assume that Φ_j is the first node of Φ ($j \geq i+1$) containing φ_2. The following diagram illustrates the known elements of nodes of Φ.

$$\cdots \quad \Phi_i \quad \Phi_{i+1} \quad \Phi_{i+2} \quad \cdots \quad \Phi_{j-1} \quad \Phi_j \quad \cdots$$
$$\varphi_1 \quad \varphi_1 U_{=c'}\varphi_2 \qquad\qquad\qquad \varphi_2$$
$$\leftarrow \quad \Sigma_{i+1 \leq k < j}\text{nextdiff}(\Phi_k)=c' \quad \rightarrow$$

Since $\varphi_1 U_{=c'}\varphi_2 \in \Phi_{i+1}$, the consistency rules ensure that $\varphi_2 \in \Phi_{i+1}$ or $\varphi_1 \in \Phi_{i+1}$ (among other things). If $\varphi_2 \in \Phi_{i+1}$ then $j=i+1$ and ($\Rightarrow$) is proven. Therefore, suppose $\varphi_1 \in \Phi_{i+1}$. The remainder of the consistency rules ensure that $O_{\sim 0}(\varphi_1 U_{=c'}\varphi_2) \in \Phi_{i+1}$ where $\sim$ is = if nextdiff(Φ_{i+1})=0 and $\sim$ is > if 0<nextdiff(Φ_{i+1})$\leq c$ and $c''=c'$-nextdiff(Φ_{i+1}). Applying the rules for connecting vertices means that $\varphi_1 U_{=c'}\varphi_2 \in \Phi_{i+2}$. Since it has now been shown that $\varphi_1 \in \Phi_{i+1}$ and $\varphi_1 U_{=c'}\varphi_2 \in \Phi_{i+2}$, this process can be repeated until Φ_j is reached.

($\Leftarrow$) For the reverse direction of the proof, it is known that $\exists j \geq i+1$ such that $\varphi_2 \in \sigma_j$ (hence $\varphi_2 \in \Phi_j$) and $\forall k, i+1 \leq k < j$ such that $\varphi_1 \in \sigma_k$ (hence $\varphi_1 \in \Phi_k$). It must be shown that $\varphi_1 U_{=c'}\varphi_2 \in \Phi_{i+1}$.

$$\cdots \Phi_i \quad \Phi_{i+1} \quad \cdots \quad \Phi_{j-2} \quad \Phi_{j-1} \quad \Phi_j \quad \cdots$$
$$\varphi_1 \qquad \varphi_1 \qquad\qquad \varphi_1 \qquad \varphi_1 \qquad \varphi_2$$

Since $\varphi_1 U_{=c}\varphi_2 \in Cl^*(\phi)$ (an initial premiss of (iv)), the rules for next and until operators in the definition of the closure set ensure that $\varphi_1 U_{=0}\varphi_2 \in Cl^*(\phi)$. It is also known that $\varphi_2 \in \Phi_j$, therefore the consistency rules can be applied to show that $\varphi_1 U_{=0}\varphi_2 \in \Phi_j$. This means that, by using the rules for connecting vertices, $O_{\sim d}(\varphi_1 U_{=0}\varphi_2) \in \Phi_{j-1}$ where d=nextdiff(Φ_{j-1}). It is also known that $\varphi_1 \in \Phi_{j-1}$ hence the consistency rules can be applied to show that $\varphi_1 U_{=d}\varphi_2 \in \Phi_{j-1}$. If $j-1=i$, the proof is complete. Otherwise, this process can be repeated to give $O_{\sim d'}(\varphi_1 U_{=d}\varphi_2) \in \Phi_{j-2}$ where d'=nextdiff(Φ_{j-2}). Working backwards through Φ it can thus be shown that $\varphi_1 U_{=c'}\varphi_2 \in \Phi_{i+1}$ where $c'=\Sigma_{i+1 \leq k < j}$nextdiff($\Phi_k$).

This completes the $\Leftrightarrow$ proof and therefore, as explained above, (ρ,i) $\models \varphi_1 U_{=c}\varphi_2$; consequently, part (iv) has been proved. The proof for the remaining (past-tense) operators of QTL can be constructed in a similar way, but will not be presented here. It can therefore be concluded that the formula ϕ is satisfiable if a fulfilling path for ϕ exists in $T(\phi)$.

10.3.2 Complexity

The above tableau method closely follows that presented in Alur & Henzinger (1990) for the logic MTL. It is stated that, for MTL, the tableau contains $O(C.2^{CN})$ states, each of size $O(CN)$ and that it can be constructed and checked for infinite paths in deterministic time exponential in $O(CN)$. It is also stated that the satisfiability problem for MTL is EXPSPACE-complete. Analysis of the complexity of the tableau method for QTL⁻ can be expected to yield similar results.

10.3.3 Worked examples

Example 1: an unsatisfiable formula
The following example illustrates the process of constructing a tableau for a QTL⁻ formula. Unfortunately, all *until* and *since* formulae generate a large number of sets that must be checked for consistency, thus making such formulae unsuitable for a worked example. Consequently, consider the formula $\phi = a \wedge \neg(a)$. Transforming this formula to remove all shorthands results in $\phi = (a \rightarrow ((a \rightarrow \text{false}) \rightarrow \text{false})) \rightarrow \text{false}$. This can be simplified to $\phi = (a \rightarrow a) \rightarrow \text{false}$. The next stage is then to construct the closure set according to the rules presented at the start of Section 10.3.1:

$$Cl(\phi) = \{(a \rightarrow a) \rightarrow \text{false}, a \rightarrow a, \text{false}, a\}$$

No subset of $Cl(\phi)$ that contains the element false can be consistent. Therefore, in this example, potential consistent subsets (vertices) are those elements of the power set of $\{(a \rightarrow a) \rightarrow \text{false}, a \rightarrow a, a\}$. Since no constant appears in the formula, $C-1$ is taken to be 0 (i.e. $C=1$), therefore the possible values for nextdiff and lastdiff are 0 or 1. Following the rules for the generation of consistent subsets (Φ) associated with *implies* formulae, it can be seen that for the given example:

$(a \rightarrow a) \rightarrow \text{false} \in \Phi$	$\Leftrightarrow$	$(a \rightarrow a) \notin \Phi \vee \text{false} \in \Phi$
$a \rightarrow a \in \Phi$	$\Leftrightarrow$	$a \notin \Phi \vee a \in \Phi$

Therefore, the subsets that must be checked for consistency are:

$\{(a \rightarrow a) \rightarrow \text{false}, a \rightarrow a, a\}$, $\{(a \rightarrow a) \rightarrow \text{false}, a \rightarrow a\}$, $\{(a \rightarrow a) \rightarrow \text{false}, a\}$, $\{a \rightarrow a, a\}$, $\{(a \rightarrow a) \rightarrow \text{false}\}$, $\{a \rightarrow a\}$, $\{a\}$ and $\{\}$

It can be seen that the first two sets fail the first forward implication of the consistency rules. Since the second forward implication is always true, no sets fail this condition. Considering now the backward implications, it can be seen that the last two sets fail the first backward implication. The second backward implication means that $a \rightarrow a$ must always be an element of the set. Consequently, the third and fifth sets fail this condition. This leaves the sets $\{a \rightarrow a, a\}$ and $\{a \rightarrow a\}$.

If time is now considered, it can be seen that there will be eight consistent subsets (vertices) since each of the above two sets will be consistent with nextdiff=0 and lastdiff=0, nextdiff=0 and lastdiff=1, nextdiff=1 and lastdiff=0, and nextdiff=1 and lastdiff=1. However, regardless of which vertices connect to other vertices, there will be no infinite path satisfying the required conditions. In particular, the first condition fails: no vertex contains the original formula ϕ. Therefore, as expected, the formula $\phi = a \wedge \neg(a)$ is unsatisfiable.

Example 2: a satisfiable formula

To provide a second example (this time featuring temporal operators), consider the formula $\phi = O_{=0}a$. As will be seen, this formula is satisfiable.

The closure set for this formula is as follows:

$$Cl(\phi) = \{O_{=0}a, a\}$$

As before, the potential consistent subsets are the elements of the power set of $Cl(\phi)$. Since zero is the largest constant in the formula, $C-1=0$ (i.e. $C=1$). Hence, nextdiff and lastdiff have the possible values of 0 or 1. The rules for the generation of consistent subsets eliminate any subsets not containing the LOTOS event a. Consequently, incorporating possible values for nextdiff ($Tdiff_i$) and lastdiff ($Tdiff_i'$), there are eight consistent subsets as follows:

$\{O_{=0}a, a, Tdiff_0, Tdiff_0'\}, \{a, Tdiff_0, Tdiff_0'\},$
$\{O_{=0}a, a, Tdiff_0, Tdiff_1'\}, \{a, Tdiff_0, Tdiff_1'\},$
$\{O_{=0}a, a, Tdiff_1, Tdiff_0'\}, \{a, Tdiff_1, Tdiff_0'\},$
$\{O_{=0}a, a, Tdiff_1, Tdiff_1'\}, \{a, Tdiff_1, Tdiff_1'\}$

It is now necessary to find which subsets can be connected. This is best illustrated diagrammatically (see Fig. 10.2).

From Figure 10.2, it can be seen that the QTL formula meets all of the conditions for satisfiability. In particular, we can find a number of fulfilling paths that meet our criteria, i.e. the first vertex contains the original formula and does not contain any $\ominus$ formulae (the third rule is met trivially as the tableau does not contain any U formulae). For example, one such fulfilling path is as follows:

$\{O_{=0}a, a, Tdiff_0, Tdiff_0'\} \rightarrow \{a, Tdiff_1, Tdiff_0'\} \rightarrow \{O_{=0}a, a, Tdiff_0, Tdiff_1'\} \rightarrow$
$\{O_{=0}a, a, Tdiff_0, Tdiff_0'\} \rightarrow \ldots$

More trivially, the following is also a fulfilling path:

$\{O_{=0}a, a, Tdiff_0, Tdiff_0'\} \rightarrow \{O_{=0}a, a, Tdiff_0, Tdiff_0'\} \rightarrow \{O_{=0}a, a, Tdiff_0, Tdiff_0'\}$
$\rightarrow \{O_{=0}a, a, Tdiff_0, Tdiff_0'\} \rightarrow \ldots$

Consequently, ϕ is satisfiable.

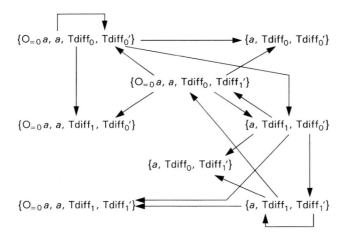

Figure 10.2 A tableau showing the connected consistent subsets.

10.4 Checking requirements against the EFSM

Having checked that there are no inconsistencies between the requirements and the real-time assumptions of the system being specified, it is now necessary to check whether each requirement ϕ_R is valid for the system being specified, that is, for each model ρ derived from the EFSM, does $(\rho,0) \models \phi_R$? Equivalently, it can be established that no model satisfies the formula $\neg\phi_R$. This latter approach is taken by an algorithmic verification technique known as model checking. With this technique, each temporal logic requirement can be checked against possible paths through a (finite) state graph description of the system. The following section describes a model checking algorithm for QTL⁻.

10.4.1 A model checking algorithm for QTL⁻

As mentioned above, in order to determine the validity of requirement ϕ_R, it is sufficient to show that no model satisfies $\neg\phi_R$.

Checking the satisfiability of $\neg\phi_R$ by constructing $T(\neg\phi_R)$

The first stage of model checking involves constructing a tableau for the *negated* requirement ϕ_R (i.e. construct the tableau $T(\neg\phi_R)$). Recall that the existence of a *fulfilling path* for $\neg\phi_R$ in the tableau $T(\neg\phi_R)$ shows that the formula $\neg\phi_R$ is satisfiable. If no such path exists, then the model checking algorithm is complete: the requirement ϕ_R is valid for any system. However, if any fulfilling paths for $\neg\phi_R$ exist, it must be shown that these (infinite) paths *cannot* occur in the system being specified.

In standard model checking techniques the system being specified is represented as a finite state graph, as defined in the following section.

A finite state graph description (G) of the system

In the verification procedure for the LOTOS/QTL approach, the LOTOS specification can be processed to produce an EFSM (see Fig. 10.1). This EFSM, denoted G in the subsequent text, consists of:

- S – a finite set of states (vertices) where each $s \in S$ includes a LOTOS event and a value for each of the data variables referred to by the requirements.
- E_S – a set of edges, each element of which connects a pair of states from S. If $(s,s') \in E_S$, then state s is said to be connected to state s'.
- $S_0 \subseteq S$ – the set of initial states.

A computation of G is defined to be an infinite sequence of states, $\sigma = s_0, s_1, s_2, ...$ such that:

- $s_0 \in S_0$ and
- $(s_i, s_{i+1}) \in E_S$ for every $i = 0, 1, 2, ...$

The following section describes how a tableau is constructed from the formula ϕ_R and how this tableau is combined with the finite state graph description of the system.

Forming the cross product $T(\neg\phi_R) \times G$

Having represented the system being specified as a finite state graph G, the next stage in the model checking algorithm involves comparing the tableau $T(\neg\phi_R)$ with G. To reach this stage, there must have existed at least one fulfilling path for $\neg\phi_R$ in $T(\neg\phi_R)$; it must therefore be shown that any such (infinite) path cannot occur in G.

To achieve this, the graph CP is defined to be the cross product $T(\neg\phi_R) \times G$ as follows (note that both $T(\neg\phi_R)$ and G are finite state directed graphs):

- Each vertex of CP is a pair (Φ, s) where Φ is a vertex of $T(\neg\phi_R)$ and s is a vertex of G (i.e. $s \in S$). Furthermore, all propositions in s must be consistent with the information in Φ. In particular, the LOTOS event in Φ must synchronize with the LOTOS event in s (following the standard LOTOS synchronization rules).
- There exists an edge from vertex (Φ_i, s_i) to (Φ_j, s_j) iff $T(\neg\phi_R)$ contains an edge from Φ_i to Φ_j and G contains an edge from s_i to s_j (i.e. $(s_i, s_j) \in E_S$).

Following the notation defined in Alur & Henzinger (1994), an infinite path through the cross product $T(\phi) \times G$ is defined to be a ϕ-path if its first projection is a ϕ-path (or fulfilling path for ϕ) through the tableau $T(\phi)$ and an *initialized ϕ-path* if, in addition, it starts at a vertex whose second projection is an initial vertex of G (i.e. the second projection is a legal computation).

As stated above, a requirement ϕ_R will be valid for G if it can be shown that any fulfilling path for the negated requirement $\neg\phi_R$ cannot occur in

G. Consequently, it is necessary to check if the cross product $T(\phi) \times G$ contains an initialized $\neg\phi_R$-path. If this is not the case, then the requirement ϕ_R is valid for the finite state graph G (derived from the original LOTOS specification). This can be proved in the same way as the above proof regarding ϕ-paths and satisfiability (a similar proof is also presented in Lichtenstein & Pnueli (1985) for a propositional linear-time temporal logic).

10.4.2   Complexity

An algorithm is presented in Lichtenstein & Pnueli (1985) for checking the satisfiability of a propositional linear-time temporal logic (PTL) formula over a finite state concurrent program. This algorithm is shown to run in a time exponential in the size of the formula being checked, but linear in the size of the checked program. PTL is equivalent to the future-tense untimed component of QTL$^-$ and hence the above complexity results will hold for this subset of QTL$^-$. Lichtenstein & Pnueli (1985) also show that the algorithm can be easily extended to include past-tense operators, but they do not discuss the effect this has on the complexity of the algorithm.

10.5   Extensions for full QTL

The above tableau method and model checking algorithm have been developed for a subset of QTL, denoted QTL$^-$, in which constraints over data variables (e.g. $x>3$ for data variable x) were not permitted. However, for the specification and verification of quality of service properties, data variables and constraints over such variables are required (as discussed in Section 9.5). Consequently, it is important to consider extensions to the above verification techniques to handle these features of QTL.

As mentioned in Chapter 9, Alur and Henzinger state that only propositional versions of temporal logics are decidable for satisfiability (Alur & Henzinger 1991). Since a constraint such as $x>3$ is an example of a predicate, it would seem likely that a logic permitting such constraints would be undecidable. This is true of the logic RTTL (Ostroff 1989) that permits constraints over data variables and is indeed undecidable. However, in real-time temporal logics, the inclusion of constraints in general *do not* imply undecidability; for example, consider the logic TPTL (Alur 1994) that permits constraints over time variables and is decidable.

In TPTL, constraints of the form $\pi_1 \leq \pi_2$ and $\pi_1 \equiv_d \pi_2$ (congruence modulo d) are permitted where $\pi ::= v+c \mid c$ and v is a timing variable and c is a constant. Comparing TPTL and QTL, the variable v in TPTL constraints is a timing variable whereas the variable in QTL constraints is a data variable. Note that time can still be referenced in QTL, but that this is achieved

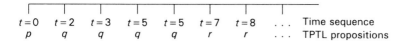

$t=0$	$t=2$	$t=3$	$t=5$	$t=5$	$t=7$	$t=8$	. . .	Time sequence
p	q	q	q	q	r	r	. . .	TPTL propositions

Figure 10.3 An example of a TPTL timed state sequence.

$t=0$	$t=2$	$t=3$	$t=5$	$t=5$	$t=7$	$t=8$	. . .	Time sequence
send1	rec1	send2	timeout	send2	rec2	send3	. . .	TPTL propositions
$x=0$	$x=1$	$x=0$	$x=1$	$x=1$	$x=2$	$x=0$	. . .	Data variable x

Figure 10.4 An example of a QTL timed state sequence.

through the use of bounded operators. Both TPTL and QTL formulae are interpreted over timed state sequences, examples of which are given in Figures 10.3 and 10.4. In the first figure, the letters p, q and r are used to denote (arbitrary) TPTL propositions while in the second figure, x is used to denote a data variable that has been defined to count the number of send events required before the corresponding rec event occurs (the value of x is incremented in the state following the occurrence of the send event and is reset in the state following a receive event).

In TPTL, time is referenced in formulae through constraints; for example, the TPTL formula $\Diamond(q \wedge t{\le}3)$ means that there is some future state in which q is true and $t{\le}3$. This is analogous to the way that data variables are referenced in QTL, as illustrated by the QTL formula $\Diamond_{>3}(\mathtt{rec2} \wedge O_{\ge0}x{=}0)$ (in some future state at a time greater than 3, $\mathtt{rec2}$ will be true and x will be zero in the next state). However, there is a significant difference between time in TPTL and data variables in QTL. The time component of the timed state sequences of TPTL is monotonic and it is proved in Alur & Henziger (1994) that relaxing this condition (to permit non-monotonic time sequences) results in an undecidable logic. In contrast, the data variable sequences in QTL's timed state sequences are non-monotonic and restricting these sequences to be monotonic would significantly reduce the expressibility of the logic with respect to the specification of quality of service parameters. Since handling a non-monotonic time sequence in TPTL results in an undecidable logic, it is conjectured that handling non-monotonic data variable sequences in QTL will also result in an undecidable logic. The proof of this conjecture is left for future work.

If the result regarding the undecidability of full QTL is proved to be correct, some other means of validation must be found in order to determine whether or not the requirements are met for a given specification. One such way of achieving this is by analyzing the traces through the (modified) extended finite state machine (resulting from stage 3 of the verification procedure). To ensure that a requirement meets the specified behaviour, the requirement must be checked against all possible traces through the state machine. However, in general it is not possible to enumerate all such traces since they may be of infinite length. It is therefore necessary to impose some condition that ensures that only finite length traces are analyzed, for example by imposing a maximum length on the traces considered. The semantics for QTL (presented in Ch. 9) can then be applied to these traces to determine if the requirement holds. Clearly, since only finite length traces have been analyzed, this process does not provide a *proof* that the requirement holds over the specified system. However, it can be used to give a level of confidence that the requirement holds where no formal proof is possible.

10.6 Tool support for checking satisfiability

A tool has been implemented to automate the checking of QTL⁻ formulae for satisfiability, based on the tableau method presented above. This tool initially reads a file that contains a list of one or more QTL⁻ formulae. Each formula is parsed and is then rewritten as a formula containing only basic temporal and binary operators. The resulting formula is then checked for satisfiability by applying the tableau method. The different stages of the tool are illustrated in Figure 10.5. This tool has been tested for a wide variety of simple QTL⁻ formulae and has been shown to produce the expected results regarding satisfiability. The results for some (very) simple Boolean examples are summarized in the first half of Table 10.1. The performance of this tool is reasonable (i.e. results produced in seconds) for untimed formulae or for formulae where the largest constant is zero.

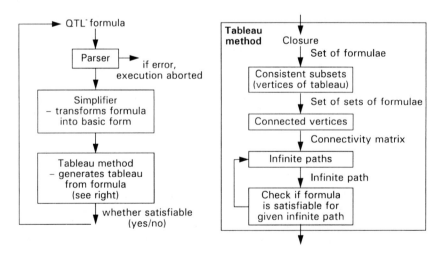

Figure 10.5 Different stages involved in the satisfiability checker.

200

Table 10.1 Results from checking the satisfiability of simple formulae.

Formula	|closure|	#vertices	#edges	Satisfiable?	Comments
true	2	4	8	Y	
false	1	0	0	N	
true→true	3	4	8	Y	
true→false	3	4	8	N	
send	1	4	8	Y	A basic LOTOS event
send ∧ (¬send)	6	8	32	N	Only one event allowed per state
send ∧ rec	6	12	72	N	" "
send ∨ rec	5	12	72	Y	" "
$O_{=0}$ true	3	8	16	Y	Proc. time – immediate
$O_{=0}$ false	2	4	0	N	" "
$\Diamond_{=0}$ true	8	64	128	Y	Proc. time – approx 5 seconds
$\Diamond_{=0}$ false	8	64	128	N	" "
$\Box_{\geq 0}$ true	12	64	128	Y	" "
$\Box_{\geq 0}$ false	11	64	128	N	" "
true $U_{=0}$ true	8	64	128	Y	" "
true $U_{>0}$ true	8	64	128	Y	" "
true $U_{<0}$ true	11	256	512	N	Constraint is <0 ∴ unsatisfiable
true $U_{=1}$ true	11	576	1728	Y	Proc. time – approx 30 seconds
true $U_{>1}$ true	11	576	1728	Y	Proc. time – approx 4 minutes
true $U_{<1}$ true	14	2304	6912	Y	Proc. time – approx 8 minutes
send→$\Diamond_{=0}$ rec	11	192	1152	Y	Proc. time – approx 5 seconds
$\Box$(send→$\Diamond_{=0}$ rec)	21	–	–	–	Memory allowance exceeded

However, for other formulae, even if the largest constant is one, the processing time runs into minutes rather than seconds (when executed on a Sparc 2). Examples that illustrate this problem are shown in the second half of Table 10.1. As these results show, it is impractical to consider the use of this tool for the examples presented in Chapters 11 and 12.

Analysis of the performance using the UNIX tool, profile, shows that approximately 40% of the processing time is spent comparing formulae. In the satisfiability checker, formulae are represented as binary trees and the comparison of formulae is achieved through a recursive search routine to compare each node. The high percentage of processing time spent in this routine suggests that a technique such as the allocation of hash numbers to formulae, or the use of a parallel machine could significantly improve the performance.

However, there remains an inherent difficulty in providing tool support for the verification process. The processing time for checking the satisfiability of QTL⁻ formulae is conjectured to be exponential in the number of operators and the value of the highest constant (based on complexity results for MTL). This means that, irrespective of how efficiently the satisfiability checker is implemented, problems will always arise with long formulae or formulae that reference large time constants.

10.7   Alternative approaches

A number of other approaches to verification are feasible. In this section, we consider alternative approaches with particular emphasis on horizontal verification.

10.7.1   Alternative model checking techniques

An alternative approach may be implemented for stages 4 and 5 above based on symbolic model checking. Instead of keeping the EFSM and the QTL assumptions separate, a timed automaton (for example, as defined in Henzinger et al. (1992)) may be generated from the modified EFSM and the QTL assumptions. Symbolic model checking (Henzinger et al. 1992) may then be employed to verify the QTL requirements. As should be apparent from the verification techniques discussed in this chapter, the main hindrance to the successful application of model checking techniques is state space explosion. Symbolic model checking represents the best current resolution of this difficulty. The idea is that rather than enumerate all the states in a model, a symbolic representation of sets of states is generated and then the set of states that satisfy a proposition is computed as a fixed point of a function on state predicates. This approach has been made possible by work on the symbolic representation of state sets using binary decision diagrams. The symbolic approach is particularly applicable in the real-time setting as temporal logic propositions referring to real-time are particularly susceptible to state explosion.

10.7.2   Approaches based on unification

A second approach is to unify behaviour, real-time assumptions and real-time requirements into a single notation and then carry out verification employing techniques for that notation. This can be achieved by unifying to a timed LOTOS or to QTL.

Unification to a timed LOTOS
With this approach, real-time assumptions and abstract behaviour would be combined to produce a timed LOTOS specification. Requirements would also be mapped to timed LOTOS and then combined with the timed behaviour. Established LOTOS verification methods could then be employed, e.g. equivalences.

The following existing research would be of value if unification into a timed LOTOS were employed. Specifically, this research relates to the problem of transforming temporal logic propositions into a process algebra behaviour.

Synthesis of CSP from temporal logic (Manna & Wolper 1984) The objective of this work is to use temporal logic as a specification language for CSP, which is considered to be a more low level (design/implementation oriented) language. In particular, they show how the synchronization part of a CSP program can be synthesized from temporal logic propositions. The temporal logic used is standard Manna and Pnueli linear time temporal logic.

The synthesis process uses tableau decision procedures. This procedure can have two possible outcomes: either it shows that the specification is unsatisfiable and thus there is no program that can satisfy the temporal logic propositions or it derives a model of the temporal logic proposition. It is relatively straightforward to derive CSP from the model. The limitation, of Manna and Wolper's work is that it does not handle time.

Synthesis of timed CSP from a timed temporal logic (Schneider et al. 1992) This work follows much the same lines as the above research, transposing a lot of the untimed CSP ideas into a timed CSP setting. The logic used is a bounded operator timed temporal logic. A semantic model for the logic is defined in terms of timed failure models. This is a different approach to the standard LOTOS labelled transition system semantics. However, failure based semantics have also been developed for LOTOS (Leduc 1990).

Importantly, this work does deal with real-time, and generally speaking the work can be seen to be close to our approach. It would offer a strong basis if unification into a timed LOTOS were undertaken.

The above related work suggests that a timed LOTOS could be synthesized from QTL propositions. In particular, transposing the above methods from CSP to LOTOS would not be difficult as the two notations are closely related apart from their handling of hiding and non-determinism. One benefit of unifying into a timed LOTOS is that further timed refinement could be undertaken within the timed LOTOS notation. However, in some senses, this represents a compromise with respect to the principle of separation of timing concerns, since the separation between functional behaviour and timing properties would only have been maintained early in system development. There is an argument, however, for such an approach, since it is only at the very early specification phases of system development that the abstraction versus time conflict is a significant issue. In addition, the design phase of system development may best be performed in a single language.

Unification into QTL

In this approach, QTL propositions would be generated from the LOTOS specification of behaviour. Verification would be carried out by investigating if each of the QTL requirements can be satisfied by the combined QTL representation of behaviour and the QTL real-time assumptions.

Again, there is some interesting research that could contribute to the development of such an approach:

Mapping LOTOS to temporal logic (Fantechi et al. 1990a,b) Fantechi et al. (1990b) derive the temporal logic formula satisfied by a given LOTOS specification. Verifying satisfaction of the requirements of the LOTOS specification (which are already expressed in temporal logic) then requires determining that the derived temporal logic formula satisfies the requirements formula. In addition, verification of equivalence of LOTOS specifications reduces to verifying logical equivalence. Automated tools can be used to relate the two formulae, such as decision procedures and theorem provers. The approach uses standard Manna and Pnueli linear time temporal logic.

Fantechi et al. (1990a) also relate the properties that can be proved with the temporal logic to the semantics that the LOTOS is expressive with respect to, i.e. the more expressive the semantics the richer the properties that can be proved. The limitations of this work are that it only uses basic LOTOS (data types are not considered).

These pieces of work could be used as the basis of unification to QTL. Additional work would be required, however, to deal with the full LOTOS language and to map to QTL.

10.7.3 Validation through simulated execution

A final approach to validation is provided by simulated execution and debugging (Harel 1992). Simulated execution for rapid prototyping has become very common, and simulation tools for most major FDTs have been developed (de Saqui-sannes & Courtiat 1989, Eertink 1992). Furthermore, sophisticated extensions to the basic approach, such as visual simulation (as performed by the Statemate tool (Harel et al. 1990a) for Statecharts), have been developed. However, real-time is generally not considered in these tools; in particular event firing times are assumed to be zero.

A number of interesting tools have been developed that enable quantitative time to be considered. For example, the EDB simulator/debugger (INT 1992b) allows the investigation of real-time properties in Estelle specifications. Importantly, quantitative timing values can be associated with execution of events in the simulator. For each simulation, parameters can be set that define the time required to determine the next transitions to execute (called the system management time) and the time transitions take to execute (called the execution time). Using these parameters, real-time assumptions can be incorporated into simulations. A complete analysis of timing behaviour, based on the timing values associated with internal delay clauses and the timing values associated with simulation time parameters, can then be obtained through simulation.

Basically, these techniques enable real-time assumptions to be resolved with abstract behaviour. However, the approaches described do not offer a complete separation of timing concerns in that there is no explicit specification or subsequent verification of real-time requirements.

10.8   Summary

This chapter has considered a verification procedure for specifications written using the LOTOS/QTL approach. More specifically, to use the terminology introduced in Chapter 8, it has considered the issue of horizontal verification, that is, proving that each requirement is satisfied by the specification of behaviour at each stage in the system development. The dual-language nature of the LOTOS/QTL approach results in a more complex verification procedure than would be necessary for a single language specification. The procedure can be divided into a number of stages that have been summarized in Figure 10.1. The two most significant of these stages relate to, first, checking each requirement against the real-time assumptions and, secondly, checking this requirement against an extended finite state machine (derived from the LOTOS specification). The first of these stages can be achieved through the construction of a tableau and then establishing the satisfiability of a formula based on one requirement and the set of real-time assumptions. A method to perform this task for a subset of QTL, denoted QTL, has been presented in Section 10.3 of this chapter. The second of these stages can be achieved through model checking techniques, an algorithm for which has been presented in Section 10.4.

As mentioned above, the tableau method presented in this chapter applies only to a subset of QTL in which constraints over data variables are disallowed. It is conjectured that, in trying to extend the restricted logic to full QTL, the decision problem becomes undecidable. An alternative means of validation based on finite length traces has then been outlined. If no formal proof is possible, this is one way to achieve some level of confidence that a specification meets a requirement.

A tool to support the checking of formulae for satisfiability has been described. However, problems with the performance of this tool for non-trivial formulae mean that it is impractical to apply it to the examples presented in the following two chapters. Finally, alternative approaches to verification have been considered.

The following chapter will illustrate the use of the LOTOS/QTL approach through a number of simple examples. A more complex example will then be considered in Chapter 12 in which the LOTOS/QTL approach will be compared with a single language approach.

PART V

Applying the LOTOS/QTL approach

This part presents examples of the LOTOS/QTL approach and consists of two chapters. Chapter 11 presents a number of simple example real-time and multimedia specifications with the LOTOS/QTL approach (corresponding to the first three scenarios introduced in Ch. 4). Chapter 12 then compares the LOTOS/QTL specification of a lip synchronization algorithm with the specification of the same system in a timed LOTOS.

Simple examples

11.1   Introduction

In this chapter, several simple examples are presented to illustrate the use of the proposed approach. The examples correspond to the first three scenarios introduced in Chapter 4 (the fourth scenario is presented in Ch. 12). In each of the examples, LOTOS is used to formally specify the abstract behaviour of the system and the real-time temporal logic QTL is used to specify both the real-time assumptions and the requirements. In addition, to aid the reader, the initial descriptions of the scenarios are repeated from Chapter 4.

Note that, due to the inherent complexity of the verification process (see Ch. 10), it is not possible in any of the examples to present a verification of the QTL requirements against the LOTOS specification and associated QTL assumptions. Similarly, it is not possible to demonstrate that the QTL requirements and assumptions can be satisfied. This illustrates the importance of tool support to mask out the complexity of such methods to the user of formal specification techniques.

11.2   Bounded invocation

11.2.1   Restatement of the problem

The first example considered is a specification of bounded invocation using a simple RPC protocol. Figure 11.1 illustrates the structure of a remote procedure call. Figure 11.1 shows two (remote) processes, the client and the server, which are connected over a communication channel. The client sends a call to the server requesting the remote execution of a procedure.

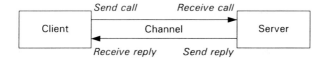

Figure 11.1 The basic concept of a remote procedure call.

Upon receiving this call, the server processes it and returns a reply containing the results of this execution.

The *assumed* behaviour of the invocation service and associated protocol can be informally described as follows:

- All communication between the client and the server is over the network (i.e. an asynchronous medium).
- The network is unreliable (hence messages may get lost) and messages may be re-ordered during transmission.
- Any successful transmission over the network (either client to server or server to client) takes a maximum of 2 ms (milliseconds).
- After receiving and executing a call, the server sends a reply back to the client; the server will take at most 1ms to process any call.
- After sending a call, the client waits for a reply. If no reply arrives within 6 ms, the client times out and re-sends the call (the timeout value is based on the estimated two-way transmission delay of 4 ms and a processing time of 1ms by the server).
- After timing out, the client takes 1ms to reset the clock and prepare to re-send the call.
- Repeated timeouts cause the client to report an error and stop execution; it is assumed that after 5 timeouts an error will be reported immediately.

In addition, the *required* behaviour of the bounded invocation service is as follows:

- The maximum response time for the protocol should be 45 ms, i.e. after sending a call, either a reply should be received or an error reported within 45 ms.
- For each distinct call sent, the server should execute the request at most once (repeated requests are ignored/discarded). This is known as *at-most-once* semantics (note that this requirement makes no reference to real-time).

These represent the *quality of service requirements* for the invocation service.

With this scenario, we would like to be able to specify the behaviour of the bounded invocation, capturing the assumptions given above. It would also be desirable to specify formally the quality of service requirements and then verify the requirements against the behaviour.

11.2.2 Structure of the specification

The structure of the specification is illustrated in Figure 11.2.

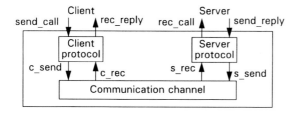

Figure 11.2 The structure of the specification.

This figure shows the service interface consisting of send_call, rec_reply, rec_call and send_reply. The protocol is then implemented in the client and server processes which communicate asynchronously using the communication channel.

11.2.3 Abstract behaviour

Considering the above informal description of the behaviour of the protocol, the abstract (untimed) behaviour of simple client and server processes may be specified using LOTOS as follows:

```
process Client [ send_call, rec_reply, c_send, c_rec, error ]
                (n:nat ) : noexit :=
  (* a timeout event is internal w.r.t. the behaviour of the
     client *)
  hide timeout in
    send_call !n; (* send call no. n from Client to Server *)
    SubClient [ c_send, c_rec, timeout, error ] ( n )
    >> rec_reply !n;      (* receive reply no. n from Server *)
      Client [ send_call, rec_reply, c_send, c_rec, error ]
            (succ (n) )
where
  process SubClient [ c_send, c_rec, timeout, error ] ( n:nat )
                  : exit :=
    c_send !call !n;
    ( c_rec !reply !n; exit
    []
    timeout;
      ( SubClient [ c_send, c_rec, timeout, error ] ( n )
      (* re-send message no. n *)
      []
```

211

```
        error !n (* report error after repeated failures *); stop
    )   )
  endproc (* SubClient *)
endproc (* Client *)

process Server[ rec_call, send_reply, s_send, s_rec ]
                : noexit :=
  hide execute_call in
    ( s_rec !call ?n:nat;  (* receive call from Client *)
      rec_call !n;
      execute_call !n;      (* the Server executes the call *)
      send_reply !n;        (* send reply from Server to Client *)
      s_send !reply !n;
      Server[ rec_call, send_reply, s_send, s_rec ]
    )
endproc (* Server *)
```

Note that to keep the specification simple, no arguments apart from the sequence number of the call are passed from the client to the server. Similarly, no values are returned to the client after the server has processed the call. These extra parameters could easily be added to the specification. The asynchronous medium can be specified as two independent simplex (unidirectional) channels, one in each direction. Both of these channels are unreliable and both may result in the re-ordering of messages. One possible LOTOS specification for such a medium is as follows. Note that in this process, the LOTOS internal event, i, is used to model the loss of a message during transmission.

```
process Medium[ c_send, c_rec, s_send, s_rec ] : noexit :=
  Simplex[ c_send, s_rec ] (* medium from Client to Server *)
  |||
  Simplex[ s_send, c_rec ] (* medium from Server to Client *)
where
  process Simplex[ send, rec ] : noexit :=
    send ?m:message ?n:nat; (* m will be a call or a reply *)
    ( ( rec !m !n; stop  (* message is transmitted successfully *)
        []
        i; stop )          (* message is lost during transmission *)
        |||
        Simplex[ send, rec ] (* allow another message to be sent *)
    )
  endproc (* Simplex *)
endproc (* Medium *)
```

This medium specifies a potentially unbounded queue. While this is valid LOTOS, there is no possibility of generating a finite state machine from

212

such a specification. Consequently, problems arise with the verification process presented in the previous chapter. To overcome this problem, however, it is possible to add another process to the specification that monitors the queue and places an upper bound on the number of messages it may hold at any one time.

The overall behaviour of the system can now be specified as follows:

```
specification RemoteProcedureCall [ send_call, rec_reply,
                rec_call, send_reply, error ] : noexit
behaviour
  hide c_send, s_send, c_rec, s_rec in
    ( ( Client [ send_call, rec_reply, c_send, c_rec, error ] ( 0 )
            (* 0 is initial message no. *)
      |||
      Server [ rec_call, send_reply, s_send, s_rec ] )
    |[ c_send, c_rec, s_send, s_rec ]|
    Medium [ c_send, c_rec, s_send, s_rec ] )
endspec
```

This shows the interleaving of the behaviour of the client and server processes, both of which synchronize on their respective sending and receiving events with the behaviour of the medium.

11.2.4   Real-time assumptions

Having considered the abstract behaviour, consider now the additional real-time information that was given in the informal description of the protocol. Note that these assumptions illustrate how a data variable can be declared to count the number of consecutive timeouts.

Maximum latency of the medium
Consider first the maximum latency of the medium, that is, the maximum time it takes for a message to be transmitted successfully between the client and the server (and vice-versa). In the informal description, the value for this was given as 2 ms. This can be written in QTL as follows (all units of time will be assumed to be ms):

- A1. Bounded latency (outward)

$$\phi_{A1}: \quad \Box(\text{s\_rec !call ?}n\text{:nat} \rightarrow \Diamond_{\leq 2} \text{ c\_send !call !}n)$$

If a call numbered n is received by the server, then at some state in the past within 2 ms, call n was sent by the client. In the premiss of the implication, the value of n is unknown, but will be instantiated when considered in conjunction with the LOTOS specification (hence ?n:nat). In contrast, the value of n in the conclusion of the implication refers to the same n as in the premiss; consequently, the value of this variable is already known (hence $!n$). Note that since messages may be lost during transmission, it is not correct to state that every c_send event is followed by an s_rec event within a certain time.

The return latency can be similarly constrained:

- A2. Bounded latency (return)

$$\phi_{A2}: \quad \Box(\ \text{c\_rec !reply ?}n\text{:nat} \rightarrow \Diamond_{\leq 2}\ \text{s\_send !reply !}n\ )$$

In these two formulae, as in all subsequent formulae, it is assumed that n will represent a rigid variable, i.e. its value remains constant through all states of a formula. Unless otherwise stated, any other variables used will be flexible variables, i.e. their value can change between different states of a formula.

Maximum processing time of the server

The second piece of real-time information stated in the informal description of the protocol referred to the response time of the server. It was stated that the server takes at most 1ms to process any call, i.e. the time between receiving a call and sending a reply is at most 1ms. This can be expressed in QTL as follows:

- A3. Maximum server response time

$$\phi_{A3}: \quad \Box(\ \text{s\_rec !call ?}n\text{:nat} \rightarrow \Diamond_{\leq 1}\ \text{s\_send !reply !}n\ )$$

This formula states that whenever call n is received by the server then, at some state in the future within 1ms, the server will send reply n.

Imposing real-time constraints on timeouts

Based on the estimate of 2 ms for the maximum (one-way) transmission delay and the assumption that the server will take at most 1ms to process a call, the estimated round trip delay can be set to 5 ms. Consequently, if a reply is not received within 6 ms of the call being sent, the client times out and re-sends the call. Alternatively, an error may cause the protocol to stop before the call is received.

- A4. Grounding a timeout in real-time

$$\phi_{A4}: \quad \Box(\ \text{c\_send !call ?}n\text{:nat} \rightarrow$$
$$(\ \Diamond_{<6}\ \text{c\_rec !reply !}n \vee \Diamond_{=6}\ \text{timeout} \vee \Diamond_{\leq 6}\ \text{error !}n\ )\ )$$

This statement means that whenever a call n is sent then either
- within 6 ms a reply (numbered n) will have been received, or
- a timeout will occur exactly 6 ms after the call was sent, or
- an error will occur within 6 ms of the call; the expression ≤ 6 is used since an error may cause the protocol to stop before time 6 is reached.

214

Constraining the reset time of the client

The informal description of the protocol behaviour states that it takes the client 1ms to reset the clock and prepare to re-send a call. This can be expressed in QTL as:

- A5. Time taken for the client to reset

ϕ_{A5}: $\Box$(timeout $\rightarrow$ ($\diamondsuit_{=1}$ c_send !call ?n:nat $\vee$ $\diamondsuit_{\leq 1}$ error ?n:nat))

This means that after a timeout, in some future state, either a call numbered n will be sent exactly 1ms after a timeout, or an error will have been reported within 1ms (thus stopping the protocol).

Constraining the error after repeated timeouts

Finally, it was stated that after repeated timeouts the client should give up trying to send its message (the medium is too unreliable or perhaps the server has crashed) and an error should be reported immediately, that is, before the next time unit. To specify this behaviour, the number of consecutive timeouts that have occurred must be counted. This can be achieved by defining a *data variable* (see Section 9.5) to count these timeouts. Let the data variable x denote the number of consecutive timeouts that have occurred up to the present time. From the informal description, five consecutive timeouts are permitted, after which an error must be immediately reported. A discussion on how the data variable x is set and incremented follows the assumption A6.

- A6. Error after repeated timeouts

ϕ_{A6}: $\Box$((timeout $\wedge$ $x=5$) $\rightarrow$ $\bigcirc_{=0}$ error ?n:nat)

This states that if a timeout is offered when the current value of x is 5, then, in the following state, an error must occur and it must occur immediately. Note that a consequence of this assumption is that the value of x will never exceed 5 (i.e. the set of possible values for x is finite).

Data variable declarations

There are a number of ways in which data variable declarations can be written. One simple method involves providing *initial*, *reset* and *increment* conditions stating the initial value of the variable, the condition (if any) that causes the variable to be reset and the condition under which the variable should be incremented, respectively. These three conditions may not be sufficient for a complex data variable declaration, hence it may be necessary to provide a more expressive set of conditions. An alternative method of writing the declarations would be to use a formal specification language such as a logic.

This section provides the data variable declarations for the previously mentioned variable x (defined to count the number of consecutive timeouts up to the current time). Two different ways of writing the declarations are presented, the first of which is the simple method described above where initial, reset and increment conditions are provided, while the second method uses a temporal logic.

Using the first method, the data variable x can be initialized, reset and incremented as follows:

Initial condition: $x=0$
Reset condition: $x=0$ immediately after event **c_rec !reply ?n:nat**
Increment condition: $x:=x+1$ on event **timeout**

If no condition can be applied in a particular state, the value of x should remain the same as in the previous state.

The second method involves using a temporal logic. As will be seen below, quantifiers are needed in the logic; consequently, a first-order logic is necessary. The logic presented below uses standard temporal operators (as in QTL) and the existential quantifier ($\exists$).

- DVD1. Initial condition

  ϕ_{DVD1}: Θ: $x=0$

  In the initial state (denoted by Θ), the value of data variable x is zero.

- DVD2. Reset condition

  ϕ_{DVD2}: $\Box$ (c_rec !reply ?n:nat $\rightarrow$ O ($x=0$ $\wedge$
  $\qquad$ O($x=0$ U Θ(c_send !call !succ(n)))))

  Every time a `reply` is received by the client, reset the value of x to zero and maintain this value until the next `send` event has just occurred (after which x will be updated).

- DVD3. Increment condition

  ϕ_{DVD3}: $\Box$(timeout $\rightarrow$ $\exists u$. ($x=u$ $\wedge$ O ($x=u+1$ $\wedge$
  $\qquad$ O($x=u+1$ U Θ (timeout $\vee$ c_rec !reply ?n:nat)))))

  For every `timeout`, a value of a *rigid* variable u can be found that is equal to the current value of x (a *flexible* variable) and, in the following state, x is set to this value plus one. This value must be maintained until the next `timeout` or `receive` event has just occurred. (Recall that a rigid variable is one that retains its value in all states of a formula whereas a flexible variable may change its value in different states.)

As can be seen, a formal definition of the data variable declarations for variable x using a first-order logic requires complex formulae. Consequently, where possible, data variable declarations will be described by initial, reset and increment conditions. However, as will be seen in Chapter 12, more complex logic declarations are sometimes required.

11.2.5   Requirements

In contrast to real-time assumptions that state the *actual* real-time behaviour of the system, requirements are concerned with expressing the *desired* properties of a system. The requirements for this example can be expressed in QTL as follows:

- R1. Maximum response time

$$\phi_{R1}: \quad \square \, (\, \text{send\_call} \, ?n\text{:nat} \rightarrow \Diamond_{<45} \, (\, \text{rec\_reply} \, !n \vee \text{error} \, !n \,) \,)$$

  Whenever a `call` numbered n is sent then, in some future state that occurs before time 45 ms, either `reply` n will be received or an `error` will be reported.
- R2. At-most-once semantics

$$\phi_{R2}: \quad \square \, (\, \text{execute\_call} \, ?n\text{:nat} \rightarrow \neg \Diamond \text{execute\_call} \, !n \,)$$

  If an "execute_call ?*n*:nat" event occurs (issued by the protocol's server process), there should be no state in the future in which this event is repeated.

Note that this statement does not say that an execute event will occur for *every* call; this would be an example of *exactly-once semantics* (which could also be expressed using QTL). Note also that mechanisms to achieve at-most-once semantics need to be incorporated into the specification to guarantee that this requirement holds. For example, a cache could be maintained of the message numbers against the results of the operations, and a look-up could be performed on this cache if a repeated message is received.

11.3   A multimedia stream

11.3.1   Restatement of the problem

The second scenario is that of a multimedia stream. As mentioned previously, a stream is a multimedia structure that links a continuous media data source and corresponding data sink. In this example, the source and the sink are assumed to be communicating asynchronously over an appropriate medium, as shown in Figure 11.3.

Suppose that the stream exhibits the following assumed behaviour (real-time values have been arbitrarily chosen):

- All communication between the data source and the data sink is asynchronous (it is assumed that the queue at the data sink is unbounded).
- The channel over which frames are transmitted is unreliable and may result in the re-ordering of messages.
- The data source repeatedly transmits data frames every 50 ms (i.e. 20

Figure 11.3 A multimedia stream.

frames per second).
- After the generation of a frame, 5 ms elapse before it is transmitted. Successfully transmitted frames arrive at the data sink between 80 ms and 90 ms after their transmission (channel latency).
- If the number of frames arriving at the data sink is not within 15 to 20 frames per second (channel throughput), then an error should be reported.
- The time taken by the data sink to process a frame is 5 ms (i.e. the time between receiving a frame and being able to play it).

The stream then has a number of *quality of service requirements* in terms of latency, jitter and throughput:
- The *end-to-end latency* should be between 90 ms and 100 ms (this requirement incorporates the acceptable jitter on latency). Consequently, a frame taking longer than 100 ms can be assumed to have been lost during transmission.
- The *end-to-end throughput* should remain between 15 and 20 frames per second.

As with the bounded invocation example, we would like to specify the behaviour and quality of service requirements formally and then verify the requirements against the behaviour.

11.3.2 Structure of the specification

Figure 11.4 illustrates the structure of the specification. It also shows the distinction between real-time assumptions and requirements: time constraints outside the box are requirements while those inside the box are real-time assumptions.

11.3.3 Abstract behaviour

A LOTOS specification of the abstract behaviour of a stream can be derived from the informal description as shown below. In addition to the source, sink and channel processes, a clock and monitor process are introduced to carry out the necessary quality of service management. Note that although a clock is explicitly included in the abstract behaviour, the *quality* of the clock is defined in the real-time assumptions. Justification for the inclusion of the clock will be given in Section 11.5.2.

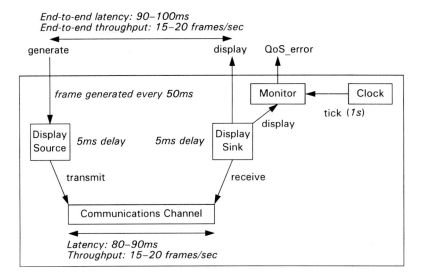

Figure 11.4   A multimedia stream.

```
specification Stream[ generate, display, QoS_error ] : noexit
behaviour
 hide transmit, receive, tick in
   ( ( Source[ generate, transmit ]
      |[ transmit ]|
      Channel[ transmit, receive ]
      |[ receive ]|
    Sink[ receive, display ] )
   |[ display ]|
   ( Clock[ tick ] ||| Monitor[ display, QoS_error ] ) )
where
 process Source[ generate, transmit ] : noexit :=
   ( generate ?frame_no:frame;
    transmit !frame_no;
    Source[ generate, transmit ] )
   |[ generate ]|
  Generator[ generate ] ( 0 )
where
 process Generator[ generate ] ( n:frame ) : noexit :=
  generate !n; stop ||| Generator[ generate ] ( succ(n) )
 endproc (* Generator *)
endproc (* Source *)
process Sink[ receive, display ] : noexit :=
  receive ?frame_no:frame;
  display !frame_no;
```

```
  Sink[ receive, display ]
  endproc (* Sink*)

  process Channel[ transmit, receive ] : noexit :=
   transmit ?frame_no:frame;
   ( ( receive !frame; stop
      (* frame is transmitted successfully *)
     []
     i; stop )      (* frame is lost during transmission *)
     |||
     Channel[ transmit, receive ] )
    (* allow another frame to be sent *)
  endproc (* Channel *)

  process Clock[ tick ] : noexit :=
   tick; Clock[ tick ]
  endproc (* Clock *)

  process Monitor[ display, QoS_error ] : noexit :=
   display ?frame_no:frame;
   ( Monitor[ display, QoS_error ]
     []
     QoS_error; stop )
  endproc (* Monitor *)
endspec (* Stream *)
```

Note that, as with the bounded invocation example, an unbounded queue has been specified. As explained in the example above, this prevents the generation of a finite state machine (in the verification process). Consequently, an extra LOTOS process can be specified which places an upper bound on the number of frames a queue may hold at any one time. This would also be necessary for the process generator, since this process generates an infinite number of frames for transmission by the data source.

11.3.4 Real-time assumptions

In this section, real-time assumptions will be presented which ground the occurrence of events from the abstract behaviour in real-time.

Generation of frames at the data source
The informal description of the real-time constraints detailed above states that the source generates frames every 50ms. This can be expressed in QTL as:

- A1. Rate of frame generaion

$$\phi_{A1}: \quad \Box(\text{generate } ?fr{:}frame \rightarrow$$
$$\bigvee_{t=0}^{50} O_{=t}(\neg(\text{generate } !fr) \ U_{=50-t} \text{ generate } ?next{:}frame))$$

This statement means that, whenever a generate event occurs, no further frame will be generated until 50 ms have passed, at which time the next frame will be generated. Note that the right-hand side of the implication specifies a choice of times (between 0 ms and 50 ms after the generate event) at which the next generate occurs.

Processing time of the data source

The second real-time assumption states that the processing time of the data source, that is the time between a frame being generated and transmitted, is 5ms.

- A2. Time taken for source to process a frame

$$\phi_{A2}: \quad \Box \ (\text{ generate ?fr:frame} \rightarrow \Diamond_{=5} \text{ transmit !fr })$$

This means that whenever a generate event occurs, this frame is transmitted in some future state that occurs 5 ms later.

Latency of the channel

This assumption states that the channel imposes a latency delay of between 80 and 90 ms on each transmission.

- A3. Latency imposed by the channel

$$\phi_{A3}: \quad \Box \ (\text{ receive ?fr:frame} \rightarrow V_{t=80}^{90}(\Diamond_{=t} \text{ transmit !fr }))$$

This logic statement means that whenever a receive event occurs, there is a choice of times for some past state (between times 80 and 90 inclusive) at which the corresponding transmit event occurred. Once again, this is not specified the other way round (e.g. in some state after a transmit, a receive will occur) since the channel is unreliable and messages may be lost during transmission.

Processing time of the data sink

The informal description above states that the data sink takes 5 ms between a frame being received and it being displayed.

- A4. Time taken for sink to process a frame

$$\phi_{A4}: \quad \Box \ (\text{ receive ?fr:frame} \rightarrow \Diamond_{=5} \text{ display !fr })$$

This means that whenever a receive event occurs, a frame is displayed in some future state that occurs 5 ms later.

Grounding the tick event in real-time

The following two real-time assumptions ensure that tick events occur every second and that the clock starts at time zero.

- A5.a Ticks occur every second

$$\phi_{A5.a}: \quad \Box \ (\text{ tick} \rightarrow V_{t=0}^{1000} \ O_{=t}(\neg(\text{tick}) \ U_{=1000-t} \text{ tick }))$$

This statement means that whenever a `tick` event occurs, no further `tick` event will occur until 1000 ms have passed, at which time the subsequent tick event will occur.

- A5.b Clock starts at time zero

$$\phi_{A5.b}: \quad \diamondsuit_{=0} \text{ tick}$$

A `tick` event will occur in some future state (possibly the current state) which occurs before the passage of time.

Channel throughput and reporting errors

Finally, it is necessary to describe the conditions under which an error should occur. The informal description states that an error must occur if the channel throughput falls outside the acceptable bounds of between 15 and 20 frames per second. For this assumption, it is necessary to define a data variable, x, to count the number of `receive` events per second.

Initial condition: $x=0$
Reset condition: $x=0$ immediately after event `tick`
Increment condition: $x:=x+1$ on event `receive?fr:frame`

The assumption governing the channel throughput and the occurrence of an error can now be specified as follows:

- A6. Throughput of the channel and reporting errors

$$\phi_{A6}: \quad \square(\,(\text{ tick} \wedge (\,x<15 \vee x>20\,)\,) \rightarrow O_{=0} \text{ QoS\_error })$$

If there is a `tick` (marking the passage of a second), and the number of `receive` events are outside the acceptable bounds, an error should be reported immediately.

11.3.5   Requirements

The requirements over the multimedia stream have been described informally above. These requirements state the desired latency, jitter and throughput, and can be specified in QTL as follows:

End-to-end latency/jitter

The QTL specification for maintaining an end-to-end latency of between 90 ms and 100 ms (i.e. incorporating acceptable jitter) is similar to the real-time assumption A3 presented for the stream above.

- R1. The latency imposed by the channel should be between 90 ms and 100ms

$$\phi_{R1}: \quad \square(\text{ display ?fr:frame} \rightarrow V_{t=90}^{100} \diamondsuit_{=t} \text{ generate !fr})$$

This formula states that for every `display` event, the associated frame was generated in some previous state which occurred at a choice of times between 90 ms and 100 ms in the past. As before, this formula only imposes latency on those messages which are successfully transmitted.

End-to-end throughput

This requirement states that there is an end-to-end throughput of between 15 and 20 frames per second. Suppose that the data variable y is used to count the number of display events (compare with the real-time assumption A6 above):

Initial condition: $y=0$
Reset condition: $y=0$ immediately after event tick
Increment condition:$y:=y+1$ on event display?fr:frame

The second requirement can now be specified by using this data variable:

• R2. Maintaining a throughput of between 15 and 20 frames per second

ϕ_{R2}: $\Box$(tick $\rightarrow$ 15≤y≤20)

For every tick, the number of display events in the last second must be between the acceptable bounds.

Considering error rates

A further requirement that may be specified for the multimedia stream example is that of end-to-end error rates. Suppose that the error rate should be no more than 10%. From the real-time assumption A1, it is known that 20 frames are sent per second (one every 50ms). Additionally, the data variable y (declared above) counts the number of frames that are displayed per second. Therefore, it is possible to state that:

$\Box$(tick $\rightarrow$ (20–y ≤ 2))

or equivalently,

$\Box$(tick $\rightarrow$ (y ≥ 18))

However, simply comparing the number of frames displayed per second against the number of frames sent per second takes no account of the number of frames currently in the channel (i.e. mid-transmission). Consequently, this method of specifying a bound on error rates does not cater for the possibility of congestion in the network. By measuring the number of frames displayed and transmitted over a broader interval (e.g. a minute), a truer indication of the error rate can be obtained.

Note that, to place a requirement such as this on the error rate, it is also necessary to constrain the non-determinism in the abstract behaviour of the channel regarding message loss. Although it would be possible to place a constraint on the number of frames received with respect to the number of frames transmitted, a better method would be to introduce probabilities into the specification technique. This would allow the specification of properties such as the probability of a successful transmission is 90% and the probability of a message being lost is 10%. This issue will be returned to in the future work section of Chapter 13.

A note on requirements
So far in this example, the requirements that have been considered are similar to a number of the real-time assumptions. This is a direct result of the abstract level at which the behaviour of the stream has been specified. However, as the specification is refined towards an implementation, the real-time assumptions reflect the more detailed nature of the specification. For example, the refined real-time assumptions may refer to the time taken in executing the transport protocol, or the delay in accessing the network from the device driver. Alternatively, the communication channel may be refined such that it incorporates compression, thus reducing the necessary bandwidth. In the following section, this refinement will be applied to the stream example to illustrate the effect refinement has on real-time assumptions and requirements. Note that this example was originally mentioned in Chapter 4.

11.4   Adding compression to the multimedia stream

11.4.1   Restatement of the problem

To illustrate a process of refinement, we consider a second stream implemented using MPEG compression and decompression as shown in Figure 11.5 (implying that a lower bandwidth channel can be used). We assume the use of MPEG compression and decompression carries an overhead of 3 ms at each end but achieves a compression ratio of, say, 200:1. All other assumptions and requirements remain as above (see Section 11.3.1).

Again, we would like to specify this refined behaviour, demonstrate that this refined behaviour is compatible with the initial behaviour and verify that the refined behaviour can still meet the requirements.

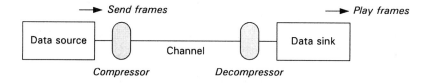

Figure 11.5   A compressed stream.

11.4.2 Refined structure of the specification

The structure of the specification remains the same as in Section 11.3.2. However, the channel is modified to include a compressor and decompressor as shown in Figure 11.6. As in Figure 11.4, the time constraints outside the box are requirements while those inside the box are the new real-time assumptions.

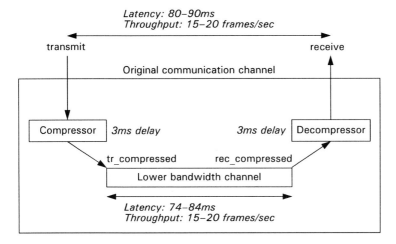

Figure 11.6 Structure of the refined communication channel.

Importantly, this figure shows how real-time assumptions at one level of refinement can become requirements at the next level of refinement. For example, the original real-time assumption governing the latency of the communication channel has become a requirement for the refined channel.

11.4.3 Refined abstract behaviour

As the above figure shows, the original communication channel now incorporates a compression and decompression process. To illustrate this, MPEG compression (Pancha & El Zarchi 1994) will be employed in the abstract behaviour. This compression technique involves the use of three types of frame: i-frames (intra-coded frames that make no reference to other frames), p-frames (forward predictive frames that represent the current frame and the closest past i-frame or p-frame) and b-frames (bidirectionally predictive frames that represent the current frame, the closest past i-frame or p-frame, and the closest future i-frame or p-frame). The refined behaviour of the communication channel is presented below:

```
process Channel[ transmit, receive ] : noexit :=
  hide tr_compressed, rec_compressed in
    ( Compressor[ transmit, tr_compressed ] ( 0, null, null )
     (* the parameters represent the initial state and the clos-
      est past and future frames (initially both set to null) *)
    |[ tr_compressed ]|
    LB_Channel[ tr_compressed, rec_compressed ]
    (* lower bandwidth channel *)
    |[ rec_compressed ]|
    Decompressor[ rec_compressed, receive ] )
where
  type Frame is
    sorts    frame
    opns     null :-> frame (* passed as parameter to compressor *)
             header:-> frame  (* passed from comp. to decomp.
                              before other frames *)
    eqns ...              (* omitted for brevity *)
  endtype (* Frame *)

  type Pic_Types is Boolean, Frame
    sorts    type_frame
    opns     i_encode : frame -> frame (* standard encoding for
                                       intra coded frames *)
             p_encode : frame, frame -> frame
                              (* forward predictive encoding *)
             b_encode : frame, frame, frame -> frame
                  (* bidirectionally predictive encoding *)
             past, future : frame -> bool
             (* test if a frame is a past or a future frame *)
    eqns ...                      (* omitted for brevity *)
  endtype (* Pic_Types *)

  process Compressor[ transmit, tr_compressed ]
          ( state:nat; closest_past, closest_future : frame )
          : noexit :=
    ( [ state eq 0 ] -> (* initial state *)
    tr_compressed !header;
    Compressor[ transmit, tr_compressed ]
              ( succ(0), closest_past, closest_future )
    [] [ state ne 0 ] ->       (* any other state *)
    transmit ?fr:frame;
    ( hide i_pic, p_pic, b_pic in
     (* to maintain abstraction in the specification, the
      choice between different types of frame is modelled using
      non-determinism *)
     ( i_pic;    (* intra coded frame *)
```

```
        tr_compressed !i_encode( fr ); exit )
    []
    ( p_pic;     (* forward predictive coded frame *)
     tr_compressed !p_encode( fr, closest_past ); exit )
    []
    ( b_pic;     (* bidirectionally predictive coded frame *)
     tr_compressed !b_encode( fr, closest_past,
                             closest_future );
     (* b_pics are never used as ref. points for further
      prediction, therefore leave closest_past and
      closest_future parameters unchanged *)
     Compressor[ transmit, tr_compressed ]
             ( state,closest_past, closest_future )
    ) )
    (* both i-pics and p_pics may be used as reference points,
    therefore change closest_past and closest_future
    parameters as necessary *)
    >> ( [ past( fr ) ] ->
          Compressor[ transmit, tr_compressed ]
          ( state, fr, closest_future )
       [] [ future( fr ) ] ->
          Compressor[ transmit, tr_compressed ]
          ( state, closest_past, fr )
   )   )
endproc (* Compressor *)

process Decompressor[ rec_compressed, receive ] : noexit :=
 rec_compressed ?fr:frame;
 (* full process omitted, but similar to compression process
 above *)
 receive !decode( fr );
 Decompressor[ rec_compressed, receive ]
endproc (* Decompressor *)

process LB_Channel[ transmit, receive ] : noexit :=
 (* The specification of this process is identical to the origi
 nal channel process above, but due to the compression only
 needs to operate at a lower bandwidth *)
 transmit ?fr:frame;
 ( ( receive !fr; stop (* frame is transmitted successfully *)
     [] i; stop ) (* frame is lost during transmission *)
  ||| LB_Channel[ transmit, receive ] ) (* allow another frame
                                       to be sent *)
 endproc (* LB_Channel *)
endproc (* Channel *)
```

11.4.4   Refined real-time assumptions

The refined real-time assumptions reflect the modified communication channel, including the compressor and decompressor processes.

Processing times of the compressor and decompressor
It is assumed that the compressor takes 3 ms to compress a frame, i.e. the time between a transmit event and the corresponding tr_compressed event is 3ms.

- A7. Processing time of the compressor

ϕ_{A7}: $\Box$(transmit ?fr:frame → $\Diamond_{=3}$ tr_compressed ?comp_fr:frame)

Whenever a transmit event occurs, the compressed frame is transmitted in some future state that occurs 3 ms later.

Similarly, the time taken in decompressing a frame is also assumed to be 3ms.

- A8. Processing time of the decompressor

ϕ_{A8}: $\Box$(rec_compressed ?comp_fr:frame → $\Diamond_{=3}$ receive ?fr:frame)

Whenever a compressed frame is received, a receive event (with the decompressed frame) occurs in some future state 3 ms later.

Throughput of the refined channel
The throughput of the refined channel must be maintained between 15 and 20 frames per second. Note that the frame rate does not change after compression; it is the bandwidth that is reduced. Note also that no error condition is incorporated into this assumption. This condition is handled in A6 above and does not change with refinement. Let data variable, z, be defined to count the number of rec_compressed events:

Initial condition: z=0
Reset condition: z=0 immediately after event tick
Increment condition: z:=z+1 on event
                                rec_compressed ?fr:frame

The above assumption can now be specified as follows:

- A9. Throughput of the refined channel

ϕ_{A9}: $\Box$(tick → 15≤z≤20)

If there is a tick, the number of rec_compressed events must be within the acceptable bounds.

Latency of the refined channel
Finally, it is necessary to define the latency of the refined channel. As shown in Figure 11.6 above, this must remain within the bounds 74 ms to 84 ms.

- A10. Latency of the refined channel

ϕ_{A10}: $\Box(\text{rec\_compressed ?fr:frame} \rightarrow V^{84}_{t=74}(\diamondsuit_{=t} \text{tr\_compressed !fr}))$

Whenever a `rec_compressed` event occurs, there is a choice of times for some past state (between 74 ms and 84 ms) at which the corresponding `tr_compressed` occurred.

11.4.5 Refined requirements

The end-to-end requirements from Section 11.3.5 above (R1 and R2) are still valid. However, in addition there are two new requirements for the refined stream.

Latency/jitter
The first requirement concerns the latency and jitter of the original channel (which now includes the compression and decompression processes); this should remain between 80 ms and 90 ms. Note that this can be viewed as *end-to-end* latency at this level of refinement. This requirement is given by:

- R3. The latency of the channel remains between 80 ms and 90 ms

ϕ_{R3}: $\Box(\text{receive ?fr:frame} \rightarrow V^{90}_{t=80}(\diamondsuit_{=t} \text{transmit !fr}))$

Whenever a `receive` event occurs, there is a choice of times for some past state (between 80 ms and 90 ms) at which the corresponding `transmit` event occurred.

Throughput
Secondly, the required throughput should be defined for the channel.

- R4. The throughput of the channel remains between 15 and 20 frames per second

ϕ_{R4}: $\Box(\text{tick} \rightarrow 15 \leq x \leq 20)$

For every `tick`, the number of `receive` events (as measured by data variable x from Section 11.3.4) must be within the acceptable bounds.
Note that these requirements are based closely on the assumptions A3 and A6 from above. This illustrates how real-time assumptions at one level of refinement can become requirements for the next level of refinement. However, the original requirements should still hold (simultaneously) over the refined behaviour.

11.5 A note on methodology

This section aims to provide some guidelines for the application of the LOTOS/QTL method. First, some general guidelines are discussed. Further considerations that relate to the examples presented in this chapter are then described.

11.5.1 General guidelines

It is important to recall that the LOTOS/QTL method is based on the principle of maintaining a separation of concerns. This means that a distinction should be drawn between the specification of behaviour and the specification of requirements, and also between the different types of time occurring in a specification.

The first of these distinctions involves identifying requirements over the system to be specified. In general, these represent end-to-end properties, and should not make reference to components or internal events of a system. The second distinction involves separating abstract behaviour from real-time assumptions. The abstract behaviour should contain no reference to real-time, but may make use of placeholders (such as tick or timeout). Semantically, these placeholders are no different from other events in the abstract specification. Where necessary, real-time assumptions should then be defined to ground these events in real-time (for example, assumption A4 from the RPC and assumption A5 from the stream). Real-time assumptions should also be defined where it is necessary to state the performance of particular components of a system (for example, assumptions A2–A4 from the stream). However, note that in addition to referencing internal events, real-time assumptions may reference external events (for example, assumptions A1, A2 and A4 from the stream). It should also be noted that there is an interesting relationship between real-time assumptions and requirements when refinement is considered. As illustrated in Section 11.4.5 above, a real-time assumption on a given component at one level of refinement may become a requirement for that component at the next level of refinement. Importantly, however, the refined requirement should still only reference external events at that level of refinement.

11.5.2 Further considerations

In addition to these general guidelines, there are a number of more subtle points that have been brought out by the examples in this chapter. These concern parts of the specification where there appears to be a choice as to whether LOTOS or QTL is used, namely in the retry count (report an error after repeated timeouts) of the RPC example and in the clock of the stream example.

The specification of the first of these, the retry count, is achieved through the declaration of a data variable. This is then incorporated into a real-time assumption that constrains the occurrence of an error. The count itself could equally well have been specified as part of the abstract behaviour, since it makes no reference to real-time. However, the intention of the example was to illustrate different features of the LOTOS/QTL approach; the retry count provided an opportunity to show how a data variable could be declared to count the number of occurrences of a particular event. Note, however, that the number of timeouts permitted before an error is reported may vary on different platforms. If the underlying network is known to be unreliable, then perhaps five timeouts are permitted; with a more reliable network, perhaps only two timeouts are permitted. Consequently, it is logical to group this information with the real-time assumptions, rather than embed it into the abstract specification.

The second consideration concerns the introduction of a clock process into the abstract behaviour of the multimedia stream. This appears to be over-specification in the abstract behaviour and it seems that it could have been handled solely in the real-time assumptions. However, it was included so as to provide an event, tick, to which the real-time assumptions could refer. This was felt to be necessary because of two characteristics of QTL and the underlying timed state sequences. First, time gaps are permitted in the timed state sequences. Consequently, if a QTL formula refers to some future state that occurs one second from now, such a state may not exist and hence the formula is false. Secondly, any number of events may occur at the same time. Since each state refers to exactly one LOTOS event, several states are permitted at the same time. In this case, if a QTL formula refers to some future state that occurs one second from now, which state should be considered? There may be several possible future states one second from now, some of which may satisfy a given condition, others of which may not. For this reason, the decision was taken to link the passage of one second with a LOTOS event, tick, thus making it clear which state was intended.

Returning to more general guidelines, decisions as to how to partition the specification into abstract behaviour, real-time assumptions and requirements fall into two categories. There are certain issues that are clear cut: they should definitely belong to one component of the specification. Other issues, like those highlighted above, are less clear cut. In these cases, time and experience is needed to develop a specification that best reflects the goal of maintaining a separation of concerns.

11.6 Summary

This chapter has provided an illustration of the use of the LOTOS/QTL approach through the specification of three simple examples. The specifications have shown the separation between the abstract behaviour, the real-time assumptions and the requirements. The first example presented a LOTOS/QTL specification of a bounded invocation service. This example shows how some fairly complex real-time assumptions can be expressed; these assumptions represent the time taken in different stages of the protocol. It was also shown how a data variable could be declared to count the number of occurrences of a particular event. In addition, requirements over the system behaviour were explicitly specified.

The second example considered the specification of a multimedia stream. This example illustrated how some typical quality of service properties such as latency, throughput and jitter could be expressed over the stream. The specification of bounded error rates was also considered. A possible refinement to the stream was then considered. This involved adding compression, thus allowing a lower bandwidth communication channel to be used. Real-time assumptions and requirements were given for the refined specification, highlighting how real-time assumptions at one level of refinement can become requirements at the next level of refinement.

Finally, some guidelines were presented for the application of the LOTOS/QTL approach. These reflected some of the considerations necessary when composing a specification in terms of abstract behaviour, real-time assumptions and requirements. A more complex multimedia example, illustrating the specification of a real-time synchronization scenario, is considered in the following chapter.

CHAPTER 12

A larger comparative example

12.1 Introduction

The purpose of this chapter is twofold: first, it aims to show the use of the LOTOS/QTL approach in the specification of a more substantial multimedia example and, secondly, it aims to compare the resulting specification with one achieved using a more traditional timed LOTOS technique. The example chosen is that of the well-known lip-synchronization problem, that is, ensuring that the presentation of independent data streams (such as voice and video) is synchronized. This example was, to the author's knowledge, first specified in the real-time programming language ESTEREL (Stefani et al. 1992) and has also been written in Temporal LOTOS (Regan 1993).

As with the previous chapter, this example is taken from the scenarios introduced in Chapter 4. To aid the reader, the problem is restated below (Section 12.2). The overall structure of the algorithm to solve the problem is then presented in Section 12.3. Following this, specifications of this problem will then be presented in both the Temporal LOTOS and the LOTOS/ QTL approach (sections 12.4 and 12.5 respectively). Comparisons will be made between the resulting specifications in Section 12.6 and, finally, the chapter will be summarized in Section 12.7.

12.2 Restatement of the problem

Suppose that there are two data streams, one carrying video frames and the other carrying voice packets, which are transmitted to a common data sink from two independent data sources. At the data sink, these two data streams must be played out in a manner such that lip-synchronization is achieved between the video and the voice. In order to meet this requirement, certain real-time constraints that relate (synchronize) the two streams must be maintained (all numbers have been kept consistent with those presented in Stefani et al. (1992) and Regan (1993)). The requirements for lip synchronization are described below.

The first requirements are that both sound and video data should be presented at regular intervals. Note that, as in Stefani et al. (1992) and Regan (1993), no jitter (variance in presentation time) is permitted on the sound presentation; however, jitter is permitted on the video presentation.

1. Sound intervals

Sound packets must be presented every 30 milliseconds (ms).

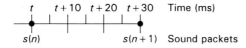

2. Video intervals

Video packets should be presented every 40 ms, but a jitter of ±5 ms is permitted (i.e. video packets must be presented between 35 ms and 45 ms after the previous packet).

The third (and final) requirement for achieving lip-synchronization is that the presentation of the sound and video data must be synchronized, that is, the presentation of one media type must not lag or precede the presentation of the other media type by more than a certain amount. The constraints on the synchronization between the sound and video presentations are described below. Note that in this example, no jitter is permitted on the sound presentation. Therefore, it is only the jitter on the video data that can cause the presentation to drift out of synchronization (for example, if video frames repeatedly arrive late).

3. Synchronization of sound and video

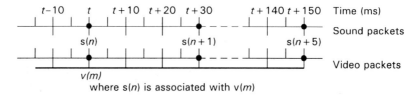

where s(n) is associated with v(m)

i. The video presentation must not lag the associated sound presentation by more than 150 ms.

ii. The video presentation must not precede the associated sound presentation by more than 15 ms.

If these real-time constraints (requirements) cannot be met or are broken at some stage in the data presentation, then lip-synchronization has not been achieved.

In this example, we would like to specify the behaviour of a lip synchronization algorithm together with a formal specification of the three requirements identified above. We would then like to verify that the algorithm meets the requirements.

12.3   Overall structure of a lip-synchronization algorithm

In this section, the overall structure of a lip-synchronization algorithm is presented. This structure is illustrated in Figure 12.1 and will be followed in both the Temporal LOTOS specification and the LOTOS/QTL specification.

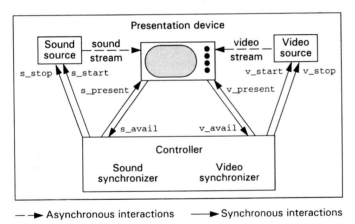

Figure 12.1   The overall structure of the lip-synchronization algorithm.

This figure shows two data sources, each of which is connected to the presentation device by a stream across which data are transmitted (asynchronously). The figure also shows a controller which has the job of monitoring the incoming data and, when the data should be presented, sends signals to the presentation device. More specifically, when a sound packet arrives at the presentation device, a message (s_avail) is sent to the controller to signal the availability of that sound packet. When appropriate, the controller returns a message (s_present) to the presentation device telling it to present the data. An identical procedure is carried out when

235

video frames arrive at the presentation device (resulting in events
v_avail and v_present). The controller is split in two sub-processes
(sound synchronizer and video synchronizer) that handle the synchronization of sound and video data respectively. The starting and stopping of a
presentation are achieved through the use of two synchronous messages
(events s_start and s_stop) transmitted from the controller to the
sound source (respectively video source). The presentation is only stopped
if an error has occurred.

12.4   Temporal LOTOS specification

An algorithm to achieve lip-synchronization is formally specified in Regan
(1993) using Temporal LOTOS, that is, a timed extension to LOTOS (see
Ch. 7). This algorithm is adapted below to follow the overall structure
presented in Figure 12.1. However, since this example aims to highlight
the specification of issues relating to real-time synchronization, only the
behaviour of the controller will be specified (i.e. the specification of the two
data sources, the two streams and the presentation device will be omitted).
This controller process has the job of maintaining lip-synchronization
between sound and video, controlling when sound packets and video
frames should be presented and when errors should be reported.

  Before considering the specification of the lip-synchronization algorithm, the extensions to LOTOS to obtain Temporal LOTOS are briefly
described. First, in Temporal LOTOS, time is introduced through two new
operators. The first operator is a delay operator, denoted σ, which represents a delay of one unit of time. The second operator is the "then" operator, denoted $\lfloor...\rfloor(...)$, which either performs events in the first parameter
immediately or delays for one time unit and then performs the events in
the second parameter. Other operators are as in standard LOTOS. Another
important feature of Temporal LOTOS is that it employs the maximal
progress assumption, that is, internal events that can occur will do so
immediately (before the passage of time). A Temporal LOTOS specification
of the lip-synchronization algorithm will now be presented. (As mentioned
above, this has been adapted from the specification given in Regan (1993).)

  Consider first the behaviour of a generic timer that will be used in the
specification. This timer takes two parameters, earliest and latest,
and it enforces a delay until the earliest time. After this initial delay,
a trigger signal may reset the timer. However, if the timer reaches the
latest time without being reset, an error is reported.

```
process TIMER [ trigger, error ] ( earliest, latest : nat )
                : exit :=
    σ^earliest ;
    ⌊trigger;
```

```
TIMER[ trigger, error ]( earliest, latest )⌋latest-earliest
       (error; exit)
endproc
```

As noted in Regan (1993), the parameterized σ action is incorrect syntax, but serves as a shorthand for a more long-winded definition.

Using this generic timer, it is possible to define timers for the sound and video presentations. For the sound presentation, no jitter is permitted and hence the earliest and latest presentation times are both set to 30 ms. However, for the video presentation, jitter is permitted; consequently, the earliest presentation time is set to 35 ms and the latest presentation time is set to 45 ms.

```
process S_TIMER[ s_present, s_late_error ] : exit :=
  s_present; TIMER[ s_present, s_late_error ]( 30, 30 )
                          (* earliest and latest times *)
endproc
```

```
process V_TIMER[ v_present, v_late_error ] : exit :=
  v_present; TIMER[ v_present, v_late_error ]( 35, 45 )
                          (* earliest and latest times *)
endproc
```

In this example, the fact that the sound presentation is anchored (i.e. no jitter is permitted) means that the presentation of video frames can be measured against the time since the sound presentation began. This time (denoted s_time) is maintained in the following process and can be accessed by synchronizing on the sound_query event.

```
process SOUND_QUERY[ sound_query ]( s_time:nat ) : noexit :=
  ⌊sound_query !s_time; SOUND_QUERY[ sound_query ]( s_time )⌋
    ( SOUND_QUERY[ sound_query ]( s_time+1 ) )
endproc
```

If a sound packet arrives before the first video frame, the sound clock can be started immediately. However, if a video frame arrives before the first sound packet, it is necessary to wait for the first sound packet before the clock can be started. In this case, the start_clock event will be used to indicate the arrival of this first frame.

```
process SOUND_CLOCK[ start_clock, sound_query ] : noexit :=
  start_clock; SOUND_QUERY[ sound_query ]( 0 )
endproc
```

The informal requirements stated that the video presentation may precede the sound presentation by at most 15 ms and may lag the sound presentation by at most 150 ms. If a video frame arrives first, the process INITIAL_SOUND_CHECK is used to ensure that the first sound packet

arrives within the required time (15 ms), otherwise an out of synchronization error is reported. (Note that after this packet has arrived, the sound
clock should be started by synchronizing with the process SOUND_ CLOCK
on event start_clock.) Similarly, if a sound packet arrives first, the process INITIAL_VIDEO_CHECK checks that the first video frame arrives
within 150 ms (in this case, the sound clock will already have been started).

```
process INITIAL_SOUND_CHECK[ s_avail, s_present, start_clock,
                             synch_error ] : noexit :=
  ⌊s_avail; s_present; start_clock;
   SOUND_SYNCHRONISER[ s_avail, s_present ]⌋¹⁵
     ( synch_error; exit )
endproc
```

```
process INITIAL_VIDEO_CHECK[ v_avail, v_present, sound_query,
                             synch_error ] : noexit :=
  ⌊v_avail; v_present;
   VIDEO_SYNCHRONISER[ v_avail,v_present, sound_query ] ( 0 )⌋ ¹⁵⁰
     ( synch_error; exit )
endproc
```

The two synchronizer processes can now be specified. Since no jitter is
permitted on the sound presentation, the sound synchronizer simply alter-
nates between receiving an s_avail signal and issuing an s_present
signal. (The sound timer handles late sound packets and will report an
s_late_error if necessary.) In contrast, the video synchronizer must
keep a check on the overall synchronization of the presentation and, if it
drifts out of the acceptable bounds, it must report an out of synchronization error. (As with the sound synchronizer, the video timer reports a
v_late_error if a video frame is late.) To achieve this, the sound clock
must be read (using event sound_query) and, depending on its value, the
video synchronizer should either report a synch_error, delay or permit a v_present signal to be sent.

```
process SOUND_SYNCHRONISER[ s_avail, s_present ] : noexit :=
  s_avail; s_present; SOUND_SYNCHRONISER[ s_avail, s_present ]
endproc
```

```
process VIDEO_SYNCHRONISER[ v_avail, v_present, sound_query ]
                           ( v_time:nat ) : noexit :=
  v_avail;
  VIDEO_CHECK[ v_avail, v_present, sound_query ] ( v_time+40 )

where
  process VIDEO_CHECK[ v_avail, v_present, sound_query ]
                     ( v_time:nat ) : noexit :=
    sound_query ?s_time:nat;
```

238

```
( [ s_time-v_time > 150 ] →
      synch_error; exit
  []
  [ v_time-s_time > 15 ] →
    σ ; VIDEO_CHECK [ v_avail, v_present, sound_query ] ( v_time )
  []
  [ not ( s_time-v_time > 150 ) and not ( v_time-s_time > 15 ) ] →
    v_present;
    VIDEO_SYNCHRONISER [ v_avail, v_present, sound_query ]
                        ( v_time )
  )
  endproc (* VIDEO_CHECK *)
endproc (* VIDEO_SYNCHRONISER *)
```

An error handler can now be defined such that, whenever an error is reported (synch_error, s_late_error or v_late_error), a stop signal is sent to both data sources.

```
process ERROR_HANDLER [ s_late_error, v_late_error,
                        synch_error, s_stop, v_stop ] : exit :=
  ( s_late_error; exit
    [] v_late_error; exit
    [] synch_error; exit )
  >>
  ( s_stop; exit ||| v_stop; exit )        (* stop sound and video
  presentations *)
endproc
```

These processes can be combined to give the behaviour of the controller. Initially, the controller must send a start signal to both data sources instructing them to start sending data to the presentation device. The subprocess SYNCHRONISER then considers the two cases where a sound packet is available first and a video frame is available first. In the first case, the SOUND_QUERY process (which keeps track of the time since the sound presentation began) is placed in parallel with the INITIAL_VIDEO_CHECK and SOUND_SYNCHRONISER processes. In the second case, the SOUND_CLOCK process (which awaits a start_clock signal before starting the sound clock) is placed in parallel with the INITIAL_SOUND_CHECK and VIDEO_SYNCHRONISER processes. The behaviour of the two timer processes and the subprocess SYNCHRONISER is then combined and, finally, the resulting behaviour is placed in parallel with the ERROR_HANDLER process.

```
process CONTROLLER [ s_start, v_start, s_avail, v_avail,
                     s_present, v_present, s_late_error,
                     late_error, synch_error, s_stop, v_stop ]
                     : exit :=
```

```
( s_start; exit ||| v_start; exit )   (* start sound and video
                                           presentations *)
  >>
 ( ( SYNCHRONISER  [ s_avail, v_avail, s_present, v_present,
                   synch_error ]
   |[ s_present, v_present ]|
   ( S_TIMER [ s_present, s_late_error ]
      ||| V_TIMER [ v_present, v_late_error ] )
  )
  |[ synch_error, s_late_error, v_late_error ]|
  ERROR_HANDLER [ s_late_error, v_late_error, synch_error,
                  s_stop, v_stop ]
 )
where
 process SYNCHRONISER [ s_avail, v_avail, s_present,
                      v_present, synch_error ] : noexit :=
   s_avail; s_present;       (* sound packet available first *)
    hide sound_query in
    ( SOUND_QUERY [ sound_query ] ( 0 )
    |[ sound_query ]|
    ( INITIAL_VIDEO_CHECK [ v_avail, v_present, sound_query,
                          synch_error ]
      |||
      SOUND_SYNCHRONISER [ s_avail, s_present ]
      ) )
  []
  v_avail; v_present;        (* video frame available first *)
    hide start_clock, sound_query in
    ( SOUND_CLOCK [ start_clock, sound_query ]
    |[ start_clock, sound_query ]|
    ( VIDEO_SYNCHRONISER [ v_avail, v_present, sound_query ] ( 0 )
      |||
    INITIAL_SOUND_CHECK [ s_avail, s_present, start_clock,
                          synch_error ]
    ) )
 endproc (* SYNCHRONISER *)
endproc (* CONTROLLER *)
```

This has completed the definition of all processes involved in the controller for the lip-synchronization algorithm. All that remains is to show the overall behaviour of the specification. In addition to the controller, this behaviour is composed of the two data sources, the two data streams and the presentation device.

```
specification LIPSYNC[ s_start, v_start, s_play, v_play,
                       s_late_error, v_late_error,
                       synch_error, s_stop, v_stop ] : exit
behaviour
  hide s_avail, v_avail, s_present, v_present, s_send, v_send,
       s_rec, v_rec in
  ( CONTROLLER[ s_start, v_start, s_avail, v_avail, s_present,
                v_present, s_late_error, v_late_error,
                synch_error, s_stop, v_stop ]
    |[ s_start, v_start, s_stop, v_stop, s_avail, v_avail,
    s_present, v_present ]|

    (* -- the specifications of the following processes have
    not been presented here -- *)
    ( ( ( SOUND_SOURCE[ s_start, s_send, s_stop ]
        |[ s_send ]|
        SOUND_STREAM[ s_send, s_rec ] )
      |||
      ( VIDEO_SOURCE[ v_start, v_send, v_stop ]
      |[ v_send ]|
        VIDEO_STREAM[ v_send, v_rec ] )
    )
    |[ s_rec, v_rec ]|
    PRESENTATION_DEVICE[ s_rec,  v_rec, s_play, v_play,
                    s_avail, v_avail, s_present, v_present ] )
)
endspec
```

Having specified the lip-synchronization algorithm in Temporal LOTOS, a specification will now be considered using the LOTOS/QTL approach.

12.5   LOTOS/QTL specification

This section describes a LOTOS/QTL specification of the lip-synchronization algorithm. First, the abstract behaviour will be presented. As above, only the behaviour of the controller process will be specified, since it is this that has the job of achieving synchronization between the sound and video streams. However, note that a LOTOS/QTL specification of a multimedia stream has been presented in the previous chapter.

12.5.1   Abstract behaviour

In contrast to the Temporal LOTOS specification given above, the LOTOS specification of the controller is specified at an abstract level, using a non-deterministic choice between different possible behaviours. Importantly, no real-time constraints are considered in this component of the specification. (Real-time will be introduced through the real-time assumptions in the following section.) However, the standard LOTOS events s_delay and v_delay are used to represent a delay (of a variable amount of time) in the specification below. The controller process can be broken down into a number of subprocesses as follows:

```
process CONTROLLER [ s_start, v_start, s_avail, v_avail,
                     s_present, v_present, s_late_error,
                     v_late_error, synch_error, s_stop, v_stop ]
                   : exit :=
  ( s_start; exit ||| v_start; exit ) (* start the sound and
                                          video presentations *)
  >>
  ( ( hide s_delay, v_delay in
    ( SOUND_SYNCHRONISER [ s_avail, s_delay, s_present,
                           s_late_error ]
      |||
        VIDEO_SYNCHRONISER  [v_avail, v_delay, v_present,
                             v_late_error, synch_error ]
    ) )
    |[ synch_error, s_late_error, v_late_error ]|
    ERROR_HANDLER [ s_late_error, v_late_error, synch_error,
                    s_stop, v_stop ]
  )
endproc
```

Comparing this to the Temporal LOTOS specification given above, the process starts in the same way by issuing start signals to the two data sources. However, the main part of the behaviour involves instantiating two synchronizer processes, one for sound and one for video. This is considerably simpler than the corresponding Temporal LOTOS since there is no need for the two timer processes, the initial sound and video check processes or the sound clock and sound query processes. An error handler is then placed in parallel with the sound and video synchronizers (to ensure that when an error is reported, a stop signal is sent to both data sources). The specification of the error handler is identical to the Temporal LOTOS specification presented above and will not be repeated here.

The sound and video synchronizer processes control the receipt of s_avail and v_avail messages and reply (after a possible delay) with s_present and v_present messages. The synchronizer processes may also report an error if an avail message is late or, in the case of the video synchronizer, a synchronization error occurs. Note that since no jitter is permitted on sound data, only video data can cause the presentation to drift out of synchronization. The sound and video synchronizer processes can be specified as shown below.

```
process SOUND_SYNCHRONISER [ s_avail, s_delay, s_present,
                             s_late_error ] : exit :=
  s_avail;
   ( s_present;
     SOUND_SYNCHRONISER  [ s_avail, s_delay, s_present,
                           s_late_error ]
   []
   s_delay; s_present;
     SOUND_SYNCHRONISER [ s_avail, s_delay, s_present,
                          s_late_error ] )
   []
   s_late_error; exit
endproc (* SOUND_SYNCHRONISER *)

process VIDEO_SYNCHRONISER [ v_avail, v_delay, v_present,
                             v_late_error, synch_error ]
                           : exit :=
  v_avail;
   ( v_present;
     VIDEO_SYNCHRONISER [ v_avail, v_delay, v_present,
                          v_late_error, synch_error ]
   []
   v_delay; v_present;
     VIDEO_SYNCHRONISER  [ v_avail, v_delay, v_present,
                           v_late_error, synch_error ] )
   []
   v_late_error; exit
   []
   synch_error; exit
endproc (* VIDEO_SYNCHRONISER *)
```

This completes the abstract behaviour of the controller process. Finally, the specification of the overall behaviour of the lip-synchronization algorithm is identical to the overall behaviour of the Temporal LOTOS specification above and thus will not be repeated.

As can be seen, the LOTOS behaviour is significantly shorter and simpler than the Temporal LOTOS specification. Clearly, however, no reference has been made to real-time and hence lip-synchronization is not achieved if this abstract behaviour is considered alone. It is therefore necessary to consider the second component of the specification in the LOTOS/QTL approach, namely the real-time assumptions.

12.5.2   Real-time assumptions

In the LOTOS/QTL approach, the real-time assumptions ground the time at which events in the abstract specification occur. The real-time assumptions for the controller process will be designed such that the lip-synchronization requirements (presented informally above) hold. More specifically, it is necessary to constrain the behaviour of events in the controller such that sound packets are presented every 30 ms, video frames are presented every 35 ms to 45 ms and video may lag the sound presentation by a maximum of 150 ms and precede it by a maximum of 15 ms. However, it is first necessary to consider some initial conditions.

Initial conditions

Consider the presentation of the initial item of data. When this data arrives at the presentation device, a signal is sent to the controller (either s_avail or v_avail) indicating the availability of data. According to the abstract behaviour presented in the previous section, after receiving an avail signal the controller may either delay or instruct the presentation device to present the data (see the two synchronizer processes). For the very first item of data, a delay should not be permitted and the signal to present the data should be issued immediately, thus ensuring that the presentation actually starts as soon as data are available. This initial condition can be specified in QTL as follows (in all formulae it will be assumed that the unit of time is one millisecond):

- A1.a Presentation of initial sound packet (if it is available before video)

$$\phi_{A1.a}: \quad \Box(\, (\, s\_avail \wedge \neg \Diamond_{\geq 0}(\, s\_avail \vee v\_avail \,)\,) \rightarrow O_{=0}\, s\_present \,)$$

   This states that if a sound packet is available now and no sound or video has previously been available (i.e. this is the first available data item) then this packet must be presented immediately.

The corresponding assumption, regarding the case when a video frame is available first, can be similarly specified:

- A1.b Presentation of initial sound packet (if it is available before video)

$$\phi_{A1.b}: \quad \Box(\, (\, v\_avail \wedge \neg \Diamond_{\geq 0}(\, s\_avail \vee v\_avail \,)\,) \rightarrow O_{=0}\, v\_present \,)$$

   If this video frame is the first available data item, then present the frame immediately.

   Note that the immediacy of the present events in the corresponding Temporal LOTOS specification is achieved through the maximal progress assumption: both s_present and v_present are hidden and hence the maximal progress assumption ensures that they occur as soon as possible (i.e. before the passage of time).

Presentation of Sound Packets

The presentation of subsequent data is governed by the requirements for lip-synchronization as described above. The presentation of sound packets will be considered first. This can be split into three parts: the case when an s_avail signal is early, when it is on time and when it is late. First, if an s_avail arrives early, the controller must delay until 30 ms have passed since the last s_present before issuing the next s_present. Note that the case must also be considered where a synch_error or a v_late_error is reported before (or at) the time of the next s_present. (For brevity, the occurrence of either of these errors is simply denoted error in A2.a and A2.b below.) The occurrence of such an error will cause the presentation to be stopped and thus the next s_present will not occur.

- A2.a Sound packet is available early

$$\phi_{A2.a}: \quad \Box\, V_{t=0}^{29}\, ((\text{s\_avail} \land \Diamond_{=t}\text{s\_present}) \rightarrow$$
$$(O_{=0}\, \text{s\_delay} \land (\Diamond_{=30-t}\text{s\_present} \lor \Diamond_{\leq 30-t}\, \text{error})))$$

In every state in which s_avail occurs and in which there has been an s_present in the last 29ms, the next event (state) must be an s_delay and must occur immediately. Furthermore, in some future state that occurs 30 ms after the previous s_present, there must be another s_present or there must be an error (either synch_error or v_late_error) before or at this time.

The second case to consider is when an s_avail arrives on time (i.e. 30 ms after the previous s_present). In this case, the next s_present should be issued immediately or an error (either synch_error or v_late_error) must occur.

- A2.b Sound packet is available on time

$$\phi_{A2.b}: \quad \Box((\text{s\_avail} \land \Diamond_{=30}\text{s\_present}) \rightarrow O_{=0}\, (\text{s\_present} \lor \text{error}))$$

In every state in which s_avail occurs and in which there has been an s_present 30 ms previously, the next event (state) must be an s_present or an error (either synch_error or v_late_error) and it must occur immediately.

The final case to consider is when an s_avail is late. Since no jitter is permitted on the sound presentation, this represents a sound late error.

- A2.c Sound packet is late

$$\phi_{A2.c}: \quad \Box((\Diamond_{\geq 0}\, (\text{s\_present} \lor \text{v\_present}) \land \Box_{\leq 30}\neg\text{s\_avail}) \rightarrow$$
$$O_{=0}\, \text{s\_late\_error})$$

The first part of this formula ensures that the presentation has started (i.e. there has already been at least one s_present or v_present). If this is the case and there has been no s_avail within the last 30 ms, then an s_late_error must occur immediately.

Comparing these real-time assumptions with the Temporal LOTOS specification, it can be seen that formulae A2.[a-c] correspond to the S_TIMER process (when synchronized with the SOUND_SYNCHRONISER process).

Presentation of video frames

Consider now the presentation of video frames. In this section, a simple strategy for the presentation of video frames will be presented. This strategy corresponds to the behaviour in the Temporal LOTOS specification above and involves presenting the video frames as soon as they become available. A more complex strategy that involves manipulating the time of the presentation to achieve the best possible lip-synchronization will be presented in Section 12.6.3 below.

The presentation of video frames is more complex than the presentation of sound packets since jitter is permitted on the video presentation. Consequently, the controller may issue a v_present signal between 35 ms and 45 ms after the previous v_present. Initially consider the early arrival of a video frame. In this case, a delay must be enforced until 35 ms at which time the video frame can be presented. However, as with the sound presentation above, note that it is necessary to consider the case when an error (either a synch_error or an s_late_error) occurs before, or at, the intended presentation time of the video frame, thus causing the presentation to be stopped. For brevity, the occurrence of one of these errors will simply be denoted error in A3.a and A3.b below.

- A3.a Video frame is available early

$$\phi_{A3.a}: \quad \Box \, V_{t=0}^{34} \, (\, (\, v\_avail \wedge \Diamond_{=t} \, v\_present \,) \rightarrow (\, O_{=0} \, v\_delay \wedge \\ (\, \Diamond_{=35-t} \, v\_present \vee \Diamond_{\leq 35-t} \, error \,) \,) \,)$$

In every state in which a v_avail occurs and in which there has been a v_present in the last 34 ms, the next event (state) must be a v_delay and must occur immediately. There must then either be a v_present signal 35 ms after the previous frame or else an error must occur before, or at, this time.

Note that it would be possible to specify this formula such that there was a non-deterministic choice of the time at which v_present occurred (between 35 ms and 45 ms after the previous v_present). However, the behaviour as presented corresponds to the behaviour of the Temporal LOTOS specification above (in which the maximal progress assumption ensures that v_present occurs as soon as possible).

The case when a video frame arrives on time (i.e. between 35 ms and 45 ms after the previous frame) will now be considered.

- A3.b Video frame is available on time

$$\phi_{A3.b}: \quad \Box \, V_{t=35}^{45} \, (\, (\, v\_avail \wedge \Diamond_{=t} \, v\_present \,) \rightarrow \\ O_{=0} \, (\, v\_present \vee error \,) \,)$$

246

If a v_avail occurs and there has been a v_present in the last 35 ms to 45 ms, then the frame must be presented immediately in the next state or else an error must occur.

The third, and final, part concerns the case when no v_avail has arrived within 45 ms of the previous frame being presented. In this case a v_late_error must occur.

- A3.c Video frame is late

$$\phi_{A3.c}: \quad \Box((\diamondsuit_{\geq 0} (s\_present \lor v\_present) \land \boxminus_{\leq 45} \neg v\_avail) \rightarrow \\ \bigcirc_{=0} v\_late\_error)$$

As with the corresponding formula for sound above, the first part of this statement ensures that the presentation has started. If this is the case and there has been no v_avail within the last 45 ms, then a v_late_error must occur immediately.

Note that, for the presentation of video frames, formulae A3.[a-c] correspond to the V_TIMER process of the Temporal LOTOS specification (when synchronized with the VIDEO_SYNCHRONISER process).

Out of synchronization error

The formulae above have considered the presentation of sound and video data, stating when delays should occur and when data should be presented. They have also considered the late arrival of data and the resulting s_late_error or v_late_error events. The final case to be considered is that of the third type of error: an out of synchronization error (event synch_error). The informal requirements stated that the video presentation should not lag the sound presentation by more than 150 ms and should not precede it by more than 15 ms. It is therefore necessary to keep a check on the cumulative drift of the video presentation from the sound presentation at all times. This can be achieved by declaring a data variable (named v_drift) to measure the drift. Note that the simple notation used in the previous chapter for data variable declarations is not sufficient to define the increment condition of the v_drift variable; a first-order logic has thus been used to specify this condition.

Initial condition: v_drift=0

Reset condition: none

Increment condition:

$$\Box \bigvee_{t=35}^{45}((v\_present \land \diamondsuit_{=t} v\_present) \rightarrow \exists u. (v\_drift = u \land \\ \bigcirc(v\_drift = u+t-40 \land \bigcirc(v\_drift = u+t-40 \; U \; \ominus(v\_present)))))$$

This states that whenever a v_present occurs and another v_present occurred between 35 ms and 45 ms in the past, then, in the next state, the current value of v_drift (i.e. u) is incremented by t–40. The variable v_drift then retains this value until the state following the next v_present (when v_drift will again be updated).

Having defined the `v_drift` variable, it is now possible to specify the formula that constrains the occurrence of an out of synchronization error.

- A4. Video presentation drifts out of synchronization

$$\phi_{A4}: \quad \Box(\,(\,\text{v\_drift}{<}{-}15 \lor \text{v\_drift}{>}150\,) \to O_{=0}\,\text{synch\_error}\,)$$

If the value of the `v_drift` variable exceeds the bounds stated in the informal requirements, then the next event (state) must be a `synch_error` and must occur immediately.

Note that it is the synchronization of the sound and video data that adds much of the complexity to the Temporal LOTOS lip-synchronization algorithm. For example, the processes SOUND_CLOCK, SOUND_QUERY, INITIAL_SOUND_CHECK, INITIAL_VIDEO_CHECK and VIDEO_SYN-CHRONISER all contribute to ensuring that the sound and video presentations remain synchronized within the permitted bounds. In contrast, this can be specified in the LOTOS/QTL approach by the declaration of a data variable to keep track of the cumulative drift of the video presentation from the sound presentation. A single formula (A4) can then be specified that provides a very concise and comprehensive statement of the level of synchronization expected before an out of synchronization error occurs.

12.5.3 Requirements

The three requirements for the lip-synchronization algorithm have been presented informally in Section 12.2 above. These will now be formally specified using QTL. Consider the first requirement that stated that sound packets must be presented every 30 ms. If a sound packet is not presented at this time, then either a `synch_error` or a `v_late_error` must have occurred previously or else an `s_late_error` must occur. This can be expressed in QTL as follows:

- R1. Sound packets presented every 30 ms

$$\phi_{R1}: \quad \Box(\,\text{s\_present} \to (\, \Diamond_{=30}\,(\,\text{s\_present} \lor \text{s\_late\_error}) \lor \\ \Diamond_{\leq30}\,(\text{synch\_error} \lor \text{v\_late\_error}\,)\,))$$

The meaning of this QTL statement follows from the description above.

The second requirement, stating that video frames must be presented between 35 ms and 45 ms after the previous frame, can similarly be expressed using QTL. As above, if no video frame is presented in the required interval and no other error has occurred in this interval, then a `v_late_error` must occur.

- R2. Video frames presented every 35 ms to 45 ms

$$\phi_{R2}: \quad \Box(\,\text{v\_present} \to (\,(V_{t=35}^{45}\,\Diamond_{=t}\,(\,\text{v\_present} \lor \text{v\_late\_error}\,)\,) \lor \\ \Diamond_{\leq45}\,(\text{synch\_error} \lor \text{s\_late\_error}\,)\,))$$

Finally, the third requirement concerning the synchronization of sound and video must be considered. This states that the video presentation must not lag the sound presentation by more than 150 ms and must not precede it by more than 15 ms. This must be true in every state or else a synch_error must occur immediately in the following state. This can be specified as follows:

- R3. Synchronization of sound and video presentation

$$\phi_{R3}: \quad \Box(\ -15 \leq v\_drift \leq 150 \ \vee \ O_{=0} \ synch\_error\ )$$

This completes the specification of the behaviour and the requirements of the lip-synchronization algorithm. In this specification, a simple strategy to obtain lip-synchronization was employed that mirrored the behaviour of the Temporal LOTOS specification. A more complex strategy will be considered in Section 12.6.3 below.

12.6   Comparison

Two specifications of a lip-synchronization algorithm have been presented above: the first used a timed extension to LOTOS, called Temporal LOTOS, and the second used the new approach proposed in this book, based on LOTOS and the real-time temporal logic QTL. This section will compare these two specifications.

12.6.1   Overall comparison

The first point (already made above) concerns the way in which the level of synchronization between the sound and video data is bounded in the two specifications. In the Temporal LOTOS specification, several processes are used to achieve this, while the equivalent information in the LOTOS/QTL approach is specified by the declaration of a data variable and a single logic formula over this variable. This formula provides a very concise and comprehensive statement of the level of synchronization expected before an out of synchronization error occurs and highlights how real-time temporal logics can be used to elegantly express real-time synchronization scenarios. A drawback, however, is that it becomes necessary for the specifier to learn two languages and, more importantly, to learn how to use them together.

A number of additional benefits arise from the separation of concerns in the LOTOS/QTL approach. Returning to the Temporal LOTOS specification, it can be seen that all real-time information is embedded into the processes that make up the lip-synchronization algorithm:

- the sound and video timers specify the time at which s_late_error and v_late_error occur;
- the initial sound (respectively video) check process ensures that the

first sound packet (respectively video frame) arrives within the permitted time interval;

- the sound query process keeps a count of the elapsed time since the first sound packet;
- the video synchronizer consults this elapsed time to determine whether it should delay by one unit of time, present the video frame or report a synchronization error.

In contrast, the real-time information in the LOTOS/QTL specification of behaviour is isolated in the real-time assumptions. These assumptions ground the events occurring in the abstract behaviour in real-time and constrain the non-determinism where necessary (for example, in choosing between presenting some data and reporting an error). One important consequence of this separation is that it results in a clear and concise specification of behaviour that is totally abstract in the sense that it does not contain any performance or implementation considerations. Furthermore, the real-time assumptions are immediately identifiable and can easily be changed if necessary. These two points mean that the specification is more portable: if the performance of the underlying system changes, no modifications are needed to the abstract behaviour and the real-time assumptions are easily identified and modified. An example of this, in which the underlying network can no longer support a jitter-free sound presentation, will be considered in Section 12.6.2 below.

To illustrate the above points, two separate modifications to the lip-synchronization algorithm will now be considered. First, the effect of permitting jitter on the sound presentation will be considered and, secondly, a more complex synchronization strategy will be specified. It is important to stress that both of these changes can be made without affecting the specification of the overall behaviour.

12.6.2 Permitting jitter on the sound presentation

Consider the effect on the two specifications of making a change to the nature of the sound presentation. Suppose that, as before, sound packets are presented every 30 ms, but that a jitter of ±1 millisecond is now permitted. In the Temporal LOTOS specification above, since the sound presentation is "anchored" (i.e. no jitter), the presentation of video frames is measured against the time since the sound presentation began. Therefore, if jitter is permitted on the sound presentation, the specification will require significant changes and restructuring. However, in the LOTOS/QTL specification, this change can easily be accommodated. For example, a new data variable, s_drift, could be defined (to measure the drift of the sound presentation from the expected time) in a similar way to the v_drift variable (see Section 12.5.2 above). The informal requirements stated that the video presentation must not precede the sound presentation by more than 15 ms and should not lag the sound presentation by more than 150 ms. Consequently, the value of v_drift-s_drift must remain within the bounds of −15 ms to 150 ms (for example, if video frames have regularly been presented early such that v_drift = −12 and sound packets have regularly been presented late such that s_drift = +4, the presentation is out of synchronization and an error should be reported). The final real-time assumption (A4) can thus be replaced as follows:

- New_A4. Video presentation drifts out of synchronization

$$\phi_{New\_A4} \colon \quad \square(\ (\ v\_drift-s\_drift<-15 \lor v\_drift-s\_drift>150\ ) \to O_{=0}\ synch\_error\ )$$

If the value of v_drift-s_drift is less than −15 or greater than 150, the next event must be a synch_error and must occur immediately.

12.6.3 Specifying a more complex lip-synchronization strategy

Consider now a more complex lip-synchronization strategy that involves manipulating the time of the presentation to achieve the best possible lip-synchronization. In this section, to keep the new strategy as clear as possible, it will again be assumed that no jitter is permitted on the sound presentation. To achieve the best possible lip-synchronization, if the video presentation is currently ahead of schedule, a delay will be enforced such that v_drift becomes as close to zero as possible. Clearly, however, since frames cannot be presented before they are available, v_drift cannot be corrected if the video presentation is currently behind schedule. In this case, frames should be presented as soon as they are available.

As with the presentation of sound packets, the presentation of video frames can be split into three parts: when a v_avail signal is early, when it is on time and when it is late. With the more complex synchronization strategy, the time at which the video frame should be presented depends

Table 12.1 Time of presentation of video frames.

	Value of v_drift: v_drift>5 (very late)	v_drift<−5 (very early)	−5≤v_drift≤5
time of v_avail (t)	General aim: present frame as soon as possible	hold up frame as long as possible	get v_drift back to zero if possible
v_avail early (t<35 ms after previous frame)	delay, then present 35 ms after previous frame	delay, then present 45 ms after previous frame	delay, then present (40−v_drift) ms after previous frame
v_avail on time (35≤t≤45 ms after frame)	present immediately	delay, then present 45 ms after previous frame	if (40−v_drift)>t then delay and present (40−v_drift) ms after previous frame, else present immediately
v_avail late (t>45ms after previous frame)		v_late_error	

on the value of `v_drift` as shown in Table 12.1.

The formulae below follow the description of behaviour given in this table and provide an alternative to the assumptions A3.[a-c] above. As above, the occurrence of a `synch_error` or an `s_late_error` will simply be denoted `error` in the formulae below.

- Alt_A3.a Video frame is available early

$$\phi_{\text{Alt\_A3.a}}: \quad \Box \, V^{34}_{t=0}(\,(\,\text{v\_avail} \wedge \Diamond_{=t} \text{v\_present}\,) \to (\, O_{=0} \text{v\_delay} \wedge$$
$$(\,\text{v\_drift}>5 \to (\Diamond_{=35-t} \text{v\_present} \vee \Diamond_{\leq35-t} \text{error}\,)\,) \wedge$$
$$(\,\text{v\_drift}<-5 \to (\Diamond_{=45-t} \text{v\_present} \vee \Diamond_{\leq45-t} \text{error}\,)\,) \wedge$$
$$(-5\leq\text{v\_drift}\leq5 \to (\Diamond_{=40-\text{v\_drift}-t} \text{v\_present} \vee \Diamond_{\leq40-\text{v\_drift}-t} \text{error}\,)\,)\,)\,)$$

In every state in which a `v_avail` occurs and in which there has been a `v_present` in the last 34 ms, the next event (state) must be a `v_delay` and must occur immediately. There must then either be a `v_present` signal (the time of which depends on the value of the `v_drift` variable) or else an error must occur.

The case when a video frame arrives on time (i.e. between 35 ms and 45 ms after the previous frame) will now be considered.

- Alt_A3.b Video frame is available on time

$$\phi_{\text{Alt\_A3.b}}: \quad \Box \, V^{45}_{t=35}(\,(\,\text{v\_avail} \wedge \Diamond_{=t} \text{v\_present}\,) \to (\,$$
$$(\,\text{v\_drift}>5 \to (\, O_{=0} \text{v\_present} \vee O_{=0} \text{error}\,)\,) \wedge$$
$$(\,\text{v\_drift}<-5 \to (\, O_{=0} \text{v\_delay} \wedge (\Diamond_{=45-t} \text{v\_present} \vee \Diamond_{\leq45-t} \text{error}))) \wedge$$
$$(-5\leq\text{v\_drift}\leq5 \to (\,$$
$$(40-\text{v\_drift}>t \to (O_{=0}\text{v\_delay} \wedge$$
$$(\Diamond_{=40-\text{v\_drift}-t}\text{v\_present} \vee \Diamond_{\leq40-\text{v\_drift}-t} \text{error}))) \wedge$$
$$(40-\text{v\_drift}\leq t \to (O_{=0}\text{v\_present} \vee O_{=0}\text{error}))\,)\,)\,))$$

If a `v_avail` occurs and there has been a `v_present` in the last 35 to 45 ms, then consider the value of the `v_drift` variable in order to determine whether to delay or present the frame immediately.

The third, and final, part concerns the case when no `v_avail` has arrived within 45 ms of the previous frame being presented. In this case a `v_late_error` must occur. This formula is identical to A3.c, but is included for completeness.

- Alt_A3.c Video frame is late

$$\phi_{\text{Alt\_A3.c}}: \quad \Box(\,(\,\Diamond_{\geq0}(\,\text{s\_present} \vee \text{v\_present}\,) \wedge \Box_{\leq45}\neg\text{v\_avail}\,) \to$$
$$O_{=0} \text{v\_late\_error}\,)$$

The first part of this statement ensures that the presentation has started. If this is the case and there has been no `v_avail` within the last 45 ms, then a `v_late_error` must occur immediately.

12.7   Summary

This chapter has presented two specifications of a lip-synchronization algorithm, one in Temporal LOTOS and the other using the proposed LOTOS/QTL approach. The simple case of jitter being permitted only on the video presentation was initially considered and some comparisons were made between the resulting specifications. This highlighted the fact that the QTL specification of the acceptable bounds on synchronization between sound and video data was very concise and comprehensive when compared with the equivalent information in the Temporal LOTOS specification. However, it was pointed out that, by specifying the real-time assumptions in QTL, it became necessary for the specifier to learn two different languages and to learn how they should be used together.

The chapter then considered the two most significant advantages of the LOTOS/QTL approach. First, by separating out the real-time assumptions, the remaining specification of behaviour is totally abstract in the sense that it does not contain any performance or implementation considerations. Secondly, the real-time assumptions are immediately identifiable and can easily be changed if necessary. As a result of these two points, the specification is more portable: if the performance of the underlying system changes, no modifications are needed to the abstract behaviour and the real-time assumptions are easily identified and modified. To illustrate this point, a change to the initial lip-synchronization problem was considered in which jitter was permitted on the sound presentation as well as on the video presentation. While this would involve significant changes and restructuring in the Temporal LOTOS specification, it was shown how the change could easily be accommodated in the LOTOS/QTL approach without altering the general behaviour.

Finally, it was shown how a more complex synchronization strategy could be incorporated easily into the specification, again without altering the general behaviour. In this strategy, the time of the presentation of video frames is manipulated to achieve the best possible lip-synchronization between sound and video.

PART VI

Conclusions

This part presents the conclusions and consists of one chapter (Ch. 13). This chapter summarises the arguments in the book and highlights the major contributions of the book. The chapter also revisits the requirements from Chapter 4 and presents some future research directions.

CHAPTER 13

Conclusions

13.1   Summary of the book

The central objective of this book has been to investigate the use of formal specification and verification techniques in the application domain of distributed multimedia systems. Particular attention has been focused on the real-time behaviour of such systems, particularly real-time quality of service parameters and real-time synchronization.

To achieve this, it was first necessary to identify the main characteristics of distributed multimedia systems (Pt II, Chs 2 to 4). By considering these characteristics, a number of requirements were identified for formal specification techniques (these will be revisited in Section 13.3 below).

Part III then contained a survey of specification techniques. Chapter 5 considered five main categories of specification techniques, namely specification logics, process algebras, finite state machines, Petri nets and synchronous languages. Chapter 6 then considered the specific languages Estelle, SDL, Esterel and LOTOS. Finally, Chapter 7 focused specifically on the process algebra LOTOS and presented an evaluation of LOTOS-based specification techniques. It initially considered some problems that arose when trying to model time constraints in standard (untimed) LOTOS. The well-known alternating bit protocol was used to provide examples where necessary. Timed extensions to LOTOS were then considered and features such as timestamps versus delay operators and maximal progress versus urgency were discussed and compared. Chapter 7 concluded with a discussion on the conflict between real-time and implementation abstraction. It was argued that, while time is necessary in a formal specification technique for the specification and verification of real-time systems, the inclusion of time in a language compromises abstraction and results in implementation dependent specifications.

Part IV then developed a new approach to the formal specification of distributed multimedia systems. Chapter 8 considered the perceived conflict between real-time and abstraction further and presented a new approach to formal specification, based on the principle of maintaining a separation of concerns. First, a separation was drawn between the specification of behaviour and the specification of requirements and, secondly, a separation was drawn between behavioural (abstract) time and real-time. To reflect this separation of concerns, the new approach was based on three specification components: the abstract behaviour, the real-time assumptions and the requirements. It was described how LOTOS could be used for the specification of the abstract behaviour and how a real-time temporal logic could be used for the specification of the real-time assumptions and requirements. An analysis of this new approach was presented, highlighting a number of benefits as well as some drawbacks. Some related work was then discussed.

In Chapter 9, the design of a real-time temporal logic for the specification of the real-time assumptions and the requirements was considered. A survey was presented that highlighted the expressiveness and decidability of different logics; it was decided to focus on a linear real-time temporal logic that utilized past-tense (as well as future-tense) operators, used a bounded operator notation to express real-time constraints, was based on a discrete time domain and permitted time addition by constant only. The syntax of a new logic, denoted QTL for quality of service temporal logic, was described; semantics (based on timed state sequences) for QTL were then provided.

The process of verification was then discussed in detail in Chapter 10. First, an overview of a verification process suitable for the new approach was presented. Each of the stages of this process were briefly described and the need for two algorithms was highlighted, one to check the satisfiability of a formula and the second to perform model checking. This chapter then detailed a tableau method for a subset of the new logic and presented a proof that, by following this method, a formula could be checked for satisfiability. A model checking algorithm, based on this tableau method, was then described. Following this, extensions to these algorithms were discussed to enable full QTL to be handled. Finally, the chapter considered some alternative techniques for model checking including symbolic model checking.

Part V then provided some examples of the LOTOS/QTL approach. First, some simple examples were presented in Chapter 11. These examples, namely a remote procedure call and a multimedia stream, demonstrated how real-time assumptions could be specified (in QTL) over the abstract behaviour (in LOTOS). Examples of requirements were also given. In Chapter 12, a more complex example was considered. This example, a lip-synchronization algorithm, was initially specified in a timed extension to LOTOS and then specified using the LOTOS/QTL approach. The two resulting specifications were compared and it was shown how extensions such as employing a more complex synchronization policy could easily be accommodated in the LOTOS/QTL approach. These two chapters served as an analysis of the new approach, highlighting benefits of the approach and also some of the drawbacks.

13.2   Contributions of the book

The first contribution of this book has been a detailed analysis of the formal specification and verification of distributed multimedia systems. While other researchers have considered distributed systems, there has been little research into the effect of multimedia on the formal specification and verification of these systems. The book has also highlighted two particularly significant characteristics of multimedia that impose requirements on formal specification techniques, namely the expression of quality of service parameters and real-time synchronization.

The principle of maintaining a separation of concerns has also been investigated in depth and it has been shown that this principle may be applied to provide a framework for the formal specification and verification of distributed multimedia systems. The potential of process algebraic techniques and logics in this framework have also been studied and an approach based on these two techniques developed.

The advantages of applying the principle of maintaining a separation of concerns have been identified:

(a) the specification of behaviour is abstract in that performance or implementation considerations are not embedded,

(b) all timing information is immediately identifiable and can easily be changed (hence, specifications are more portable),

(c) different specification techniques can be used as and where they are most appropriate,

(d) requirements are formally specified (using a temporal logic), and

(e) by using standard LOTOS for the abstract behaviour, existing tools can be used as part of the verification process.

However, some of the drawbacks of the approach are that it is necessary to learn two languages and to understand how they are integrated. More significantly, the overall verification process is considerably more complex than for a single language approach.

13.3   Requirements revisited

Table 13.1 shows how the requirements identified in Chapter 4 have been addressed:

Table 13.1   Summary of requirements.

Requirement:	Addressed by:
Usability and naturalness	Enhanced by maintaining a separation of concerns
Concurrency	Use of LOTOS
Interaction	Use of LOTOS
Openness/inter-operability	Use of LOTOS (through its standardization)
Implementation independent	Provided by maintaining a separation of concerns
Object-based techniques	Only briefly discussed
Dynamic reconfiguration	Only briefly discussed
Co-existence of different languages for different ODP viewpoints	Not addressed
Specification of real-time constraints	Use of QTL (real-time temporal logic)
Specification of probabilistic constraints	Not addressed
Real-time constraints easily identified and changed	Provided by maintaining a separation of concerns
Verification, including real-time constraints	A verification process has been presented for the LOTOS/QTL approach, although problems with data variables have been highlighted

To summarize, LOTOS is recognized as a mature technique providing the necessary features for the specification of concurrent, interacting systems. The use of a separation of concerns also aids the naturalness of specifications by enabling requirements and behaviour to be written in the most appropriate language. The lip synchronization specification provides the best illustration of this point. In addition, the use of standard LOTOS encourages the development of open and interoperable systems. The use of LOTOS also allows the adoption of other results from the LOTOS community, for example object-based techniques and dynamic reconfiguration. The use of QTL then provides a unified way to specify a range of real-time constraints, including both quality of service parameters and real-time synchronization as well as other non real-time constraints. The principle of maintaining a separation of concerns permits the abstract (implementation independent) specification of behaviour and the isolation of all real-time constraints. The issue of verification has also been addressed although some problems remain unresolved. The final two requirements regarding ODP viewpoints and probabilities have not been addressed and will be discussed in the following section.

13.4   Directions for future research

13.4.1   Introducing probabilities

A first direction for future research concerns the introduction of probabilities into a dual language framework. In Hansson (1991), a number of reasons are presented for the inclusion of probabilities in formal specification techniques, including:

- most existing formal techniques only permit the concept of *unreliability* to be specified as a possibility of failure; probabilities are required to accurately model this unreliability;
- probabilities can be used to model *fairness*, for example by interpreting a fair choice between two alternatives as "there is a non-zero probability for each alternative"; and
- by combining the use of real-time and probabilities, *performance properties* such as "the probability of an event occurring within 2 seconds is 98%" can be specified.

It would therefore be interesting to consider how probabilities could be incorporated into the LOTOS/QTL approach. Applying the principle of maintaining a separation of concerns, probabilities can also be isolated from the abstract behaviour of a system. One way to achieve this would be to develop a real-time probabilistic logic, similar to TPCTL (Hansson 1991), to replace the use of QTL.

A further reason for the introduction of probabilities is the potential of deriving performance models directly (rather than using another notation, such as queueing models). Future work could consider the derivation of such models from an extended LOTOS/QTL approach.

Note that early work addressing the above topics is reported in Lakas et al. (1996a,b). In particular, their work describes probabilistic and stochastic extensions to QTL and associated procedures either to derive performance models for simulation, or to carry out model checking. Interestingly, the inclusion of probabilities and stochastic distributions removes the need for data variables and enables a more correct specification of error rates (overcoming two of the limitations of QTL).

13.4.2   Further development of verification tools

A second valuable direction would be to extend the tools for the LOTOS/QTL approach. As mentioned in Chapter 10, a tool has already been developed to check the satisfiability of a formula (based on the tableau method). However, because of problems highlighted with data variables, this tool (and the underlying technique) only applies to a subset of QTL, denoted QTL$^-$. From the examples in Chapters 11 and 12, it can be seen that data variables are required for the specification of quality of service and real-time synchronization constraints; however, their inclusion appears to make QTL undecidable. Further research is therefore needed to try and resolve the conflict between the expressibility and the decidability of QTL.

It would also be interesting to develop a tool to perform the model checking component of the LOTOS/QTL verification process. However, this relies on the construction of a tableau from the QTL formula, as in the satisfiability check, and hence runs into the same problems detailed above.

Given the theoretical difficulties with verification, an alternative approach to model checking would be to develop a tool based on the analysis of finite length traces as discussed in Section 10.5. Clearly, such an approach cannot generate a formal proof, but may give some level of confidence that a given property holds over a specification.

A further area of research would be to develop a simulation tool based on a probabilistic extension to the LOTOS/QTL approach as discussed above. Such a tool would provide a pragmatic approach to the validation of quality of service and real-time synchronization constraints in distributed multimedia systems.

13.4.3 Relationship of the new approach with ODP

Chapter 8 (Section 8.3.2) presented a brief discussion on applying the new approach to the specification of ODP systems from a computational perspective. It would also be interesting to consider the impact of the dual language techniques on the other ODP viewpoints. However, this raises issues of the consistency of a system specification across different viewpoints (Bowman et al. 1996b). In particular, the consistency problem is significantly complicated by the possibility of different viewpoints being specified in different languages, e.g. the computational viewpoint in LOTOS and the information viewpoint in Z.

Initial work on this topic has clarified the basic interpretation of cross-viewpoint consistency (Bowman et al. 1996a, b) and shown that, in a formal setting, consistency relationships across language boundaries can be defined. For example, it is shown in Derrick et al. (1996) how to relate LOTOS and Z specifications. In terms of multimedia, the work on consistency has identified two specific requirements that must be addressed in ODP:

    i. to provide a uniform treatment of quality of service across ODP viewpoints, and

    ii. to integrate this treatment with consistency checking in a formal setting.

The LOTOS/QTL approach provides a valuable starting point for this research.

13.5   Concluding remarks

Formal specification techniques have played an important role in the development of communication protocols and distributed systems. However, these techniques must now evolve to meet the new challenge of distributed multimedia computing. This book has investigated the implications of multimedia for formal specification and verification techniques. A new approach to formal specification has been developed, based on the principle of maintaining a separation of concerns, and a number of benefits and drawbacks have been identified. A number of crucial areas of future research have also been identified.

APPENDIX A

Some notes on terminology

A.1 Introduction

As computer systems have become more complex (through the incorporation of such properties as concurrency, distribution and real-time), classification of the properties of systems and especially the correctness properties of systems has become important. The correctness properties of traditional computing were straightforward: (1) are the correct results being output?, and (2) will the program terminate? Succinct mathematical theories to express the properties of traditional systems and assess whether they meet these two criteria have been developed, e.g. denotational semantics (Stoy 1977), axiomatic semantics (Hoare 1969, Dijkstra 1975, de Bakker 1980) and operational semantics (Pagan 1981). A wealth of semantic models for more complex modern systems have been developed, for example, labelled transition systems (Keller 1976), extended finite state machines (Danthine 1982) and Petri nets (Reisig 1985). Associated with these new theories is terminology to classify systems and their correctness properties. This terminology is however not used uniformly and many researchers use terms rather idiosyncratically. This appendix seeks to define precisely the terms that are used in this book to classify systems and their correctness properties.

A.2 System classifications

A.2.1 Functional and non-functional

This distinction is used inconsistently throughout the literature. In fact, there are two clearly different usages. The first is a literal interpretation in terms of *mathematical functions* and the second is a non-literal interpretation, which categorizes different classes of system description. We will distinguish these here as *strong functional* and *weak functional* respectively.

Strong functional
This distinction is obtained from elementary mathematical theory. *Strong functional* in a computational sense means adhering to the properties of mathematical functions:

Definition 1:   Strong functional

> *A computation is strong functional if it can be directly modelled as a mathematical function, i.e. the results of the computation are uniquely determined by its data inputs.*

In particular, this definition requires that the top level behaviour of a system must be directly expressible as a mathematical function from the inputs of the system to its outputs. Such a top level function will classically be defined itself in terms of functions, which express how a computation changes from state to state.

- Example
  Systems that can be modelled using Scott/Strachey (Stoy 1977) denotational semantics are strong functional in nature, since the heart of the Scott/Strachey approach is to model computation as mathematical functions from program states to program states. Thus, programs written in simple sequential programming languages such as Pascal and Algol 60 are strong functional.

Definition 2:   Non-strong functional

> *A computation is non-strong functional if it cannot be modelled directly as a mathematical function.*

- Example
  A non-deterministic system cannot be directly modelled as a function and is more appropriately viewed as a mathematical relation (we will return to this point shortly).

Weak functional
This alternative interpretation is commonly used in the distributed systems environment. The distinction is between a computation that can be expressed solely in terms of ordering and one which cannot be so expressed. By ordering, we mean specification in terms of the relative order of system events, i.e. using operators such as sequence, choice, concurrency, etc. Importantly this class of specification does not contain quantitative time

constraints; it is purely in terms of qualitative time. What we call ordering is often called temporal ordering, e.g. in the name LOTOS (Language Of Temporal Ordering Specification) or temporal logic. However, we will avoid this term as the word temporal causes confusion with quantitative time specification.

Definition 3:   Weak functional

A computation is weak functional if it can be modelled purely in terms of ordering.

- Example
  Many concurrent and distributed systems are weak functional, e.g. the dining philosophers' problem or mutual exclusion problem.

Definition 4:   Non-weak functional

A computation is non-weak functional if it cannot be modelled purely in terms of ordering.

- Example
  All real-time systems are non-weak functional in nature, since quantitative time constraints must be incorporated into a complete description of the system.

Parts of systems can be weak functional, while other parts can be non-weak functional. As a reflection of this, the development of the weak functional part of a complex system is frequently separated from the development of the non-weak functional part.

As suggested by the names we have used, all strong functional systems are weak functional, but not the other way around. An illustration of this is that the weak functional category includes non-deterministic computation, while such computations are not directly expressible as a function. The distinction between strong and weak functional is depicted in Figure A.1.

In order to remain consistent with the majority of workers in distributed systems, in the main text of this book we have used the terms functional and non-functional in the typical distributed systems sense. So, any reference to functional and non-functional in the main body of the book means weak functional in the sense of this subsection. In order to facilitate comparison between the different interpretations of functional and other classes of system, we will use the terms strong functional and weak functional throughout the remainder of this appendix.

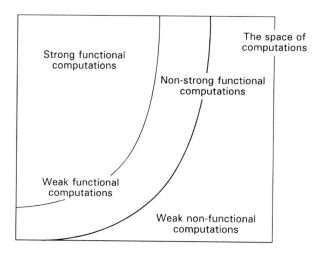

Figure A.1   The relationship between weak and strong functional.

A.2.2   Deterministic and non-deterministic

The terms non-functional and non-deterministic are often used inter-changeably. However, although they are related, they have very different meanings. Non-deterministic is correctly defined as follows:

Definition 5:   Deterministic

> *A computation is deterministic if it yields the same results for the same set of inputs whenever it is performed.*

The behaviour of a deterministic system does not vary on repeated execution, i.e. a system will produce the same result for a particular set of inputs on every "run" (every time at which the inputs are made) of the system.

Definition 6:   Non-deterministic

> *A computation is non-deterministic if it does not satisfy definition 5.*

- Example
  A flight simulator may non-deterministically decide either to alter the wind speed affecting the plane or to simulate a snow storm.

Typically, in formal models of concurrency, the interplay between the observer (or environment) of a system and the system itself characterizes the deterministic or non-deterministic nature of the computation. If all possible choices between alternative paths through a computation are under the control of the external observer, then the system is deterministic. However, if the choice between certain alternative paths is hidden from the observer, i.e. is internal to the computation, then the system is non-deterministic. Such non-determinism classically manifests itself by an observer performing a particular interaction with the system (e.g. pressing an input button) and the system choosing internally and, hence, non-deterministically, to behave in one of a number of alternative ways. This, for example, is the interpretation of deterministic and non-deterministic choice employed in process algebras.

Most end systems do although need to be deterministic. Therefore, the main value of non-determinism is in system development. Specifically, non-determinism is used by system designers in order to give *abstraction* and particularly abstraction away from implementation issues (Hoare 1985). A classic example of use of non-determinism is in modelling a communications medium. Such systems offer complex internal behaviour that, if completely specified, would be enormously complex and would probably require the physical laws of noise and attenuation on signals to be described. Thus, specifications are typically abstracted away from this complexity by modelling loss and duplication of messages as internal non-deterministic options. The observers of the medium, the sender and receiver processes, interact with the medium by sending respectively receiving messages, but they have no influence over whether the medium relays the message correctly, loses it or duplicates it.

Non-deterministic computation is non-strong functional, as a particular input to a non-deterministic system may have distinct images (non-deterministic computation can be more appropriately viewed in terms of mathematical relations). However, it is not the case that all non-strong functional systems are non-deterministic. For example, Petri nets define non-strong functional concurrent computation but are deterministic. In fact, most concurrent and distributed systems are deterministic. The justification for concurrent systems being non-strong functional is that they inherently involve *ongoing* interaction between parallel components and their environment (which may be another component). Thus, they are not naturally viewed as simple state transforming functions.

In contrast, non-deterministic behaviour can be expressed as ordering, as is typical in a process algebra, so weak functional behaviour can be non-deterministic. Figure A.2 depicts the relationship between determinism and functionality.

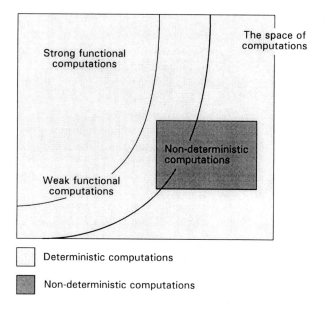

The space of computations

Strong functional computations

Non-deterministic computations

Weak functional computations

☐ Deterministic computations

▦ Non-deterministic computations

Figure A.2   The relationship between functionality and determinism.

A.2.3   Transformational and reactive

A distinction closely related to the above, is that between transformational and reactive systems. These terms were coined by Manna and Pnueli and their book (Manna & Pnueli 1992) presents an in-depth discussion of the terms.

Definition 7:   Transformational

> *A transformational system produces a final result at the end of a terminating computation, i.e. the system possesses a predefined final state.*

- Example
  Simple sequential programs are transformational; for example, a sequential program written in Pascal to evaluate factorial n and then terminate is transformational.

Crucially, transformational programs are evaluated in three consecutive parts. First, the environment and program interact by instantiating inputs to the program. Secondly, the program computes, completely independently of the environment, until it terminates. Thirdly, and finally, the environment and program interact once again, by passing the program results to the environment.

Definition 8:   Reactive

> *Reactive systems maintain an ongoing interaction with their environ-*
> *ment. Reactive systems cannot be specified in terms of a relationship*
> *between initial state and final state (even if it were a non-deterministic*
> *relationship).*

- Example
  Good examples are real-time control systems, such as a power station
  control system or an avionics system. Operating systems are also
  examples of reactive systems.

Reactivity can also be explained in terms of concurrent behaviour. In
these terms a program is said to be transformational if the program and the
environment act sequentially, while a program is said to be reactive if program and environment act concurrently. This close relationship between
concurrency and reactivity will be emphasized further in the next section.

A.2.4   Concurrency, distribution and real-time

Many different types of system are being developed by the modern computer scientist. Some of the most interesting are concurrent systems, distributed systems and real-time systems. All three of these system types are
relevant to this book. Thus, this section seeks to highlight the characteristics of these different types of system, by relating them to the terms highlighted in the previous three sections. This section will be structured as
a series of examples of different types of computation, the characteristics
of which will be highlighted. The level of complexity of computation
increases through the examples.

- Example 1
  A sequential program to evaluate $n!$ and then terminate is *strong func-*
  tional and *transformational*.
- Example 2
  Consider a parallel program to evaluate $n!$ using divide and conquer
  as a black box where the parallel process communicates via shared
  memory. The behaviour of the complete program is transformational
  and strong functional, because its external behaviour should be the
  same as Example 1. However, the internal behaviour is not so simple.
  The internal communication between parallel processes required to
  realize this computation implies that the program is inherently reactive and thus not transformational or strong functional.
- Example 3
  Consider a solution to the dining philosophers problem where there is
  some interaction between the system and its environment (perhaps a

signal is passed to the environment whenever the bowl of rice needs to be replenished). This is a distributed system containing ongoing communication between concurrent components both internally and externally. Thus, the behaviour of this system can be viewed to be in all senses reactive.

- Example 4

Consider the dying dining philosophers problem (Stankovic & Ramamritham 1988). This is an example of a concurrent computation with communication that also possesses real-time characteristics. Specifically, if philosophers do not eat according to a specified time constraint, they die. Such a system is reactive, but in addition its reactivity is time constrained. Thus, if it does not respond to interaction with its environment in a timely manner, its behaviour is unsatisfactory, e.g. Aristotle dies. This is an example of a reactive, non-weak functional system.

A.3   True concurrency and interleaving

The semantics of formal description languages are defined by mapping the operators in the language to a model of concurrent systems; there are many such underlying models. These models can be classified according to the means by which they model choice and the means by which they model concurrency.

There are three classes of concurrency model (in increasing order of expressiveness): *linear time*, *branching time* and *true concurrency* models[1]. Linear time models express semantics as the set of all computations of a given program, where each computation is expressed as a linear sequence of states the program can pass into on execution. Branching time models express semantics as a tree of states, where each node (representing a state) has as direct descendants all states derivable from the state on execution. These two forms of semantics are similar in the sense that they both model concurrency as *interleaving*, by expressing parallel execution as a choice of possible interleaved executions. However, they are distinguished by their interpretation of choice. Linear time semantics cannot distinguish different classes of branching point (classically varieties of deterministic and non-deterministic choice) while branching time semantics can.

Since both linear time and branching time models express concurrency as choice and sequence (through interleaving) neither distinguishes these distinct phenomena. True concurrency semantics have thus been developed in order to realize such a distinction. True concurrency models typically use a structure of states over which two relations are defined, one

---

1. Note time here has no relation to quantitative time.

precedence (which constrains events to occur only following other events), the other conflict (which is true for events that cannot occur within the same execution). In such models events that are not related (by precedence or conflict), i.e. are independent, are seen as concurrent. Such independence distinguishes concurrency from choice and sequence, which are represented using conflict and precedence.

Definition 9: Interleaving

Interleaving models concurrency as a choice of possible sequential executions.

Definition 10: True concurrency

In true concurrency approaches, parallelism is modelled independently of sequence and choice. In a typical approach two relations, precedence and conflict, are incorporated; events that are not related are seen as concurrent.

True versus interleaved modelling of concurrency has fuelled the debate between the *intensionalists* and *extensionalists* in concurrency theory. The latter approach has been advocated by a number of notable researchers (Hoare 1985, Milner 1989, Manna & Pnueli 1992) on the grounds that the meaning of concurrent systems should be expressed in terms of how a system can be observed by a notional environment, i.e. a system observational or experimental behaviour. This interpretation also relates to the view of reactive systems as passive until operated upon. Such an observational interpretation prompts an interleaved interpretation of concurrency.

However, the intensionalists argue that viewing concurrency as choice and sequence represents over-specification of the actual behaviour of the system. Partial order semantics enable causal relationships (dependence and independence of events) to be represented explicitly, and causally independent events are not mapped into a linear timescale. Importantly, concurrency is represented independently of choice. It should be noted that the fair transition systems of Manna & Pnueli (1992) represent a compromise between interleaving and true concurrency. Specifically, they use fairness criteria (justice and compassion) to constrain pure interleaving, only allowing certain, more realistic, interleaved traces.

A.4 Synchronous and asynchronous

The distinction between synchronous and asynchronous (applied to systems and models of concurrency and distribution) is used extensively in writings on the subject. However, the terms are not used completely consistently. The following subsection seeks to address this confusion.

A.4.1 Definitions

There are two clear and distinct circumstances in which the terms synchronous and asynchronous can be applied:
1. in communication; and
2. in parallel behaviour (order of process execution).
The two cases will be considered in turn.

A.4.1.1 Communication

Communication between independently (and concurrently) executing processes can be either synchronous or asynchronous. Synchronous communication occurs if there is an instant of common interaction between the communicating parties, i.e. the exchange of communication forces a common computation time instant. Under asynchronous communication no such common interaction point is enforced and there is an indeterminable delay (buffering) involved in sending a message. This distinction is summarized below:

Definition 11: Synchronous communication

In synchronous communication, there is a common interaction point between the sender and receiver; at this instant they exchange data.

Definition 12: Asynchronous communication

In asynchronous communication, the sender places data into a buffer; at some point in the future, the receiver can obtain the data from this buffer.

Synchronous communication is also often called rendezvous communication. This however is not a completely satisfactory usage since the term rendezvous (as found in ADA) refers to a very different communication semantics (remote procedure call style interaction). In agreement with Andrews (1991), we use the above definitions.

According to these descriptions it should be apparent that the communication mechanism offered by LOTOS is synchronous and the communication mechanism offered by ESTELLE and SDL is asynchronous.

A.4.1.2   Parallel behaviour

Many different parallel execution orders can be found in concurrent systems. The terms synchronous and asynchronous can be used to define two particular classes of parallel behaviour:

1. Synchronous parallel behaviour

   In this class of behaviour (also called lock step), concurrent threads are tied and the order of event execution in parallel processes is synchronized. Execution of events is simultaneously initiated in parallel processes and the events complete simultaneously. Thus, as with synchronous communication, synchronous parallel behaviour implies waiting between processes if parallel events execute at different speeds. This class of parallel behaviour generally implies a common (global) clock according to which event execution is determined, i.e. parallel processes execute time dependent upon one another.

2. Asynchronous parallel behaviour

   In this class of behaviour, concurrent threads execute completely independently of one another. There is no relationship between the ordering and time of execution of processes/events that are found in different parallel threads. Asynchronous parallel behaviour often implies absence of a common (global) clock that determines timing; parallel threads possess their own localized notion of time.

The use of the terms synchronous and asynchronous parallel behaviour is captured below:

Definition 13:   Synchronous parallel behaviour

Synchronous execution implies that concurrent events are simultaneously initiated and simultaneously completed according to a global clock.

Definition 14:   Asynchronous parallel behaviour

Asynchronous execution implies that concurrent events execute independently of each other.

ESTELLE offers both asynchronous and synchronous parallel behaviour. Asynchronous behaviour arises between systems and synchronous behaviour occurs when the attribute process is associated with modules on the same level.

The LOTOS parallel operators (| |, | [..] | and | | |) define asynchronous parallel behaviour. In fact, process algebras generally define asynchronous parallel behaviour. An exception is SCCS (Milner 1983) that incorporates the × synchronous parallel behaviour operator.

A.4.2   Variations on a theme I

In the literature there is a further use of the terms asynchronous and synchronous execution in the realm of programming real-time systems. A number of researchers interested in real-time system design have called their programming languages synchronous (Berry & Gonthier 1988). This term has been used since their languages are based upon what they call the *synchrony hypothesis*. This hypothesis states that all events occur instantaneously and no time passes between events occurring. Thus all events are notionally synchronized in time, although they may be distinguished by ordering. This concept has been found to be of value in real systems in which certain portions of the system evaluate so quickly as compared to other parts of the system that such a hypothesis can be applied. This use of the term synchronous is summarized below:

Definition 15:   Synchrony hypothesis

With the synchrony hypothesis, all events occur instantaneously and no time passes between events occurring.

Asynchronous within this domain is used to describe parts of systems that cannot be made to satisfy the synchrony hypothesis. These parts exhibit unpredictable latency, i.e. it is impossible to give a precise time bound within which a communication will complete. This clearly has a close relationship to the classical asynchronous communication definition. However, the usage has been arrived at from a different direction to that in classical usage. Berry et al. use the synchronous/asynchronous distinction as a means of classifying the characteristics of a class of computer systems (distributed real-time systems) that they are trying to build. One of many mechanisms could be used to build these systems. In particular, either asynchronous or synchronous parallel behaviour may be used or asynchronous or synchronous communication.

A.4.3   Variations on a theme 2

The terms asynchronous and synchronous message passing are sufficient to describe most models of distributed systems. However, in distributed multimedia systems, it is necessary to add an extra term to capture the style of message passing associated with continuous media. With continuous media, it is important to preserve certain temporal properties of the data across a communication. These properties are known as quality of service parameters and include the throughput, jitter and latency on the communication. Continuous media communications are not synchronous as there is a delay between the sending and the receiving of data. However, this is not asynchronous communication as there is an implicit timing relationship between the two parties. We introduce the following term to cover continuous media communications:

Definition 16:   Isochronous communication

> *Isochronous communication means that, in spite of asynchronous networks, you retain a strict real-time relationship between the end points of the transmission.*

This reflects the situation in, for example, a video conference where the video frames captured at one end of a communication must be played out at precisely the same rate at the other end of the communication.

Strictly speaking, this is not possible in a communications network owing to variable delays, packet loss, etc. Therefore, continuous media communications aim for this ideal but accept that variations will occur. The term isochronous is however in standard usage in the distributed multimedia community for this approximation to the ideal.

A.5   Correctness properties

As indicated at the beginning of this appendix, the correctness properties of traditional sequential programs are easy to define, consisting of two elements: the correctness of the final results and the termination properties. However, the correctness properties of the more complex systems being considered in this book are not so straightforward to express. A number of classes of correctness property have been highlighted in the literature. This section seeks to review and clarify the terminology associated with these classes.

The classic work on defining the classification properties of concurrent systems arose within the temporal logic community and very succinct and elegant expressions of these properties can be made in temporal logic. However, the discussion presented here will avoid such formalisms and only intuitive expressions of these properties will be made.

A.5.1   Safety and liveness properties

These two classes of correctness property have gained wide acceptance in the field of concurrent and distributed programming. However, it should be noted that a different categorization was used in Manna & Pnueli (1992). We will, however, concentrate on the classic safety/liveness distinction.

Definition 17: Safety

If a property P is true at all points in a computation, it is a safety property.

The intuitive characterization of a safety property is that "nothing bad will ever happen". The following are all examples of safety properties:
1. Partial correctness
   The classic partial correctness property from sequential computing is a safety property. It states that every terminating computation terminates in the required state.
2. Guaranteeing mutual exclusion
   Mutual exclusion is concerned with ensuring that the *critical sections* of concurrently executing processes that execute shared objects are not executing at the same time. Guaranteeing mutual exclusion is a safety property.

Definition 18: Liveness

If a property is true at least once, infinitely many times or continuously from a certain point in a computation then it is a liveness property.

The intuitive characterization of liveness properties is that "something good will eventually happen". Examples of liveness properties include:
1. Total correctness
   The sequential computing property of total correctness is a liveness property. Total correctness states that every computation terminates in the required state.
2. Fairness properties
   These are a classic example of liveness properties. Fairness defines conditions on the progress of parallel processes, i.e. that all processes will eventually progress. A number of fairness properties exist, some are highlighted below.
3. Justice (or weak fairness)
   This is the minimal level of attention that needs to be paid to a process to avoid starvation. A computation is *just* if it is not the case that a process is continually, beyond some point, in a state where it wishes to proceed without being taken. Manna and Pnueli use justice to distinguish between non-determinism and concurrency; justice applies to concurrent processes, but not to non-deterministic processes.
4. Compassion (or strong fairness)
   A computation is compassionate if it is not the case that a process is infinitely often in a state where it wishes to proceed without being taken. Compassion is a stronger form of fairness since the continuously enabled has been replaced by the infinitely often enabled.

5. Freedom from starvation

This property is an expression of fairness within the domain of shared resources. Specifically, freedom from starvation strengthens mutual exclusion by adding the condition that any process that wants to will eventually be able to access the shared resource.

A.5.2 Timeliness properties

Safety and liveness are classic correctness criteria for concurrent and distributed systems. However, such criteria are not sufficient when real-time systems are being considered. In such environments, a notion of timeliness must also be incorporated. A fundamental classification of timeliness properties (such as safety/liveness) has not been accepted within the real-time domain. Thus, the definition in this section is necessarily less precise than those appearing in the previous section.

Definition 19: Timeliness

> *If a property is true at a specific instance of time, within or throughout a specified period of time in a computation then it is a timeliness property.*

The form of both liveness and safety can be taken by timeliness properties. In fact, Alur & Henzinger (1991) even suggest that equivalent propositions expressed in two different real-time logic notations could resemble a liveness property in one and a safety property in the other.

Two commonly highlighted forms of timeliness properties are, *bounded-response* properties and *bounded-invariance* properties. The former assert that "something good" will happen within a specified period of time, while the latter assert that "nothing bad" will happen during a specified period of time. The following are examples of these two forms of timeliness property:

1. If the condition that, if Aristotle does not eat within 20 hours of last eating he will die, is added to the classic dining philosophers problem, the resulting dying dining philosophers (Stankovic & Ramamritham 1988) is a real-time problem. A solution to this problem may concern itself with the following kinds of assertion:

   i. Aristotle will always restart eating within 20 hours of stopping eating.

   ii. Whenever fork 1 is picked up it is not requested by another philosopher during the next 25 minutes (the time it takes for a philosopher to eat a sufficiency).

   (i) is an example of a bounded-response property, while (ii) is an example of a bounded-invariance property.

2. Timeliness properties can be highlighted from the failure of the London ambulance control system.

    i. An ambulance will always pick up the patient within 20 minutes of the corresponding 999 call.

    ii. Whenever a 999 call is received it is not the case that all ambulances are unavailable during the next 5 minutes.

    (i) is an example of a bounded-response property, while (ii) is an example of a bounded-invariance property.

With regard to validation, validation of non-real-time systems is concerned with *safety* and *liveness* properties, while validation of real-time systems is also concerned with *timeliness* properties.

A.5.3   Maximal progress/urgency

In timed concurrency models the relationship between event occurrence, especially communication events, and the passage of time is crucial. In particular, it is important that the passage of time has a lower priority than the acceptance of a communication. If this were not the case it would be possible for a process to continue to idle even though it could perform a communication.

The concepts of *maximal progress* and *action urgency* are two possible mechanisms by which the passage of time can be given a lower priority than the occurrence of events. This is a very natural property for a timed concurrency model to possess. However, the semantic models of a number of FDTs have been found not to possess such a property. This is particularly the case with the interleaving models of concurrency underlying classical untimed process algebras. In these models it is possible for events to be facilitated and yet not be selected. This can make it very difficult (and often impossible) to model real-time behaviour (see Ch. 7).

Definition 20:   Maximal progress

> *Internal events, that is those that can no longer be influenced by the environment, occur "as soon as possible".*

Note that maximal progress is also sometimes referred to under the names maximal parallelism, minimum delay or the ASAP (as soon as possible) principle. Importantly, maximal progress applies only to internal (or hidden) events; their execution is not unnecessarily delayed. The view is taken that observable events can always be influenced (e.g. delayed) by the environment and consequently their occurrence cannot be forced.

An alternative approach to maximal progress is provided by the concept of *action urgency*. There are two distinct ways in which urgency can be applied to a specification. The first of these is detailed in Leduc & Léonard

(1993). In this approach, *all* actions (except those that *explicitly* permit time to pass) must occur before the next delay action. A second approach, proposed in Bolognesi & Lucidi (1992), allows a more flexible specification of urgent actions. A new operator called *urgency*, denoted $\rho(U)$ (where U is a list of event gates) is introduced to express the fact that each of the given actions (or interactions) in U must be performed urgently, as soon as all the involved parties are ready. Note that, unlike maximal progress, action urgency can be applied to internal and external events alike.

A.6 Summary

The areas of concurrent, distributed and real-time programming are fraught with terminology difficulties. This is a major problem for workers in the field. To minimize the terminology difficulties for this book, this appendix has defined a set of terminology to be used throughout. Terminology has been introduced for various system properties, for styles of communication and execution and, finally, for correctness properties. These definitions are summarized in Table A.3.

Table A.3 Summary of terminology

Term	Definition
1. Strong functional	A computation is strong functional if it can be modelled as a mathematical function, i.e. the reults of the computation are uniquely determined by its data inputs.
2. Non-strong functional	A computation is non-strong functional if it cannot be modelled as a mathematical function, i.e. the results of the computation are uniquely determined by its data inputs.
3. Weak functional	A computation is weak functional if it can be modelled purely in terms of ordering.
4. Non-weak functional	A computation is non-weak functional if it cannot be modelled purely in terms of ordering.
5. Deterministic	A computation is deterministic if it yields the same results for the same set of inputs whenever it is performed.
7. Non-deterministic	A computation is non-deterministic if it can yield different results on different executions with the same inputs.
8. Reactive	Reactive systems maintain an ongoing interaction with their environment and cannot be specified in terms of a relationship between initial state and final state.
9. Interleaving	Interleaving models concurrency as the choice of possible interleaved sequential executions.
10. True concurrency	True concurrency is typically defined by two relations: precedence and conflict; events that are not related by either are interpreted as concurrent.
11. Synchronous communication	In synchronous communication, the sender and receiver meet at some point in time and at that instant exchange data.
12. Asynchronous communication	In asynchronous communication, the sender places data into a buffer; at some point in the future, the receiver can obtain the data from this buffer.
13. Synchronous execution	Synchronous execution implies that concurrent events are simultaneously initiated and simultaneously complete according to a global clock.
14. Asynchronous execution	Asynchronous execution implies that concurrent events execute independently of each other.
15. Synchrony hypothesis	With the synchrony hypothesis, all events occur instantaneously and no time passes between events occurring.
16. Isochronous communication	Isochronous communication means that, in spite of asynchronous networks, you retain a strict real-time relationship between each end of the transmission.
17. Safety property	If a property P is true at all points in a computation then it is a safety property.
18. Liveness property	If a property is true at least once, infinitely many times or continously from a certain point in a computation then it is a liveness property.
19. Timeliness property	If a property is true at a specific instance of time, within or throughout a specified period time in a computation then it is a timeliness property.
20. Maximal progress	Internal events, that is, those that can no longer be influenced by the environment, occur "as soon as possible".

Multimedia stream specifications

B.1. Multimedia stream in Estelle

This specification of the stream is limited due to space considerations. In particular, the error behaviour is unsatisfactorily expressed. A manager could be incorporated that restarts the stream transmission and handles the error behaviour. In addition, the behaviour of the sink process is not optimal. Specifically, when transition T8 fires, we would like not only to move into state RECEIVE and wait for the current frame to arrive, but also to start a timer associated with the arrival of the next frame. This timer would count down 50 ms from the point T8 fires. The next frame should arrive within 10 ms of this 50 ms timer expiring. This is difficult to do and would require dynamic creation of parallel threads. Thus, we have taken a simpler, but non-optimal, solution, which is to start the 50 ms timer from the point we go back into WAITING, i.e. when T9 fires. According to this solution the allowed interval of arrivals could drift out with regard to the jitter constraint on latency.

```
specification Stream;
{ This is a multimedia stream specification in Estelle. }
{ The timescale we are using is milliseconds. }

default individual queue;

const maxtrans = 20;      {the maximum number of transmissions
                           that could possibly be in the queue
                           at one time.}

channel SourceOut (sender,receiver);
  by sender : frame (frno : integer);
```

```
channel intracchannel (cha,transfr);
 by cha : requesttrans (frno : integer);
 by transfr : finishedtrans (frno : integer);

channel SinkIn (sender,receiver);
 by sender : frame (frno : integer);

{------------------ source ------------------------}

module source systemprocess;

ip Outchannel : Sourceout (sender);
end;

body sourcebody for source;

state START, SENDING;
var fr_no : integer;
initialize to START
 begin end;

trans
from START
 to SENDING
  delay(5)        {Delay in generating first frame}
   name T0 : begin
    output Outchannel.frame(1);    {Send first frame}
     fr_no:=2
   end;
from SENDING
 to SENDING
  delay(50)          {Frame delay}
   name T1 : begin
    output Outchannel.frame(fr_no);   {Send a frame}
     fr_no:=fr_no+1
    end;

end;    {module source}

{--------------- cchannel ---------------------}

module cchannel systemprocess;

ip inchan : SourceOut (receiver);   outchan : SinkIn (sender);
end;

body cchannelbody for cchannel;

  {-------------- child process of cchannel -------------}
  module transmitfr process;
```

```
  ip chan : intracchannel (transfr);
  export done:boolean;
end;

body transmitfrbody for transmitfr;
state WAITING,SENDING;
var fr_no:integer;
initialize to WAITING
 begin
   done:=false
 end;

trans
from WAITING
 to SENDING
   when chan.requesttrans(frno)
     name T2 : begin
       fr_no:=frno
     end;

from SENDING
 to WAITING
   delay(80,90)   {the latency value imposed on the channel}
     name T3 : begin
       output chan.finishedtrans(fr_no);
       done:=true  {indicate process can be released}
     end;

   end;   {of module transmitfr}

{ Main body of the cchannel module starts here }

ip subchan : array[1..maxtrans] of intracchannel (cha);

modvar transf:transmitfr;

state TRANSMIT;
var i: integer;

initialize to TRANSMIT
 begin
   i:=1;
 end;

trans
from TRANSMIT to same
 when inchan.frame(frno)
   name T4 : begin
     init transf with transmitfrbody;
```

```
      connect subchan[i] to transf.chan;
      output subchan[i].requesttrans(frno);
      all transmitfrbody:transmitfr do
      if transmitfrbody.done then release transmitfrbody;
      if (i=maxtrans) then i:=1 else i:=i+1;
    end;

from TRANSMIT to same
  any j:1..maxtrans do
    when subchan[j].finishedtrans(frno)
      name T5 : begin
        output outchan.frame(frno);
      end;

end;    {of module cchannel}

{------------------ Sink ------------------------}

module sink systemprocess;

ip Inchannel : Sinkin (receiver);
end;

body sinkbody for sink;

state START, WAITING, RECEIVE, ERRORSTATE;
initialize to START
  begin  end;

trans
from START
 to WAITING
   when Inchannel.frame(frno)
     name T6 : begin
       {wait 5ms and play frame frno}
     end;

 to ERRORSTATE
   delay(95)
     name T7 : begin
       {latency error on first transmission}
     end;

from WAITING
 to RECEIVE
   delay(50)    {wait until next frame is needed}
     name T8 : begin
       {need a frame now or in the next 10ms}
```

```
    end;

from RECEIVE
 to WAITING
   when Inchannel.frame(frno)
     name T9 : begin
       {wait 5 ms and play frno}
     end;

 to ERRORSTATE
   delay(10)
     name T10 : begin
       {timeout the frame has arrived too late}
     end;

from ERRORSTATE
 to ERRORSTATE
   name T11 : begin
     {notify error and wait for restart}
   end;

end;    {of module sink}

{------------------ Main body --------------------}

modvar   sourcenode:source;  chnl:cchannel;   sinknode:sink;

initialize
begin

   init sourcenode with sourcebody;
   init chnl with cchannelbody;
   init sinknode with sinkbody;

   connect sourcenode.Outchannel to chnl.inchan;
   connect chnl.outchan to sinknode.Inchannel;

end;

end.
```

B.2.   Multimedia stream in SDL

Owing to space limitations a number of aspects of the full stream specification have not been incorporated. First, we have not implemented the 5 ms processing delays in the sink and source; it would be straightforward to extend the specification with timers to incorporate these two delays. In addition, the allowed interval of arrivals could drift out with regard to the jitter constraint on latency, for the same reason that it can in the Estelle specification.

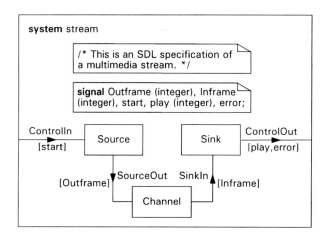

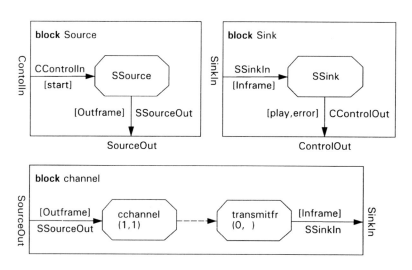

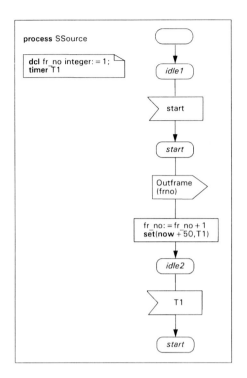

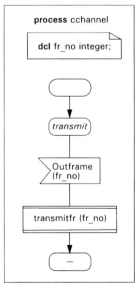

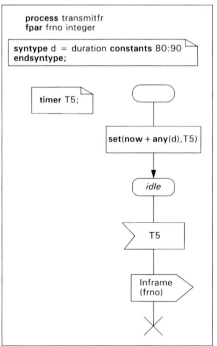

289

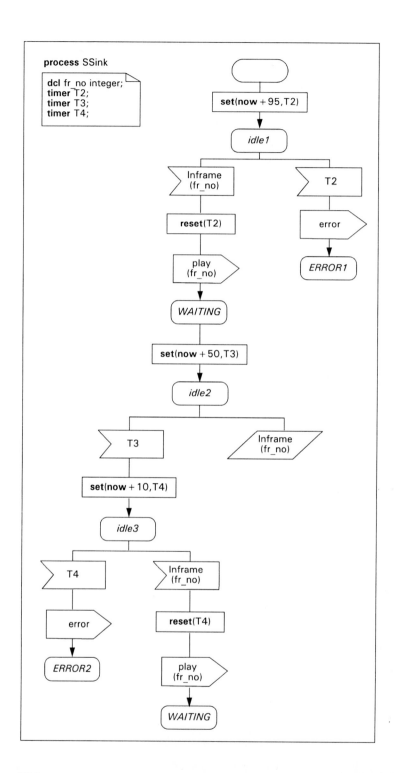

290

B. 3.   Multimedia stream in Esterel

Once again we have not implemented the 5 ms processing delays in the sink and source and the allowed interval of arrivals could drift out with regard to the jitter constraint on latency.

```
% --------------- source ----------------------

module source :

type elt_type;

function elt (integer): elt_type;

input   CLOCKTICK;           % One CLOCKTICK = one millisecond

output  SourceOut (elt_type);    % The output signal with value
frame no+

% behaviour of source

var fr_no := 2: integer in
  emit SourceOut (elt (1));         %send first frame
  every 50 CLOCKTICK do
    emit SourceOut (elt (fr_no)); %send a frame
    fr_no := fr_no + 1
  end   %every block
end     %var block
      %end of source module

% --------------- channel ----------------------
module channel:
constant TRUE: boolean, FALSE: boolean;
type elt_type, queue_elem, queue_type;
input CLOCKTICK, SourceOut (elt_type);
output SinkIn (elt_type);

function new_queue (): queue_type; % These are externally
                        %defined data manipulation functions
function top (queue_type): queue_elem;
function add_last (queue_elem, queue_type): queue_type;
function remove_top (queue_type): queue_type;
function empty (queue_type): boolean;
function calc_delay (queue_elem, integer): integer;
function make_pair (elt_type, integer): queue_elem;
function fst (queue_elem): elt_type;

                                  % THREAD 1
signal CurrentDate (integer) in [   % This thread issues a
                                  % signal defining the
```

```
                                    % current time
  var cur: integer in [            % according to some external
                                    % CLOCKTICK signal
   every CLOCKTICK do cur := cur + 1; emit CurrentDate (cur) end
  ] end % var
  ||                                % THREAD 2
  signal UpdateQueue, RemoveTop,    % This thread places input
                                    % frames into the queue
    TopQueue (queue_elem), NextWait (integer) in [
   every SourceOut do emit UpdateQueue end % every
    ||                              % THREAD 3
    var queue: queue_type, NewWait: boolean in [
                                    % This thread handles the
                                    % queue manipulation and
     queue := new_queue ();         % evaluating when the
     every UpdateQueue do [         % next frame should be emitted
      NewWait := FALSE;
      present SourceOut then
        if (empty (queue)) then NewWait := TRUE end; % if
        queue := add_last (make_pair (?SourceOut, ?CurrentDate),
        queue);
      end; % present
      present RemoveTop then
        queue := remove_top (queue);
        if (not (empty (queue))) then NewWait := TRUE end; % if
      end; % present
      if (NewWait) then
        emit TopQueue (top (queue));
 (*)    emit NextWait (calc_delay (?TopQueue, ?CurrentDate))
      end % if
     ] end % every
    ] end % var
    ||                              % THREAD 4
    var ToBeSent: elt_type in [     % This thread emits frames
                                    % from the channel
     loop
      await immediate NextWait;
      ToBeSent := fst (?TopQueue);
      await (?NextWait) CLOCKTICK;
      emit UpdateQueue; emit SinkIn (ToBeSent); emit RemoveTop
     end % loop
    ] end % var
  ] end % signal
] end % signal
```

292

```
%--------------------- sink ----------------------
module sink:

type elt_type;

input   CLOCKTICK, SinkIn (elt_type);
output  Play (elt_type), ERROR;

% behaviour of sink

 do
  await SinkIn;
  emit Play (?SinkIn)
 watching 95 CLOCKTICK timeout emit ERROR end;

  await 50 CLOCKTICK;
  loop
   do
    await SinkIn;
    emit Play (?SinkIn)
   watching 10 CLOCKTICK timeout emit ERROR end % frame too late
  end % loop
   % end of module sink

%------------------- stream ----------------------
module stream :

type elt_type;

input   START, STOP, CLOCKTICK; % start the stream transmission
output  Play (elt_type);        % play a frame

% behaviour of stream (this is the top level behaviour of the
% specification)

await START;
do
 trap error in
  signal SourceOut (elt_type), SinkIn (elt_type), ERROR in
  [
   copymodule source
   ||
   copymodule channel
   ||
   copymodule sink
   ||
   [ await ERROR; exit error ]
  ]
```

293

```
    end    %signal block
    handle error do  nothing end % resolve error
  watching STOP
    % module stream
```

B.4.   Multimedia stream in LOTOS

```
specification stream [start,play,error]:noexit
library  Boolean,NaturalNumber  endlib
type BBuffer is NaturalNumber
sorts buffer
opns
    nil : -> buffer
    add : Nat , buffer -> buffer
    fst : buffer -> Nat
    rmv : buffer -> buffer
eqns forall x,y : Nat,   z : buffer
    ofsort Nat
    fst(nil) = 0;
    fst(add(x,nil)) = x;
  fst(add(x,add(y,z))) = fst(add(y,z));

    ofsort buffer
    rmv(nil) = nil;
    rmv(add(x,nil)) = nil;
  rmv(add(x,add(y,z))) = add(x,rmv(add(y,z)));
endtype

behaviour
hide SourceOut,framedelay,latencydelay,SinkIn,
     timeout1,timeout2,timeout3 in
  ( start;
    ( source[SourceOut,framedelay](succ(0))
     |[SourceOut]|
      channel[SourceOut,latencydelay,SinkIn](nil)
     |[SinkIn]|
      sink[SinkIn,play,timeout1,timeout2,timeout3,error] )    )
  where

    (* ----------- source ------------------------ *)
  process source[SourceOut,framedelay](fr_no:Nat):noexit:=
   generation_delay!fr_no; (* Indicates delay in generating
                                   frame. *)
```

```
    SourceOut!fr_no;
    framedelay; (* Indicates 50 ms delay *)
    source[SourceOut,framedelay] ( succ(fr_no) )
  endproc (* source *)

  (* ----------- channel ------------------------- *)
  process channel[SourceOut,latencydelay, SinkIn]
                 (buf:buffer):noexit:=
    (SourceOut?fr_no:Nat;
     channel[SourceOut,latencydelay,SinkIn](add(fr_no,buf)) )
    []
    [fst(buf) ne fst(nil)] ->
       (latencydelay!fst(buf);    (* Indicates 80 ms to 90 ms
                                      latency delay *)
       SinkIn!fst(buf);
       channel[SourceOut,latencydelay,SinkIn](rmv(buf)))
  endproc (* channel *)

  (* ----------- sink ------------------------- *)
  process sink[SinkIn,play,timeout1,timeout2,timeout3,
               error]:noexit:=

    ( SinkIn?fr_no:Nat; (* first frame arrived *)
      processingdelay!fr_no; (* time involved in processing
                                frame *)
      play!fr_no;
      waiting[SinkIn,play,timeout2,timeout3,error]
    []
      timeout1;error;stop     (* latency error *)
    )
    where
      process waiting  [SinkIn,play,timeout2,timeout3,
                        error]:noexit:=
      timeout2;    (* ready to receive a frame *)
       (SinkIn?fr_no:Nat;
        processingdelay!fr_no;
        play!fr_no;
        waiting[SinkIn,play,timeout2,timeout3,error]
       []
        timeout3; error; stop   (* frame too late *)
        )
    endproc (* waiting *)
  endproc (* sink *)

endspec
```

B.5.   Multimedia stream in LOTOS-T

In the following specification we assume that all actions that are not timed behave as ordinary LOTOS actions, i.e. they are offered continuously from the point they become enabled. The specification fully reflects the assumptions and requirements laid out (except it may let the allowed interval of arrivals drift out with regard to the jitter constraint on latency).

```
specification stream [start,play,error]:noexit
library  Boolean,NaturalNumber  endlib
timedef sort Nat
 opns  + for +
         0 for 0
         > for gt
enddef

behaviour
hide SourceOut,SinkIn in
 ( start;
    ( ( SourceOut!0 {5}; source[SourceOut](succ(0))
     ||| sink[SinkIn,play,error]  )
    |[SourceOut, SinkIn]|
       channel[SourceOut,SinkIn]  )  )
  where

   (* ------------ source ----------------------- *)
   process source[SourceOut](fr_no:Nat):noexit:=
    SourceOut!fr_no {50}; (* transmit frame with delay 50 ms. *)
    source[SourceOut]( succ(fr_no) )
   endproc (* source *)

   (* ------------ channel ---------------------- *)
   process channel[SourceOut,SinkIn]:noexit:=
    SourceOut?fr_no:Nat;
    ( ( choice t:Nat [] [79<t< 91] -> i {t}; SinkIn!fr_no; stop )
      |||
      channel[SourceOut,SinkIn]   )
   endproc (* channel *)

   (* ------------ sink ------------------------- *)
   process sink[SinkIn,play,error]:noexit:=
    ( SinkIn?fr_no:Nat;       (* first frame arrived *)
     ( play!fr_no {5}; stop
      |||
       waiting[SinkIn,play,error]  )  )
    []
```

```
    i {95}; error; stop       (* latency error *)
  where
   process waiting[SinkIn,play,error] :noexit:=
    i {50};       (* delay before inputting next frame *)
     ( SinkIn?fr_no:Nat; ( play!fr_no {5}; stop
                            |||
                           waiting[SinkIn,play,error] )
      []
       i {10}; error; stop  )   (* frame too late *)
    endproc (* waiting *)
   endproc (* sink *)

endspec
```

Bibliography

Abrial, J. R. 1996. *The B-book: assigning programs to meanings.* Cambridge: Cambridge University Press.

Accetta, M., R. Baron, D. Golub, R. Rashid, A. Tevanian, M. Young 1986. *Mach: a new kernel foundation for UNIX development.* Technical report, Department of Computer Science, Carnegie Mellon University.

Ahuja, S. R., J. R. Ensor, D. N. Horn 1988. The rapport multimedia conferencing system. In *Proceedings of the Conference on Office Information Systems (COIS '88)*, R. B. Allen (ed.), 1–8. New York: ACM.

Alur, R. & T. A. Henzinger 1989. A really temporal logic. In *Proceedings of the Thirtieth Annual Symposium on Foundations of Computer Science*, Z. Galil (ed.), 164–69. Los Alamitos, Calif.: IEEE Computer Society Press.

Alur, R. & T. A. Henzinger 1990. Real-time logics: complexity and expressiveness. *Proceedings of the Fifth Annual IEEE Symposium on Logic in Computer Science*, 390–401. Philadelphia: IEEE Computer Society Press.

Alur, R. & T. A. Henzinger 1991. Logics and models of real time: a survey. In *REX workshop on real-time: theory in practice*, J. W. deBakker, C. Huizing, W. P. de Roever, G. Rozenberg (eds), 74–106. Berlin: Springer.

Alur, R. & T. A. Henzinger 1994. A really temporal logic. *Journal of the ACM* **41**(1), 181–204.

Alur, R., C. Courcoubetis, D. L. Dill 1990. Model checking for real-time systems. In *Proceedings of the Fifth Annual IEEE Symposium on Logic in Computer Science*, 414–25. Philadelphia: IEEE Computer Society Press.

Alur, R., T. Feder, T. A. Henzinger 1991. The benefits of relaxing punctuality. In *Proceedings of the Tenth Annual ACM Symposium on Distributed Computing*, L. Logrippo, 139–52. New York: ACM

Anderson, D. P., Y. Osawa, R. Govindan 1992. A file system for continuous media. *ACM Transactions on Computer Systems* **10**(4), 311–37.

Andreu, M., M. Haziza, C. Jard, J-M. Jezequel 1993. Analyzing a space protocol: from specification, simulation to experimentation. In *Proceedings of the Fifth International Conference on Formal Description Techniques (FORTE '92)*, M. Diaz & R. Groz (eds), 195–206. Amsterdam: Elsevier.

Andrews, G. R. 1991. *Concurrent programming: principles and practice.* Redwood, California: Benjamin Cummings.

APM 1993. *ANSAware 4.1 application programming in ANSAware.* Document RM.102.02. Cambridge: APM Cambridge Ltd.

Baguette, Y. 1992. *TPX Specification.* OSI 95 report, ULg-5/R/V1, University of Liège, Belgium.

Bannon, L. & K. Schmidt 1991. CSCW: Four characters in search of context. In *Studies in computer supported cooperative work. theory, practice and design,* J. M. Bowers & S. D. Benford (eds), 3–16. Amsterdam: North Holland.

Bates, P. C. & M. E. Segal 1990. Touring machine: a video telecommunications software testbed. In *Proceedings of the First International Workshop on Network and Operating System Support for Digital Audio and Video (NOSSDAV '90).* University of California, Berkeley.

Beckwith, R., D. G. Jameson, W. Tuck 1990. Distance learning and LiveNet. *The Computer Bulletin* **2**(5), 2–4.

Bentley, R., J. Hughes, D. Randall, T. Rodden, P. Sawyer, I. Sommerville, D. Shapiro 1992. Ethnographically informed systems design for air traffic control. In *Proceedings of CSCW '92,* M. Mantel, R. Baecker (eds), 123–9. New York: ACM.

Benveniste, A., & P. L. Guernic 1991. Synchronous programming with events and relations: the signal language and its semantics. *Science of Computer Programming* **16**, 103–49.

Bergstra, J. A. & J. W. Klop 1986. Process algebra: specification and verification in bisimulation semantics. In *Mathematics and computer science II, CWI Monographs* **4**. M. Hazewinkel, J. K. Lenstra, L. G. L. T. Meertens (eds), 61–94. Amsterdam: North Holland.

Berners-Lee, T., R. Cailliau, A. Luotonen, H. F. Nielsen, A. Secret 1994. The worldwide web. *Communications of the ACM* **37**(8), 76–82.

Berra, P. B., C. Y. R. Chen, A. Ghafoor, C. C. Lin, T. D. C. Little, D. Shin 1990. Architecture for distributed multimedia database systems. *Computer Communications* **13**(4), 217–31.

Berry, G. & G. Gonthier 1988. *The ESTEREL synchronous programming language: design, semantics, implementation.* INRIA report 842, Institute Nationale de Recherche en Informatique et Automatique (INRIA).

Berryman, S. 1993. *Modeling and evaluating timing constraints in real-time systems.* PhD thesis, Department of Computing, University of Lancaster.

Blair, G. S., A. Campbell, G. Coulson, F. García, D. Hutchison, A. Scott, W. D. Shepherd 1993. A network interface unit to support continuous media. *IEEE Journal of Selected Areas in Communications (JSAC)* **11**(2), 264–75.

Blair, G. S., J. Gallagher, D. Hutchison, D. Shepherd (eds) 1991. *Object-oriented languages, systems and applications.* London: Pitman.

Blair, L., G. S. Blair, H. Bowman, A. Chetwynd 1995. Formal specification and verification of multimedia systems in open distributed processing. *Computer Standards and Interfaces* **17**, 413–36.

Blair, G. S., L. Blair, J.-B. Stefani 1996. A specification architecture for multimedia systems in open distributed processing. *Computer Networks and ISDN Systems,* in press.

Blattner, M. M. & R. B. Dannenberg (eds) 1992. *Multimedia interface design.* New York: ACM.

Blattner, M. 1994. *In our image: interface design in the 1990s.* IEEE Multimedia **1**(1), 25–36.

Bolognesi, T. & E. Brinksma 1988. Introduction to the ISO specification language LOTOS. *Computer Networks and ISDN Systems* **14**(1), 25–59.

Bolognesi, T. & F. Lucidi 1991. Timed process algebras with urgent interactions and a unique powerful binary operator. In *REX workshop on real-time: theory in practice,* J. W. deBakker, C. Huizing, W. P. deRoever, G. Rozenberg (eds), LNCS 600, 124–48. Berlin: Springer.

Bolognesi, T. & F. Lucidi 1992. LOTOS-like process algebras with urgent or timed interactions. In *Proceedings of the Fourth International Conference on Formal Description Techniques (FORTE '91),* K. R. Parker & G. A. Rose (eds), 249–64. Amsterdam: Elsevier.

Bolognesi T., E. Brinksma, C. A. Vissers (eds) 1992. *Proceedings of the Third LotoSphere workshop and seminar,* unpublished.

Bolognesi, T., F. Lucidi, S. Trigila 1990. From timed petri nets to timed LOTOS. In *Tenth International IFIP Symposium on Protocol Specification, Testing and Verification,* L. Logippo, R. Probert, H. Ural (eds), 395–408. Amsterdam: Elsevier.

Bolognesi, T., F. Lucidi, S. Trigila 1994. Converging towards a timed LOTOS standard. *Computer Standards and Interfaces* **16**, 87–118.

Borenstein, N. 1993. MIME: a portable and robust multimedia format for internet mail. *Multimedia* **1**(1), 29–36.

Bowman, H., G. S. Blair, L. Blair, A. G. Chetwynd 1994. Time versus abstraction in formal description. In *Proceedings of the Sixth International Conference on Formal Description Techniques (FORTE '93),* R. L. Tenney, P. D. Amer, M. Ü. Uyar (eds), 467–82. Amsterdam: Elsevier.

Bowman, H., G. S. Blair, L. Blair, A. G. Chetwynd 1995a. Formal description of distributed multimedia systems: an assessment of potential techniques. *Computer Communications* **18**(12).

Bowman, H., J. Derrick, P. Linington, M. W. A. Steen 1995b. FDTs for ODP. *Computer Standards and Interfaces* **17**, 457–79.

Bowman, H., E. A. Boiten, J. Derrick, M. W. A. Steen 1996a. Viewpoint consistency in ODP, a general interpretation. In *Proceedings of the First IFIP Workshop on Formal Methods for Open Object-based Distributed Systems,* E. Najm & J-B. Stefani (eds), 191–206. Paris: Ecole Nationale Supérieure des Télécommunications (ENST).

Bowman, H., J. Derrick, P. Linington, M. W. A. Steen 1996b. Cross viewpoint consistency in open distributed processing. *Software Engineering Journal* **11**(1), 44–57.

Brailsford, D. F. & R. J. Beach 1989. Electronic publishing – a journal and its production. *The Computer Journal* **32**(6), 482–93.

Bricker, A., M. Gien, M. Guillemont, J. Lipkis, D. Orr, M. Rozier 1991. Architectural issues in microkernel-based operating systems: the CHORUS experience. *Computer Communications* **14**(6), 347–57.

Brookes, S. B., C. A. R. Hoare, A. W. Roscoe 1984. A theory of communicating sequential processes. *Journal of the Association of Computing Machinery* **31**(3), 560–99.

Budkowski, S. & P. Dembinski 1987. An introduction to Estelle: a specification language for distributed systems. *Computer Networks and ISDN Systems* **4**, 3–23.

Bulterman, D. C. & R. van Liere 1992. Multimedia synchronisation and UNIX. In *Proceedings of the Second International Workshop on Network and Operating System*

Support for Digital Audio and Video (NOSSDAV '91), R. G. Herrtwich (ed.), 108–19. Berlin: Springer.

Campbell, A., G. Coulson, F. García, D. Hutchison 1992. A continuous media transport and orchestration service. *ACM SIGCOMM Computer Communications Review* **22**(4), 99–110. New York: ACM.

CCITT 1988. *Recommendation Z.100: specification and description language SDL*. AP IX -35. Geneva: International Consultative Committee for Telephony and Telegraphy.

Chen, P. M., E. K. Lee, G. A. Gibson, R. H. Katz, D. A. Patterson 1994. RAID: High-performance, reliable secondary storage. *ACM Computing Surveys* **26**(2), 145–85.

Chesson, G. 1988. XTP/PE overview. In *Proceedings of the Thirteenth IEEE Conference on Local Computer Networks*, 292–6. Los Alamitos: IEEE.

Christodoulakis, S. & S. Graham 1988. Browsing within time-driven multimedia documents. In *Proceedings of the ACM Conference on Office Information Systems*, R. Allen (ed.), 219–27. New York: ACM.

Christodoulakis, S., M. Theodoridou, F. Ho, M. Papa, A. Pathria 1986. Multimedia document presentation, information extraction, and document formation in MINOS: a model and a system. *ACM Transactions on Office Information Systems* **4**(4), 345–83.

Clark, D. D., M. L. Lambert, L. Zhang 1987. NETBLT: A high throughput transport protocol. *Computer Communication Review* **17**(5), 353–9.

Clark, D. D. et al. 1991. *The AURORA gigabit testbed:*. Internal report, Bellcore, New Jersey.

Clark, R. G. 1992. *LOTOS design-oriented specifications in the object-based style*. Technical report TR 84, Department of Computing Science and Mathematics, University of Stirling.

Clarke, E. M., E. A. Emerson, A. P. Sistla 1986. Automatic verification of finite state concurrent systems using temporal logic specifications. *ACM Transactions on Programming Languages and Systems* **8**(2), 244–63.

Coolahan, J. E. & N. Roussopoulus 1983. Timing requirements for time-driven systems using augmented Petri nets. *IEEE Transactions on Software Engineering* **9**(5), 603–16.

Coulson, G. , G. S. Blair, P. Robin 1994. Micro-kernel support for continuous media in distributed systems. *Computer Networks and ISDN Systems* **26**, 1323–41.

Coulson, G., G. S. Blair, N. Davies, N. Williams 1992. Extensions to ANSA for multimedia computing. *Computer Networks and ISDN Systems* **25**, 305–23.

Coulson, G., G. S. Blair, F. Horn, L. Hazard, J. B. Stefani 1995. Supporting the real-time requirements of continuous media in open distributed systems. *Computer Networks and ISDN Systems* **27**(8).

Courtiat, J.-P. 1989. A petri net based semantics for Estelle. In *The formal description technique Estelle*, M. Diaz, P-P. Ansart, J-P. Courtiat, P. Azema, V. Chari (eds), 353–71. Amsterdam: Elsevier.

Crowley, T., E. Baker, H. Forsdick, P. Milazzo, R. Tomlinson 1990. MMConf: an infrastructure for building shared multimedia applications. In *Proceedings of the Conference on Computer Supported Cooperative Work (CSCW '90)*, F. Halasz (ed.), 329–42. New York: ACM.

Danthine, A. A. S. 1982. Protocol representation with finite state models. *Computer network architectures and protocols*, P. E. Green Jr (ed.), 579–606, New York: Plenum.

Davies, J. 1993. Specification and proof in real-time CSP. In *Distinguished dissertations in computer science*. New York: Cambridge University Press.

Davies N. A. & J. R. Nicol 1991. A technological perspective on multimedia computing. *Computer Communications* **14**(5), 260–72.

de Bakker, J. W. 1980. *Mathematical theory of program correctness*. London: Prentice-Hall.

de Boer, F. & J. Hooman 1992. The real-time behaviour of asynchronously communicating processes. In *Proceedings of the Second International Symposium on Formal Techniques in Real-Time and Fault-Tolerant Systems*, J. Vytopil (ed.), 451–72. Berlin: Springer.

de Prycker, M. 1989. Evolution from ISDN to B-ISDN: a logical step towards ATM. *Computer Communications* **12**(3), 141–6.

de Prycker, M. 1991. *Asynchronous transfer mode: solution for broadband ISDN*. New York: Ellis Horwood.

Derrick, J., E. A. Boiten, H. Bowman, M. W. A. Steen 1996. Supporting ODP – translating LOTOS to Z. In *Proceedings of the First IFIP Workshop on Formal Methods for Open Object-based Distributed Systems*, E. Najm & J-B. Stefani (eds), 419–34. Paris: Ecole Nationale Supérieure des Télécommunications (ENST).

de Saqui-sannes, P. D. & J. P. Courtiat 1989. Rapid prototyping of an Estelle simulator: ESTIM. In *The formal description technique Estelle*, M. Diaz, P-P. Ansart, J-P. Courtiat, P. Azema, V. Chari (eds), 353–71. Amsterdam: Elsevier.

Dijkstra, E. W. 1975. Guarded commands, non-determinacy, and formal derivation of programs. *Communications of the ACM* **18**(8), 453–7.

Dijkstra, E. W. 1976. *A discipline of programming*. Englewood Cliffs, New Jersey: Prentice-Hall.

Dourish, P. & S. Bly 1992. Portholes: supporting awareness in a distributed work group. In *Proceedings of CHI '92 (Human factors in computing systems)*, May 3–7, P. Bauersfeld, J. Bennett, G. Lynch (eds), 541–7. New York: ACM.

Drayton, L., A. Chetwynd, G. S. Blair 1991. An introduction to LOTOS through a worked example. *Computer Communications* **15**(2), 70–85.

Eertink, H. 1992. Executing LOTOS specifications: the SMILE tool. In *Proceedings of the third LOTOSPHERE workshop and seminar*, vol 1.T. Bolognesi, E. Brinksma, C. A. Vissers (eds).

Ehrig, H. & B. Mahr 1985. *Fundamentals of algebraic specification 1*. Berlin: Springer.

Ellis, C. A. & S. J. Gibbs 1989. Concurrency control in groupware systems. *ACM SIGMOD Record* **18**(2), 399–407.

Emerson, E. A. 1990. Temporal and modal logic. In *Handbook of theoretical computer science (vol. B)*, J. van Leeuwen (ed.) 995–1072. Amsterdam: Elsevier.

Emerson, E. A. & J. Y. Halpern 1986. "Sometimes" and "not never" revisited: on branching versus linear time temporal logic. *Journal of the ACM* **33**(1), 151–78.

Emerson, E. A., A. K. Mok, A. P. Sistla, J. Srinivasan 1991. Quantitative temporal reasoning. In *Second International Conference on Computer-Aided Verification (CAV '90)*, LNCS 531, 136–45. Berlin: Springer.

Eriksson, H. 1994. MBONE: The multicast backbone. *Communications of the ACM* **37**(8), 54–60.

Ernberg, P., T. Hovander, F. Monfort 1993. Specification and implementation of an ISDN telephone system using LOTOS. In *Proceedings of the Fifth International Con-*

ference on Formal Description Techniques (FORTE '92), M. Diaz & R. Groz (eds), 179–94. Amsterdam: Elsevier.

Fahlén, L. E., C. G. Brown, O. Stahl, C. Carlsson 1993. A space based model for user interaction in shared synthetic environments. In *Proceedings of InterCHI '93*, S. Ashlund, A. Henderwson, E. Hollnagel, K. Mullet, T. White (eds), 43–8. Amsterdam: IOS Press.

Fantechi, A., S. Gnesi, C. Laneve 1990a. An expressive temporal logic for basic LOTOS. In *Proceedings of the Second International Conference on Formal Description Techniques (FORTE '89)*, S. T. Vong (ed.), 383–99. Amsterdam: Elsevier.

Fantechi, A., S. Gnesi, G. Ristori 1990b. Compositional logic semantics and LOTOS. In *Proceedings of the Tenth International IFIP Symposium on Protocol Specification, Testing and Verification (PSTVX)*, L. Logrippo, R. L. Probert, H. Ural (eds), 365–78. Amsterdam: Elsevier.

Færgemand, O. & A. Olsen 1992. New features in SDL-92. Presented as a tutorial at the *Fifth International Conference on Formal Description Techniques (FORTE '92)*, M. Diaz & R. Groz (eds).

Fernandez, J. C. & L. Mournier 1990. *ALDÉBARAN: user's manual*. Internal report, Laboratoire de Genie Informatique, Institut IMAG. Grenoble, France.

Fernandez, J., D. Vazquez & J. Vinyes 1992. Io: An Estelle simulator for performance evaluation. In *Proceedings of the Fourth International conference on Formal Description Techniques (FORTE '91)*, K. R. Parker & G. A. Rose (eds), 51–66. Amsterdam: Elsevier

Ferrari, D., J. Ramaekers, G. Ventre 1993. Client-network interactions in quality of service communication environments. In *Proceedings of the Fourth IFIP Conference on High Performance Networking*, A. Danthine & O. Spaniol (eds), e1–1, e1–14. University of Liege, Amsterdam: Elsevier.

Fidge, C. J. 1992. Specification and verification of real-time behaviour using Z and RTL. In *Proceedings of the Second International Symposium on Formal Techniques in Real-Time and Fault-Tolerant Systems*, J. Vytopil (ed.), 393–409. Berlin: Springer.

Fish, R. S. 1989. Cruiser: a multi-media system for social browsing. *The ACM SIGGRAPH Video Review Supplement to Computer Graphics* **45**(6), videotape. New York: ACM.

Fredlund, L. & F. Orava 1992. Modelling dynamic communication structures in LOTOS. In *Proceedings of the Fourth International Conference on Formal Description Techniques (FORTE '91)*, K. R. Parker & G. A. Rose (eds), 185–200. Amsterdam: Elsevier.

Garavel, H. 1990. *CÆSAR reference manual*. Internal report, Laboratoire de Genie Informatique, Institut IMAG.

Garey, M. R. & D. S. Johnson 1979. *Computers and intractability: a guide to the theory of NP-completeness*. San Francisco: W. H. Freeman.

Garfinkel, D., P. Gust, M. Lemon, S. Lowder 1989. *The sharedX multi-user interface user's guide, version 2.0*. Report STL-TM-89-07, Hewlett-Packard Laboratories. Palo Alto, California.

Gautier, T., P. L. Guernic, A. Benveniste, P. Bournai 1986. Programming real-time with events and data flow. In *Information Processing 86*, H-J. Kugler (ed.), 469–74. Amsterdam: Elsevier.

Gaver, W., T. Moran, A. MacLean, L. Lovstrand, P. Dourish, K. Carter, W. Buxton 1992. Realising a video environment: EuroPARC's RAVE system. In *Proceedings of*

CHI '92 (Human Factors in Computing Systems), P. Bauersfeld, J. Bennett, G. Lynch (eds), 27–35. Monterey, California.

Gelman, A. D. , H. Kobrinski, L. S. Smoot, S. B. Weinstein, M. Fortier, D. Lemay 1991. A store and forward architecture for video-on-demand services. In *Proceedings of the IEEE International Conference on Communications (ICC '91)*, 842–6. Piscataway, New Jersey: IEEE Press.

Goldberg, M., J. Robertson, G. Bélanger, N. D. Georganas, J. Mastronardi, S. Cohn-Sfetcu, R. Dillon, J. Tombaugh 1989. A multimedia medical communication link between a radiology department and an emergency department. *Journal of Digital Imaging*, vol. 2(2), 92–8.

Gordon, M. J. C. & T. F. Melham (eds) 1993. *Introduction to HOL: a theorem proving environment for higher-order logic*. Cambridge: Cambridge University Press.

Govindan, R. & D. P. Anderson 1991. Scheduling and IPC mechanisms for continuous media. *Thirteenth ACM Symposium on Operating Systems Principles*. Pacific Grove, California, SIGOPS, **25**, 68–80.

Groote, J. F. 1990. Specification and verification of real time systems in ACP. In *Proceedings of the Tenth International IFIP Symposium on Protocol Specification, Testing and Verification (PSTV X)*, L. Logrippo, R. L. Probert, H. Ural (eds), 261–74. Amsterdam: Elsevier.

Hager, R., A. Klemets, G. Q. Maguire, M. T. Smith, F. Reichert 1993. MINT – a mobile internet router. In *Proceedings of 43rd IEEE Vehicular Technologies Conference (VTC '93)*. Secaucus, New Jersey: IEEE Computer Society Press.

Halasz, F. & M. Schwartz 1994. The Dexter hypertext reference model. *Communications of the ACM* **37**(2), 30–39.

Halbwachs, N., D. Pilaud, F. Ouabdesselam 1990. Specifying, programming and verifying real-time systems using a synchronous declarative language. In *Automatic Verification Methods for Finite State Systems*, J. Sifakis (ed.), 213–31. Berlin: Springer.

Hanko, J. G., E. M. Keurner, J. D. Northcutt, G. A. Wall 1992. Workstation support for time critical applications. In *Proceedings of the Second International Workshop on Network and Operating System Support for Digital Audio and Video (NOSSDAV '91)*, R. G. Herrtwich (ed.), LNCS 614, 4–9. Berlin: Springer.

Hansson, H. 1991. *Time and probability in formal design of distributed systems*. PhD thesis. Department of Computer Systems, Uppsala University, Sweden.

Hansson, H. 1992. Modelling timeouts and unreliable media with a timed probabilistic calculus. In *Proceedings of the Fourth International Conference on Formal Description Techniques (FORTE '91)*, K. R. Parker & G. A. Rose (eds), 67–82. Amsterdam: Elsevier.

Harel, D. 1987. Statecharts: a visual formalism for complex systems. *Science of Computer Programming (North-Holland)* **8**, 231–74.

Harel, D. 1992. Biting the silver bullet: towards a brighter future for systems development. *IEEE Computer* **25**, 8–20.

Harel, D., H. Lachover, A. Naamad, A. Pnueli, M. Politi, R. Sherman, M. Trachtenbrot 1990a. STATEMATE: a working environment for the development of complex reactive systems. *IEEE Transactions on Software Engineering* **16**, 403–14.

Harel, D., O. Lichtenstein, A. Pnueli 1990b. Explicit clock temporal logic. In *Proceedings of the Fifth Annual IEEE Symposium on Logic in Computer Science*, 402–13. Philadelphia: IEEE Computer Society Press.

Hayter, M. & D. McAuley 1991. The desk area network. *ACM Operating Systems Review* **25**(4), 14–21.

Hehmann, D. B., M. G. Salmony, H. J. Stüttgen 1990. Transport services for multimedia applications on broadband networks. *Computer Communications* **13**(4), 197–203.

Hehmann, D., B. Kohler, N. Luttenberger, L. Mackert, W. Schulz, H. Stüttgen 1991. Implementation experience with a communication subsystem prototype for B-ISDN. In *Proceedings of the Third IFIP Conference on High Speed Networking*. Spaniol & A. Danthine, 257–71. Amsterdam: North Holland.

Hehmann, D. B., R. G. Herrtwich, W. Schulz, T. Schuett, R. Steinmetz 1992. Implementing HeiTS: architecture and implementation strategy of the Heidelberg high speed transport system. In *Proceedings of the Second International Workshop on Network and Operating System Support for Digital Audio and Video (NOSSDAV '91)*, R. G. Herrtwich (ed.), LNCS 614, 33–44. Berlin: Springer.

Henzinger, T. A., Z. Manna, A. Pnueli 1990. An interleaving model for real-time. In *Fifth Jerusalem Conference on Information Technology*, J. Maor & A. Peled (eds), 717–30. Washington: IEEE Computer Society Press.

Henzinger, T. A., X. Nicollin, J. Sifakis, S. Yovine 1992. Symbolic model checking for real-time systems. In *Proceedings of the Seventh IEEE Symposium on Logic in Computer Science*, 394–406. Los Alamitos, Calif.: IEEE Computer Society Press.

Hoare, C. A. R. 1969. An axiomatic basis for computer programming. *Communications of the ACM* **12**(10), 576–80.

Hoare, C. A. R. 1985. *Communicating sequential processes.* London: Prentice-Hall.

Hoare, C. A. R. 1987. Communicating sequential processes. *Communications of the ACM* **21**(8), 666–77.

Holzmann, G. J. March 1992. Practical methods for the formal validation of SDL specifications. *Computer Communications* **15**(2), 129–34.

Hopper, A. 1990. Pandora – an experimental system for multimedia applications. *Operating Systems Review* **24**(2), 19–34.

Huitema, C. 1989. The challenge of multimedia mail. *Computer Networks and ISDN Systems* **17**, 324–27.

Hutchison, D., G. Coulson, A. Campbell, G. S. Blair 1994. Quality of service management in distributed systems. In *Network and distributed systems management*, M. Sloman (ed.), 273–302. Reading, Mass.: Addison-Wesley.

IEEE 802.6 1990. *IEEE standards for local and metropolitan area networks: distributed queue bus (DQDB) subnetwork of a metropolitan area network.* Piscataway, N. J.: IEEE Press.

INT 1992a. *Estelle simulator/debugger Edb (version 3.0): user reference manual.* Reference Manual Institut National des Telecommunications (INT), Departement Systemes et Reseaux, Evry, Framce.

INT 1992b. *Estelle-to-C compiler (version 3.0): user reference manual.* Reference manual, Institut National des Telecommunications (INT), Departement Systemes et Reseaux, Evry, France.

ISO 1987. *Estelle – a formal description technique based on an extended state transition model.* ISO/TC97/SC21/WG1/DIS9074.

ISO 1988. *LOTOS: a formal description technique based on the temporal ordering of observational behaviour.* ISO DP 8807.

ISO/IEC 10746-2 | ITU Recommendation X.902 1995. *Open distributed processing –*

reference model – part 2: foundations.

ISO/IEC 10746-3 | ITU Recommendation X.903 1995. *Open distributed processing – reference model – part 3: architecture.*

ISO/IEC CD 10746-1 | ITU Recommendation X.901 1995. *Open distributed processing – reference model – part 1: overview.*

ISO/IEC CD 10746-4 | ITU Recommendation X.904 1995. *Open distributed processing – reference model – part 4: architectural semantics.*

ISO/IS 10021-1 | ITU-T Recommendations X.400 1988. *Message handling: system and service overview.*

ISO/IS 8824 | ITU-T Recommendations X.208 1988. *Information processing systems – open systems interconnection – specification of abstract syntax notation one (ASN.1).*

ISO/IS 8825 | ITU-T Recommendations X.209 1987. *Information processing systems – open systems interconnection – specification of basic encoding rules for abstract syntax notation one (ASN.1).*

ISO October 1994. *Working draft on enhancements to LOTOS.* ISO/IEC JTC1/SC21/ WG1 N1349.

Jahanian, F. & A. Mok 1986. Safety analysis of timing properties in real-time systems. *IEEE Transactions on Software engineering* **12**(9), 890–904.

Jensen, K. 1990. *Coloured Petri nets: a high level language for system design and analysis.* Report DAIMI PB-338, Department of Computer Science, Aahus University, Denmark.

Johnson, D. S. 1990. A catalog of complexity classes. In *Handbook of theoretical computer science (vol. A)*, J. van Leeuwen (ed.), 67–161. Amsterdam: Elsevier.

Jones, C. B. 1990. *Systematic software development using VDM.* Englewood Cliffs, New Jersey: Prentice-Hall.

Keller, R. M. 1976. Formal verification of parallel programs. *Communications of the ACM* **19**(7), 371–84.

Koch, T., B. Krämer, N. Völker 1994. Modelling dynamic ODP-configurations with LOTOS. In *Proceedings of the IFIP TC6 WG6.1 International Conference on Open Distributed Processing (ICODP '93)*, J. de Meer, B. Mahr, O. Spaniol (eds), 346–51. Amsterdam: Elsevier.

Koo, R. 1989. A model for electronic documents. *SIGOIS Bulletin* **10**(1), 23–33.

Koymans, R. 1990. Specifying real-time properties with metric temporal logic. *Real-Time Systems* **2**, 255–99.

Kretz, F. 1990. Multimedia and hypermedia information objects coding. *Proceedings of the Third IEEE Comsoc International Workshop on Multimedia Communication (Multimedia '90).*

Lakas, A., G. S. Blair, A. G. Chetwynd 1996a. Specification and verification of real-time safety and liveness properties. In *Proceedings of the Eighth International Workshop on Software Specification and Design*, 75–84. Paderborn.

Lakas, A., G. S. Blair, A. G. Chetwynd 1996b. Specification of stochastic properties in real-time systems. In *Proceedings of the Eleventh UK Performance Engineering Workshop for Computer and Telecommunication Systems*, M. Merabti, M. Carew & F. Ball (eds), 202–16. London: Springer.

Lamport, L. 1980. Sometimes is sometimes "not never" – on the temporal logic of programs. In *Proceedings of the Seventh Annual ACM Symposium on Principles of Programming Languages*, 174–85. New York: ACM Press.

Leduc, G. & L. Léonard 1993. A timed LOTOS supporting a dense time domain and including new timed operators. In *Proceedings of the: Fifth International Conference on Formal Description Techniques (FORTE '92)*, M. Diaz & R. Groz (eds), 87–102. Amsterdam: Elsevier.

Leduc, G. 1990. *On the role of implementation relations in the design of distributed systems using LOTOS*. PhD thesis, Faculté des Sciences Appliquées, Université de Liège, Belgium.

Leggett, J. J. & J. L. Schnase 1994. Viewing Dexter with open eyes. *Communications of the ACM* **37**(2), 76–86.

Léonard, L. & G. Leduc 1994. An enhanced version of timed LOTOS and its application to a case study. In *Proceedings of the Sixth International Conference on Formal Description Techniques (FORTE '93)*, R. L. Tenney, P. D. Amer, M. Ü. Uyar (eds), 483–98. Amsterdam: Elsevier.

Leopold, H., K. Frimpong-Ansah, N. Singer 1994. From broadband services to a distributed multimedia support environment. In *Proceedings of Cost 237: Multimedia Transport and Teleservices*, D. Hutchinson, A. Danthine, H. Leopold, G. Coulson (eds), LNCS 882, 47–68. Berlin: Springer.

Leveson, N. G. & J. L. Stolzy 1987. Safety analysis using Petri nets. In *IEEE Transactions on Software Engineering*, vol 13, 386–97. New York: IEEE.

Lichtenstein, O. & A. Pnueli 1985. Checking that finite state concurrent programs satisfy their linear specification. In *Proceedings of the Twelfth Annual ACM Symposium on Principles of Programming Languages*, 97–107. New York: ACM.

Linington, P. 1995. RM-ODP: the architecture. In *Open distributed processing, experiences with distributed environments, Proceedings of ICODP 94, Third International Conference on Open Distributed Processing*, K. Raymond & L. Armstrong (eds), 15–33. England: Chapman & Hall.

Little, T. D. C. & A. Ghafoor 1990. Synchronisation properties and storage models for multimedia objects. *IEEE Journal On Selected Areas in Communications* **8**(3), 413–27.

Little, T. D. C. & A. Ghafoor 1991. Multimedia synchronisation protocols for broadband integrated services. *IEEE Journal on Selected Areas in Communications* **9**(9).

Little, T. D. C. & D. Venkatesh 1994. Prospects for interactive video-on-demand. *IEEE Multimedia* **1**(3), 14–24.

Liu, C. L. & J. W. Layland 1973. Scheduling algorithms for multiprogramming in a hard real-time environment. *Journal of the Association for Computing Machinery*, **20**(1), 46–61.

Liu, P. (ed.) 1994. ISO standards from an information infrastructure perspective. *IEEE Multimedia* **1**(1), 89–90.

Lougher, P. & D. Shepherd 1993. The design of a storage server for continuous media. *The Computer Journal* **36**(1), 32–42.

Loveria, G. & D. Kinstler 1990. Multimedia: DVI arrives. *BYTE IBM Special Edition (Guideposts for the 90's)*, **15**(11), 105–8.

Lunn, A., A. C. Scott & W. D. Shepherd 1994. A minicell architecture for networked multimedia workstations. In *Proceedings of the IEEE International Conference on multimedia computing and systems*. S. Stevens & R. Steinmetz (eds), 285–94. Los Alamitos, Calif.: IEEE Computer Society Press.

Manna, Z. & A. Pnueli 1992. *The temporal logic of reactive and concurrent systems*. New York: Springer.

Manna, Z. & A. Pnueli 1989. The anchored version of the temporal framework. In *REX workshop on linear time, branching time and partial order in logics and models for concurrency*, J. W. de Bakker, W.-P. de Roever, G. Rozenberg (eds), LNCS 354, 201–84. Berlin: Springer.

Manna, Z. & P. Wolper 1984. Synthesis of communicating processes from temporal logic specifications. *ACM Transactions on Programming Languages and Systems* 6(1), 68–93.

Mañas, J. A. September 1992. Getting to use LITE. In *Proceedings of the Third LOTOSPHERE Workshop*, T. Bolognesi, E. Brinksma, C. A. Vissers (eds) Unpublished.

Mavridis, A. & A. Weser May 1990. TELEMED: first results from Europe's largest broadband communications project in telemedicine. In *Proceedings of the International Conference on Integrated Broadband Services and Networks*, 126–35. Los Alamitos, Calif.: IEEE Computer Society Press.

Mayr, T. 1989. Specification of object-oriented systems in LOTOS. In *Proceedings of the First International Conference on Formal Description Techniques (FORTE '88)* K. J. Turner (ed.), 107–119. Amsterdam: Elsevier.

Merlin, P. & D. J. Farber 1976. Recoverability of communication protocols – implications of a theoretical study. *IEEE Transactions on Communications* 24, 1036–43.

Miguel, C., A. Fernandez, L. Vidaller 1993. Extending LOTOS towards performance evaluation. In *Proceedings of the Fifth International Conference on Formal Description Techniques (FORTE '92)*, M. Diaz & R. Groz (eds), 103–18. Amsterdam: Elsevier.

Miguel, C. 1991. *Extended LOTOS definition*. OSI 95 (Esprit project 5341), report number OSI95/DIT/B5/8/TR/R/V0, Depto. Ingeniería de Sistemas Telemáticos, Universidad Politécnica de Madrid. Madrid, Spain.

Milne, G. J. 1985. CIRCAL and the representation of communication, concurrency and time. *ACM Transactions on Programming Languages and Systems* 7(2), 270–98.

Milner, R. 1980. *A calculus of communicating systems*. LNCS 92. Berlin: Springer.

Milner, R. 1983. Calculi for synchrony and asynchrony. *Theoretical Computer Science* (2), 267–310.

Milner, R. 1986. Process constructors and interpretations. In *Information Processing 86*, H. J. Kugler (ed.). Amsterdam: Elsevier.

Milner, R. 1989. *Communication and concurrency*. Englewood Cliffs, New Jersey: Prentice-Hall.

Milner, R., J. Parrow, D. Walker 1992. A calculus of mobile processes, parts I and II. *Information and Computation* 100(1), 1–77.

Miloucheva, I., O. Bonnesz, H. Buschermohle 1993. *XTPX based multimedia transport system for flexible QoS support*. Internal report, Department of Computer Science, Technical University of Berlin.

Mullender, S. (ed.) 1994. *Distributed Systems*. Reading, Mass.: Addison-Wesley.

Najm, E. & J.-B. Stefani 1992. Dynamic configuration in LOTOS. In *Proceedings of the Fourth International Conference on Formal Description Techniques (FORTE '91)*, K. R. Parker & G. A. Rose (eds), 201–16. Amsterdam: Elsevier.

Nicola, R. D. 1986. Transition systems and testing preorders: an alternative to Petri nets for system specification. In *Information processing 86*, H.-J. Kugler (ed.). Amsterdam: Elsevier.

Nicolaou, C. 1991. *A distributed architecture for multimedia communication systems*.

PhD thesis, University of Cambridge Computer Laboratory.

Nicollin, X. & J. Sifakis 1991. An overview and synthesis on timed process algebras. In *Proceedings of the Third Workshop on Computer-Aided Verification (CAV '91)*, K. G. Larsen & A. Skou, Report IR-91-4/5, 501–12. Aalborg University, Denmark.

Nicollin, X., J.-L. Richier, J. Sifakis, J. Voiron 1990. ATP: an algebra for timed processes. In *Proceedings of the IFIP TC 2 Working Conference on Programming Concepts and Methods*, M. Broy & C. B. Jones (eds), 402–29. Amsterdam: North Holland.

Nieh, J., J. N. Northcutt, J. G. Hanko 1994. SVR4 UNIX scheduler unacceptable for multimedia applications. In *Proceedings of the Fourth International Workshop on Network and Operating System Support for Digital Audio and Video (NOSSDAV '93)*, D. Shepherd, G. Blair, G. Coulson, N. Davies & F. Garcia (eds), 41–53, LNCS 846. Berlin: Springer.

Nirschl, H., J. Blanchard, B. Loyer 1993. LOTOS in Alcatel. In *Proceedings of the Fifth International Conference on Formal Description Techniques (FORTE '92)*, M. Diaz & R. Groz (eds), 27–35. Amsterdam: Elsevier.

Olson, M. H. & S. A. Bly 1991. The Portland experience: a report on a distributed research group. *International Journal of Man Machine Studies* **34**(2), 211–28.

Ostroff, J. S. 1989. *Temporal logic for real-time systems*. Taunton, England: Research Studies Press.

Ostroff, J. S. 1990. A logic for real-time discrete event processes. *IEEE Control Systems Magazine* **10**(4), 95–102.

Ostroff, J. S. 1992a. Verification of safety critical systems using TTM/RTTL. In *REX workshop on real-time: theory in practice*, J. W. de Bakker, C. Huizing, W. P. de Roever, G. Rozenberg (eds), 573–602, LNCS 600. Berlin: Springer.

Ostroff, J. S. 1992b. Formal methods for the specification and design of real-time safety critical systems. *The Journal of Systems and Software* **18**(1), 33–60.

Ousterhout, J. & F. Douglis 1989. Beating the I/O bottleneck: a case for log-structured file systems. *Operating Systems Review* **23**(1), 11–28.

Pagan, F. G. 1981. *Formal specification of programming languages: a panoramic primer*. New Jersey: Prentice-Hall.

Pancha, P. & M. El Zarchi 1994. MPEG coding for variable bit rate video transmission. *IEEE Communications Magazine*, Vol. 32(5), 54–66.

Patterson, J. F. & R. D. Hill 1990. Rendezvous: an architecture for synchronous multi-user applications. In *Proceedings of CSCW '90*, F. Halasz (ed.), 317–28. New York: ACM.

Peterson, J. L. 1981. *Petri net theory and the modelling of systems*. Englewood Cliffs, New Jersey: Prentice-Hall.

Pinto, P. F. & P. F. Linington 1994. A language for the specification of interactive and distributed multimedia applications. In *Proceedings of the International Conference on Open Distributed Processing (ICODP '93)*, J. de Meer, B. Mahr & O. Spaniol (eds), 217–34. Amsterdam: Elsevier.

Pnueli, A. 1977. The temporal logic of programs. In *Proceedings of the Eighteenth Annual Symposium on Foundations of Computer Science*, 46–57. Los Alamitos, Calif.: IEEE Computer Society Press.

Pnueli, A. 1985. Linear and branching structures in the semantics and logics of reactive systems. In *Proceedings of the Twelfth International Colloquium on Automata, Languages and Programming*, W. Brauer (ed.), LNCS Vol. 194, 15–32. Berlin: Springer.

Postel, J. B., G. G. Finn, A. R. Katz, J. K. Reynolds 1988. An experimental multimedia mail system. *ACM Transactions on Office Information Systems* **6**(1), 63–81.

Quemada, J., D. Frutos, A. Azcorra 1991. *TIC: a timed calculus.* Internal report, Depto. Ingeniería de Sistemas Telemáticos, Universidad Poletécnica de Madrid. Madrid, Spain.

RACE Project Number 1078 1994. *European museums network.* Brussels, Belgium: European Commission.

RAISE Language Group 1992. *The RAISE specification language.* Englewood Cliffs, New Jersey: Prentice-Hall.

Reed, G. M. & A. W. Roscoe 1988. A timed model for communicating sequential processes. *Theoretical Computer Science* **58**, 249–61.

Reed, G. M., A. W. Roscoe, S. A. Schneider 1991. CSP and timewise refinement. In *Fourth Refinement Workshop.* J. M. Morris & R. C. Shaw (eds), 258–80. Berlin: Springer.

Regan, T. 1991. *Process algebra for timed systems.* PhD thesis, Department of Computer Science, University of Sussex.

Regan, T. 1993. Multimedia in temporal LOTOS: a lip-synchronisation algorithm. In *Proceedings of the Thirteenth International IFIP Symposium on Protocol Specification, Testing and Verification (PSTV XIII),* A. Danthine, G. Leduc & P. Wolper (eds), 127–42. Amsterdam: Elsevier.

Reisig, W. 1985. *Petri nets.* Berlin: Springer.

Reynolds, J. K., J. B. Postel, A. R. Katz, G. G. Finn, A. L. De Schon 1985. The DARPA experimental multimedia mail system. *IEEE Computer,* **18**(10), 82–9.

Richier, J. L., C. Rodriguez, J. Sifakis, J. Voiron 1987. Verification in XESAR of the sliding window protocol. In *Proceedings of the Seventh International IFIP Symposium on Protocol Specification, Testing and Verification (PSTV VIII),* H. Rudin & C. H. West (eds), 235–48. Amsterdam: Elsevier.

Ritchie, I. 1989. HYPERTEXT – moving towards large volumes. *The Computer Journal* **32**(6), 516–23.

Root, W. R. 1988. Design of a multimedia vehicle for social browsing. In *Proceedings of the Conference on Computer-Supported Cooperative Work (CSCW '88),* L. Suchman (ed.) 25–38. New York: ACM.

Ross, F. E. July 1990. FDDI – A LAN among MANs. *ACM Computer Communication Review* **20**(3), 16–31.

Rudkin, S. 1992. Inheritance in LOTOS. In *Proceedings of the Fourth International Conference on Formal Description Techniques (FORTE '91),* K. R. Parker & G. A. Rose (eds), 409–23. Amsterdam: Elsevier.

Ruston, L., G. Coulson, N. Davies, G. S. Blair 1992. Integrating computing standards and the telecommunications industry: a tale of two architectures. In *Proceedings of the Second International Workshop on Network and Operating System Support for Digital Audio and Video (NOSSDAV '91),* R. G. Herrtwich (ed.), 57–68. Berlin: Springer.

Sasnett, R., J. R. Nicol, V. Phuah, S. Gutfreund 1994. Experiences of developing distributed multimedia business applications. In *Proceedings of the IEEE International Conference on Multimedia Computing and Systems,* L. Belady (ed.), 363–74. Los Alamitos, Calif.: IEEE Computer Society Press.

Schneider, S., J. Davies, D. M. Jackson, G. M. Reed, J. N. Reed, A. W. Roscoe 1992. Timed CSP: theory and practice. In *REX Workshop on Real-Time: theory in practice,*

J. W. de Bakker, C. Huizing, W. P. de Roever, G. Rozenberg (eds), 640–75, LNCS 600. Berlin: Springer.

Scholler, E. M. & S. L. Casner 1989. A packet-switched multimedia conferencing system. *SIGOIS Bulletin* **10**(1), 12–22.

Schot, J. 1992. *The role of architectural semantics in the formal approach of distributed systems design.* PhD thesis, Tele-Informatics Group, University of Twente, The Netherlands.

Shepherd, W. D. & M. Salmony 1990. Extending OSI to support synchronisation required by multimedia applications. *Computer Communications* **13**(7), 399–406.

Sijelmassi, R. & P. Gaudette 1989. An object-oriented model for Estelle. In *Formal Description Techniques*, K. J. Turner (ed.), 91–106. Amsterdam: Elsevier.

Spears, D. R. 1988. Broadband ISDN service visions and technological realities. *International Journal of Digital and Analog Cabled Systems* **1**, 3–18.

Spivey, J. M. 1989. *The Z notation: a reference manual.* Englewood Cliffs, New Jersey: Prentice-Hall.

Stankovic, J. A. & K. Ramamritham 1988. *Tutorial: hard real-time systems.* Philadelphia: IEEE Computer Society Press.

Stefani, J.-B. 1993. Some computational aspects of QoS in an object based distributed architecture. In *Proceedings of the Third International Workshop on Responsive Computer Systems*.

Stefani, J.-B., L. Hazard, F. Horn 1992. Computational model for distributed multimedia applications based on a synchronous programming language. *Computer Communications (Special Issue on FDTs)* **15**(2).

Stefik, M., G. Foster et al. 1987. Beyond the chalkboard: computer support for collaboration and problem solving in meetings. *Communications of the ACM* **30**(1), 32–47.

Steinmetz, R. 1994. Data compression in multimedia computing – standards and systems. *ACM Multimedia Systems* **1**(5), 187–204.

Stirling, C. May 1991. *Modal and temporal logics.* Internal report ECS-LFCS-91-157, Laboratory for Foundations of Computer Science, Department of Computer Science, University of Edinburgh.

Stoy, J. E. 1977. *Denotational semantics: the Scott–Strachey approach to programming language theory.* Cambridge, Mass.: MIT Press.

Tanenbaum, A. 1989. *Computer networks.* Englewood Cliffs, New Jersey: Prentice-Hall.

Tanenbaum, A. S., R. van Renesse, H. van Staveren, S. J. Mullender 1988. *A retrospective and evaluation of the amoeba distributed operating system.* Technical report, Department of Mathematics and Computer Science, Vrije Universiteit, Amsterdam.

Tennenhouse, D. L. 1990. Layered multiplexing considered harmful. *Protocols for High-Speed Networks.* Amsterdam: Elsevier.

The Object Management Group 1991. *The common object request broker: architecture and specification.* OMG Document 91.12.1, revision 1.1, draft 10, The Object Management Group, Framington, MA.

The Open Software Foundation 1992. *Distributed computing environment.* The Open Software Foundation, Cambridge, MA.

Thomas, M. 1993. Translator tool for ASN.1 into LOTOS. In *Proceedings of the Fifth International Conference on Formal Description Techniques (FORTE '92)*, M. Diaz &

R. Groz (eds), 49–64. Amsterdam: Elsevier.

Tofts, C. 1988. *Temporal ordering for concurrency.* Internal report, Laboratory for Foundations of Computer Science, Department of Computer Science, University of Edinburgh.

Tofts, C. 1990. Timed concurrent processes. In *Semantics for Concurrency – Proceedings of the International BCS-FACS Workshop,* M. Z. Kwiatkowska, M. W. Shields, R. M. Thomas (eds), 281–94. University of Leicester.

Turner, K. J. 1990. A LOTOS-based development strategy. In *Proceedings of the Second International Conference on Formal Description Techniques (FORTE '89),* S. T. Vuong (ed.), 117–32. Amsterdam: Elsevier.

Turner, K. J. 1993. *Using formal description techniques, an introduction to Estelle, LOTOS and SDL.* Chichester: John Wiley.

van Hulzen, W. H. P., P. A. Tilanus, H. Zuidweg 1990. LOTOS extended with clocks. *Proceedings of the Second International Conference on Formal Description Techniques (FORTE '89),* S. T. Vuong (ed.), 179–94. Amsterdam: Elsevier.

Vin, H. M. & P. V. Rangan 1993. Designing a multi-user HSTV storage server. *IEEE Journal on Selected Areas in Communications* **11**(1), 153–64.

Vissers, C. A., G. Scollo, M. van Sinderen, E. Brinksma 1991. Specification styles in distributed systems design and verification. *Theoretical Computer Science* **89**, 179–206.

Vogel, A. 1994. On ODP architectural semantics using LOTOS. In *Proceedings of the First International Conference on Open Distributed Processing (ICODP '93),* J. de Meer, B. Mahr & O. Spaniol (eds), 340–45. Amsterdam: Elsevier.

Walker, J. & B. R. Gardner 1990. Cellular radio. In *Mobile information systems,* J. Walker (ed.), 59–104. Norwood, MA: Artech House.

Walter, B. 1983. Timed petri-nets for modelling and analyzing protocols with real-time characteristics. In *Proceedings of the Third International IFIP Symposium on Protocol Specification, Testing and Verification (PSTV III),* H. Rudin & C. H. West (eds), 149–59. Amsterdam: Elsevier.

Wegner, P. 1987. Dimensions of object-oriented language design. In *Proceedings of the Conference on Object-Oriented Programming Systems, Languages and Applications (OOPSLA '87), SIGPLAN Notices* **22**, 168–82.

Williams, N. & G. S. Blair 1994. Distributed multimedia applications: a review. *Computer Communications* **17**(2), 119–32.

Winskel, G. 1989. Event structures. In *REX workshop on linear time, branching time and partial order in logics and models for concurrency,* J. W. Bakker, W-P. de Roever, G. Rozenberg (eds), 364–97, LNCS 354. Berlin: Springer.

Wolfinger, B. & M. Moran 1992. A continuous media data transport service and protocol for real-time communication in high speed networks, In *Second International Workshop on Network and Operating System Support for Digital Audio and Video (NOSSDAV '91),* R. G. Herrtwich (ed.) 171–82. Berlin: Springer.

Wolper, P. 1985. The tableau method for temporal logic: an overview. *Logique et Analyse* **28**, 119–36.

Yi, W. 1990. Real-time behaviour of asynchronous agents. In *Proceedings of CONCUR '90 (Theories of Concurrency: Unification and Extension),* J. C. M. Baeton & J. W. Klop (eds), 502–20, LNCS 458. Berlin: Springer.

Yi, W. 1991. *A calculus of real time systems.* PhD thesis, Department of Computer Science, Chalmers University of Technology, Gothenberg, Sweden.

Index